The Washington Post

NEW UPDATED EDITION

REDSKINS

A HISTORY OF WASHINGTON'S TEAM

THOMAS BOSWELL • LIZ CLARKE • ANTHONY COTTON • KEN DENLINGER
WILLIAM GILDEA • RICHARD JUSTICE • TONY KORNHEISER • MARK MASKE
SHIRLEY POVICH • DAVID SELL • LEONARD SHAPIRO • MICHAEL WILBON

Published by
Washington Post Books
1150 15th Street, N.W.
Washington, D.C. 20071

Second Edition

The text of this book is composed in Palatino,
with the display in Futura Extra Black.

Manufactured by Chroma Graphics, Largo, Md.,
in association with Alan Abrams
ISBN: [1-930691-01-7]

Publisher and Editor: Noel Epstein
Graphic Designer: Robert Barkin, Barkin & Davis
Project Coordinators: Elissa Leibowitz, Susan Breitkopf
Trivia Editors: Martie Zad, Gene Wang

Cover Photograph by Rich Lipski, The Washington Post

CONTENTS

Tales of the Faithful Fan

By Thomas M. Boswell

My father, who jokingly described himself as "a fifth-string quarterback, but on a championship team," moved to Washington in 1937. He found it easy to remember the date: It was the year the Redskins also moved to town and won their first World Championship to boot.

For nearly 60 seasons, from Sammy Baugh through Sonny Jurgensen to Joe Gibbs, my mild-mannered dad, the government librarian and artist, turned into a tiger on Redskins Sundays. Though hardly a sports fan at all, he was — like countless Washingtonians — utterly devoted to the Redskins. Taciturn to a fault, he'd talk about the team with people to whom he otherwise would never have spoken.

Like many men who'd come up hard through the Depression and World War II, he seldom showed emotion. Except when an open Redskins receiver dropped a touchdown pass. Or an official blew a call. Then he showed so much "emotion" that my mother would come in from the kitchen and say, "Paul, someday I'm going to come in and find you dead on the floor, all because of the silly Redskins." Then she'd sit down and watch, too.

Passionate about politics, my father made only one blanket exception. Redskins coaches — provided they were winners — could be as Republican as they pleased. He adored George Allen, with whom, I like to think, he might have disagreed on every subject except The Team.

For a lifelong Washingtonian, the Redskins creep into every corner of your life. I first met my wife in the old Duke Ziebert's restaurant. She doesn't know it (yet), but the first time I looked at her face, the Super Bowl trophy, which the Redskins had won the previous season, was just a few feet behind her in the glass case where it was displayed in those days. She particularly piqued my interest that first day when she said, perplexed, "Who is this Joe Theismann?" Of course, I knew my Redskins trash can would no longer be part of the decor.

When our son was born, it didn't escape my notice that the Redskins immediately won the next Super Bowl. He's already a huge fan, and, by Washington birthright, an ardent critic. By the time he was 12 and the team started a season 0-7, Russell pleaded, "Come on, dad. Make them fire Norv Turner." When my son is my current age, our family will have been Redskins fans for 100 years.

You see, in the Washington area, we inevitably mark arrivals and vital meetings, births and marriages, perhaps even deaths (or at least jokes about them) with the Redskins. The team is this itinerant town's one trans-generational reference point. All over the world, millions assume that people who live near The Nation's Capital measure time by "the Kennedy Years" or "the Reagan Era." Not much. Not regular people. But plenty of us refer to the Gibbs Years or the Allen Era or perhaps, if things work out for the team's new owner, the Danny Days.

In reading this book, though, it's important to keep in mind that before there was a Joe Theismann, Doug Williams or Mark Rypien in the Super Bowl, there was Al Dorow, Ralph Guglielmi and Norm Snead. Before there was John Riggins, Larry Brown and Earnest Byner, there was Johnny Olszewski, Joe Don Looney and Don Bosseler. Before there were Smurfs, Hogs and The Posse, there was the Papoose Backfield. Before Vince Lombardi, there was Mike Nixon.

The history of sports franchises, even distinguished ones, seldom resembles a glorious, upward-sloping line. Instead, a team's progress often looks more line a sine curve, oscillating slowly over the decades. What goes up not only comes down but often stays down for a while. When it does, you should know what it is that you love and why you love it.

Long before the days of Redskins glory under Allen and Gibbs, there was a solid quarter century of ignominy under 10 different coaches. Some of us grew up in those spinach days, when the Redskins had dismal records like 4-12, 3-13 and 6-10. Ooops, sorry. Those records were from the 1990s. Actually, the Redskins of my son's formative fan years weren't much different from the Redskins of my childhood in the 1950s and 1960s, when Washingtonians loved a team that was never good enough to break your heart but sure taught you how to kick the TV.

When you first fall in love with a team when it's bad, or even mediocre, you fall hardest. The glory days merely cement the bond. I'm actually glad that, in the first six years that my son and I watched Redskins games together, they never made the playoffs and, all told, lost 23 more games than they won. Some of us know how we got where we are as fans. For better or worse — and with Dan Snyder in charge, it sure looks like better is back — the Redskins are ours. We like it that way. We don't "hail" them so much as we have inhaled them since childhood. When they're bad or bizarre or even boring, they're still as much ours as family. And when they finally do get back to the Super Bowl, when they draft stars of the future like Champ Bailey, Jon Jansen, Lavar Arrington and Chris Samuels, we feel doubly exhilarated. We weren't just on board from the beginning of the golden days. We were there before the beginning.

My earliest memory of the Redskins actually has to do with a white football. You don't see them much anymore, especially the ones made of rubber with a black circle painted around each end. But they were still in vogue in the mid-1950s. The Los Angeles Rams used them in night games on the West Coast, where such balls supposedly were easier to see under the rudimentary arc lights. Some snazzy, early NFL films show Norm Van Brocklin throwing bombs to Tom Fears and Crazy Legs Hirsch, heaves that seemed to travel farther than should be humanly possible, in part because the white ball stood out starkly in the night.

My white football was a source of shame to me. No such animal was ever seen in my haunts — the playgrounds and alleys of Northeast Washington. Not all families had TV sets yet. For sure, nobody was watching Ram games at 1 a.m.; all you got then was a test pattern, not Van Brocklin. Like any omniscient 9-year-old, my assumption was that my father, who had given me "Whitey" for Christmas, was a hopeless square. He also was modest (such men still existed in the 1950s, though the breed now seems extinct), so he didn't bother to mention that he'd been on a state high school championship team. He hadn't been especially good, so he didn't deem it worth comment.

So the ball was disdained, used only when no other ball on the block was available. If it rolled into 6th Street, none of us would risk our lives darting into traffic, as we would have for a real football. "Let it go," we'd yell, as "Whitey" took another shot from a passing Packard.

Then one day, probably in 1956, I saw my first football card of a real Washington Redskin: quarterback Eddie LeBaron. Only one thing about the talismanic card of The Little General was obviously a mistake: The ball was white! If it had been possible to apologize formally to an inanimate object, every kid within five blocks would have gotten down on one knee in front of my ball. "Whitey," now perilously close to the end of its days, was raised to place of honor. And my connection to the Redskins was made. For life, it appears.

By November 10, 1957 — my 10th birthday — my destiny was sealed. My father took me to Griffith Stadium to see the Redskins in person. Still have the ticket stubb; never forget anything about that day. The rookie backfield of Jim Podoley, Don Bosseler and Ed Sutton — yes, The Papoose Backfield, known to others as The Lollypops — led the way. The Skins beat the Baltimore Colts on a field goal from midfield by Sam Baker. I've told about that kick at intervals throughout my life. Yet I noticed several years ago that the record books say that the Colts won, 21-17. My only reaction is amazement that the NFL could be so popular despite such shoddy record keeping in its formative years. Don't tell me that Baker's kick put the Redskins ahead but that the Colts marched down the field to score last and win. No, that couldn't have been it. I was there.

One of youth's worst misfortunes is to grow up in a town represented by excellent athletic teams. All the wrong values are taught. Fortunately, my gang was spared this fate. We were exposed to baseball's Washington Senators, who hadn't won a pennant in more than 20 years and hadn't even finished in the first division in more than a decade. The Redskins were dependably mediocre, with a slight bias toward defeat. A kid could count on them. If the Skins won one week, you could bet your allowance on them to lose the next week. And if they lost one week, they'd probably pull one out the next time.

In the 10 years before they registered on my consciousness in 1956, the Redskins had won 49, lost 67 and tied 1. No titles were predicted or expected. In fact, for 25 consecutive seasons — from 1946 until 1971 — the Redskins never played a post-season game.

Yes, those were my Redskins. Still are. From the time I was 10 until I was a senior in high school, the Redskins never beat the New York Giants. Our gang hated the Giants. We hated their linebacker Sam Huff, who to us was a late-hit, pile-on artist. We hated when they beat us by 53-0 or 45-14. Once we tied 'em, 24-24. We lived off that for years.

In the course of all this, we learned that if you love something or someone, it must be unconditional and permanent or it's nothing much at all. About 10 of us gathered every Saturday for years to play touch football and, of course, pretend that we were the latest quarterback prospect for the Redskins, like George Izo, Dick Shiner or Eagle Day.

Wherever we went, for an RC Cola and a Lemon Pie or those tiny, syrup-filled wax bottles that you'd chew, somebody in the group would casually drop the football on the ground and yell, "Fumble!" Everybody had to dive on it, even in the street; good for your technique. If you got a couple in a row, you'd claim you were Gene Brito or Andy Stynchula. We may have been out of our minds, but, so far, only one of us has gotten a divorce. We learned lessons in fidelity as Redskins fans.

The key to our affection — an excellent childhood lesson — was to accept them exactly as they were. Because they definitely weren't going to get any better in those days. Our hero LeBaron was 5 feet, 7 inches — not much bigger than we were as kids and smaller than many of us as older boys. He had to throw jump passes on routes over the middle. Not because it was stylish but so he could see his receivers. His claim to NFL fame was his faking. Faking! Is this scraping the barrel to find distinction, or what? Yet throughout my own mundane quarterbacking days, I took pride in my deceptive ball handling. Although no evidence exists that anyone was ever faked out.

By the time Huff became a Redskin in 1964, we assumed that he had to be nearing the end of his career or Washington never would have gotten him. However, because we had passed our Redskins catechism, we saw life as it was. Most of our Redskins, after all, were deeply flawed, including some butter-fingered wide receivers who had a habit of dropping perfectly thrown bombs, or defensive backs like Jim Steffen, whose calling card was the bone-crushing, downfield, cross-body-block tackle — after he'd allowed another 20-yard completion. It didn't change our view of Huff because he suddenly wore burgundy and gold. We just accepted him. He was our own.

Old habits die hard, even faced with the prospect of more pleasant ones. Once you've decided that football heaven is watching Sonny Jurgensen pass Washington to a 42-37 defeat — a loss more glorious to me and my buddies than the banal 17-14 wins of other teams — it's hard to turn your head around. For example, when Vince Lombardi left the executive suite in Green Bay to coach the Redskins, my friends and I found it at least as ridiculous as it was inspiring. America worshipped the Packers, us included. So we were slightly embarrassed for him. What next? Would Einstein show up in our high school to teach algebra? It was positively peculiar watching him on the Redskins sidelines, in a golf visor, on a 90-degree day in early September.

Lombardi was a watershed nonetheless. Franchises have an interior image of themselves, like a mirror turned inward. No matter what they project to the world, they can't escape how they view themselves. Lombardi shattered that negative, self-mocking mirror just by signing on board. After that, anything was possible. Even five Super Bowl trips and three world titles.

Reading this book can have a similar effect, especially when you're reminded of how extraordinary successful the Redskins were when they first arrived in Washington in 1937. There is Ray Flaherty, the first Washington Redskins coach, accumulating a winning record of more than 73 percent, the best in team history, before the Redskins' long dry spell began. The idea of the Redskins winning 73 percent of their games would have been incomprehensible to my gang.

All across America we have heard the refrain in recent years that "Washington fans are spoiled." They expect a contender every year. They won't tolerate a bad record. Which fans are those? Many of us subsisted for years on a few elegant interceptions by Paul Krause and an occasional crushing tackle by Chris Hanburger. We can wait if we must. We paid the dues for all the Johnny-come-lately celebrities now in the owner's box. We put in the hard time for all the talk-show hotshots.

All this may help explain why the beginning of a new Redskin Millennium has such a special feeling for die-hard Washington football fans. The Redskins new owner, Dan Snyder, actually appears to be One of Us. Time will tell if the bond is genuine. But Snyder is not only a native of the Washington area but was born in 1965 — the perfect moment to become a lifelong burgundy-and-gold addict.

By the time Snyder was 6 years old, Lombardi was the Redskins coach and that quarter century of lousy teams was about to end. When Snyder was 7, Allen's Over-The-Hill Gang went to the Super Bowl. If you're looking for the "Rose-bud" in Snyder's biography, search no further. The town talked nothing but Redskins. No doubt, somebody was in the Oval Office in 1972, but I've already forgotten his name.

Until Snyder was 12, Allen stayed in town, licking his thumb, saying his corny huddle prayers and creating the distinct impression that a Redskins win was more important than disarmament. Finally, when Snyder was 15, who came to town but Gibbs. For 12 glittering years, the capital of the free world was a town called Washington Redskins. The only flaw in Snyder's resume is that, while he was certainly bitten in his youth by the Redskins bug, he was never inoculated by the kind of decade-of-defeat that teaches patience.

No wonder that a self-made, 30-something fellow with millions in his pockets could imagine no greater challenge, nor any bigger fun, than owning the Redskins and restoring their glory. The Washington Redskins are about tradition and continuity in a city that supposedly has neither. Snyder, like many of us, knows differently. The day he bought the team, Snyder talked about a belt buckle he wore everywhere when he was a kid. It said, "Redskins." That's the way it should be. But isn't often.

CHAPTER I
In the Beginning

Instant Love, Instant Greatness

By William Gildea

The expression on the face of the team's general manager was in keeping with his surroundings. The Redskins, opening business in Washington after five years in Boston, had moved into an office on 9th Street N.W. Boxes were stacked, furniture was being rearranged, and a black telephone was on the floor. Jack Espey, the general manager, glanced about the room, his chin cupped in his right hand, his tie open at the collar. It wasn't the disarray in the room that troubled him. It was August 16, 1937. The Washington Redskins' first practice, in the Anacostia neighborhood of Southeast Washington, was scheduled in eight days. Where was the coach?

Ray Flaherty was missing. Espey didn't know where he was. Redskins owner George Preston Marshall, who had inherited the Palace Laundry headquartered at the corner of 9th and H streets, N.W., hadn't heard from Flaherty in weeks. Even though it might cost more than a dollar, Espey took it on himself to get the long-distance operator to put in a call to Flaherty's parents in Spokane, Washington. But no one answered.

Ray (Red) Flaherty had been a broad-shouldered, 6-foot end at Gonzaga University in Spokane and then a regular for the powerful New York Giants, where he had absorbed the thinking of renowned coach (Stout) Steve Owen. Flaherty began thinking like a coach himself. In the National Football League's 1934 championship game, played on an icy surface at the Polo Grounds, he suggested using basketball shoes. Donned at halftime, the shoes offered the traction the Giants needed to upset the heavily favored Chicago Bears.

Flaherty served as an assistant coach with the Giants in 1935 as well as a player, before Marshall named him head coach of the Boston Redskins. Marshall had been the principal proprietor and then sole owner of the team since 1932, and Flaherty became its fourth coach in five years. In 1935, the Redskins had lost eight games while winning only two and tying one. They were a financially troubled franchise, usually playing almost in privacy — to relatives, friends and diehards — at Fenway Park. As Boston football fans watched popular games at Harvard, Boston College and nearby Holy Cross, Flaherty reconstructed the Redskins in his first year and, with 11 rookies, led the pro team to the NFL's 1936 Eastern Division title with a 7-5 record. He could coach.

Flaherty also had a mind of his own, and in early August of 1937 he was preoccupied with the coming season. It hadn't occurred to him to write or call Espey or Marshall. He was busy working. Flaherty wanted to win the 1937 league title as much as the owner did. Marshall, known for his volubility and salesmanship, had been telling everyone he encountered, including passersby on Washington streets, of the Redskins' fabulous prospects for 1937, all the while trying to peddle tickets to anyone he could. It was the circumspect Flaherty, though, who had to make the championship happen.

Presumed missing, he was aboard a train from Spokane to Chicago, on a mission: He was headed to see Sammy Baugh. "Slingin' Sammy," the passing master out of Texas Christian University, would be playing for the College All-Stars in Chicago against the NFL champion Green Bay Packers, who had beaten the Boston Redskins, 21-6, in the 1936 title game.

At the NFL's college draft that year, five teams incomprehensibly had passed up the opportunity to take Baugh: Brooklyn, Pittsburgh (the team that later would let Johnny Unitas go), Philadelphia, the Chicago Cardinals and the Giants. The Redskins had been able to snare him, an extraordinary stroke of luck. Indeed, the first telegraphic message ever sent, out of Washington, could have applied to the Redskins' fortunes that draft day: "What hath God wrought?" Baugh would become a football giant and the cornerstone of the Washington franchise.

So Flaherty went to pay a courtesy call in Chicago. He also wanted to throw in a few words of friendly persuasion so that Baugh would sign a contract soon. He knew that Baugh already had signed to play pro baseball as well, with a promise that he could pursue a gridiron career during football season. (See profile on Page 37.)

Baugh was a special football talent in good part because of his college coach. To be sure,

Baugh was a natural who could do more things well on a football field — pass, kick, run, tackle — than any other player. But TCU's Dutch Meyer told him things he'd never forget. Even when Baugh was in his eighties at his home in Rotan, Texas, few days went by when he didn't think of Meyer, who had gathered the finest passers at TCU. Two years behind Baugh was Davey O'Brien, an immense talent of diminutive stature who stepped into the college spotlight after Baugh relinquished it. Later, O'Brien starred for the Eagles.

"We were just high school kids. We didn't know a damn thing," Baugh recalled. "Dutch Meyer taught us. All the coaches I had in the pros, I didn't learn a damn thing from any of 'em compared with what Dutch Meyer taught me. He taught the short pass. The first day we go into a room and he has three S's up on a blackboard; nobody knew what that meant. Then he gives us a little talk and he says, 'This is our passing game.' He goes up to the blackboard and he writes three words that complete the S's: 'Short, Sure and Safe.' That was his philosophy — the short pass.

"Everybody loved to throw the long pass. But the point Dutch Meyer made was, 'Look at what the short pass can do for you.' You could throw it for seven yards on first down, then run a play or two for a first down, do it all over again and control the ball. That way you could beat a better team."

Flaherty knew what made Sammy tick, and he knew that opposing rushers would be out to all but break his passer's neck. So Flaherty would invent a version of the screen pass to save that prize neck. Beginning in the mid-1940s in the rival All-American Football Conference, coach Paul Brown of the Cleveland Browns employed the screen pass with great effectiveness; Otto Graham threw it to Marion Motley and other backs. But Flaherty invented the play almost a decade before, not from the T formation of later times but from the single-wing and double-wing formations the Redskins then employed. Baugh would receive the snaps at tailback, and the line would shift right or left to set up a screen for a receiver.

When Flaherty arrived in Chicago for the September 1 College All-Stars game with the Packers, he already was visualizing Sammy in a burgundy Redskins jersey. Flaherty visited Baugh and two other Redskins draftees at the collegians' camp. They sat and talked about the forward pass. The All-Stars' coach knew something of the subject as well. He was Gus Dorais, who as Notre Dame's quarterback in 1913 surprised Army with a new element in the game, the forward pass. Knute Rockne was Dorais' principal pass-catcher.

At game time, Flaherty wore a straw hat in the hot, humid weather and smoked cigarettes as he sat among 84,500 fans in Soldier Field. As he expected, he was pleased. The final score was 6-0, the first time in the annual series the collegians beat the pro champions. Baugh produced the lone score, a 20-yard pass that Gaynell Tinsley, out of Louisiana State, carried another 28 yards across the goal line. Baugh and Tinsley held their own against Green Bay's fabled passing combination of Arnie Herber and Don Hutson. And one time after Green Bay had been stopped at the All-Stars' three-yard line, Baugh punted out of trouble.

Dorais predicted that Baugh "will do until some supernatural passer comes along." And this: "That ball he threw to Tinsley for the touchdown was floating so lightly that a babe could have plucked it." And more: "Outside of his passing, his best point is his defensive play. He's a dream guy as a safety man. Cagey, smart and fast, and they stay tackled when Sammy hits 'em."

The next morning, Flaherty took a train — not to Washington but to New York. He wanted to make a trade with the Giants for a former Gonzaga player named Max Krause, and he did. Krause may not live large in Redskins history, but he played a few roles. Most importantly, he was a blocking back; Flaherty would surround Baugh with blockers, hoping to protect him like a priceless artifact.

Then Flaherty boarded a train to Washington, arriving as Espey stewed eight days before training. "Thought you might have forgotten we moved and taken the train to Boston," Espey said.

"I admit I aimed a little higher than the capital, but no higher than New York," Flaherty said.

More than 1,000 fans flocked to Fairlawn Field in Anacostia to watch the first practice. Marshall sat on a sideline, and Flaherty took calisthenics with 25 players. Baugh had another all-star game commitment, but Washington's top running back, Cliff Battles, joined up after a one-day holdout. As much laundry as Marshall had been taking in, he hoarded his dollars and cents even from the likes of Battles, a barrel-chested runner who was an early version of Larry Brown.

Marshall also played coy about Baugh. "I wouldn't say that Baugh proved himself out there in Chicago," Marshall told a reporter. "The All-Stars were playing a bunch of tired guys." A few days later, though, Baugh would lead another college group, the

Prelude to greatness: Ray Flaherty, the coach with the highest winning percentage in Redskins history, on his first team outing in 1937.

Southwest All-Stars, to victory over the Chicago Bears in Dallas.

In the meantime, Flaherty took most of his players on a bus to Frederick, Maryland, to play an exhibition game against the American Legion All-Stars. But just before Rockville, the bus driver was pulled over by a policeman and charged with reckless driving for crossing a solid line while passing a car. At length, the team made it to Frederick and dressed. Then a downpour hit, and the game was postponed. The next day, the Redskins went back and won, 50-0. Marshall, selling tickets in the flush of the victory (such as it was, given the opponent), debunked baseball. "That's a commonplace game," he said. "You have one every day." He declared pro football "the national pastime."

On Wednesday, September 8, 1937, Baugh finally stepped off an Eastern Air Lines plane in Washington, and there to shake his golden passing hand were Marshall and Flaherty. A sculpted version of Baugh's hand would come to occupy a place on Marshall's desk. But for now the loquacious promoter signed the taciturn Texan for a single season. Eight days later, on a Thursday night, the Redskins were to begin their long-playing run in Washington with a game against the Giants at Griffith Stadium.

On the Anacostia practice field, Battles, 255-pound all-league tackle Turk Edwards, big back Erny Pinckert and other veterans warmly welcomed the rookie Baugh. No surprise: They would need him against the Giants. On Thursday afternoon, the Senators drew a smattering to Griffith Stadium for a 4-3 loss to the Detroit Tigers. That night, 24,492 welcomed the Redskins.

Ten minutes before the game Flaherty addressed his players. Shirley Povich of *The Washington Post* was inside the locker room to take down the words. Flaherty almost had a Rockne flair:

"All right, you guys. You've got a football game out there. What are you going to do about it? You're gonna kick hell out of those Giants, that's what. You've got to. You've moved into a new town, you and me and all of us. And the future of pro football in Washington depends on this game tonight, here. You've got pretty good jobs, all of you. And me, too. And we want to keep those jobs. And that means we've got to win this ball game. Not only that, there's a hell of a crowd out there tonight. They've come out to see what pro football is like. Well, show 'em.

"I want 60 minutes of the best that's in you. I won't take anything less. Sixty minutes of 100 percent effort. Those Giants are going to be tough tonight. You know how they hate us. And I'll tell you something, I've found out that they're out to get Erny Pinckert. I want you guys to give Erny plenty of protection. I don't want anybody standing around when they start to give Erny the works. You've got hands, use 'em. You're as big as they are. And I think you're tougher. Understand?"

Then came the crux of the message:

"For three years now you guys who've been with the Redskins have been complaining that you haven't had a passer. Well, we've gone out and got you one. And I want plenty of protection for Sammy Baugh. You know damn well those Giants will be out to cut Sammy down the first chance they get and try to get him out of there. Well, what are you going to do about that? You know damn well what I want you to do. I don't want to see a Giant get to Sammy. Don't let 'em get to Sammy, understand?"

The Giants watched Sammy. The crowd watched Sammy. Wearing number 33, he was Number 1 in home fans' hearts before he had touched a ball and Number 1 on opponents' hit lists. As it turned out, the quarterback in the wing formations, Riley Smith, an all-American at Alabama and the Redskins' No. 1 draft pick of 1936, scored all of Washington's points in a 13-3 victory. He kicked an 18-yard field goal in the first period. He broke a 3-3 tie in the fourth period with another 18-yarder.

But Baugh played a part. Among other things, his passes to Wayne Millner, Charley Malone and Bob McChesney set up Smith's second field goal. Then Smith clinched the game by intercepting a pass and running 60 yards for a touchdown. And he kicked the point after.

Later in the season Smith kicked a 27-yard field goal with 25 seconds remaining to play to beat Philadelphia, 10-7. Against the Cleveland Rams, he scored 10 points in the third period to clinch another victory. With the ball tucked under his left arm, he was the cover boy on the program (10 cents would buy it) on November 28, 1937 when the Redskins beat the defending champion Packers, 14-6, at Griffith Stadium. "He told me," said his son, Riley Smith, a businessman in Mobile, Alabama, "that when he'd walk into the Shoreham, the band would break into 'Hail to the Redskins.' "

Smith was awestruck by the attention he and the team received in Washington. The love affair between the city and the Redskins began instantly. Good football was being played then at Georgetown, George Washington and Catholic University, so it wasn't a matter of filling a vacuum. The Senators had won the pennant as recently as 1933. Washingtonians simply liked their sports, and there was keen interest in this pro league that brought together an array of standouts from the college ranks. For Washington and the Redskins, it was a perfect match: instant love from the fans, instant greatness on the gridiron.

For Marshall, it was all he could ask for. He loved sitting back at halftime at Griffith Stadium and basking in the glory of the games and the increased ticket sales and the shows he put on. He had a band, the first in league history, and a team song and halftime surprises galore.

Corinne Griffith, the silent screen star and Marshall's second wife, wrote the words to "Hail to the Redskins." They had been married in 1936, and she had no choice but to get involved with the team if she were to keep much of his attention. In her book *My Life With the Redskins*, Griffith (no relation to the baseball family) wrote that sitting with Marshall at a game could try her patience. He always was jumping up, yelling at an official and sometimes even rushing down to the field to confront an official or a Redskins coach, to whom he would "suggest" plays and personnel changes. Griffith wrote, "A pair of flying coattails whipped me smartly in the face as George clambered over the railing to the field, en route for a man-to-man chat with the referee."

Marshall tried one of these talks once with Flaherty. Jim Barber, a former tackle who lives in Spokane and is the only living player from the original Washington Redskins team besides Baugh, recalled, "Marshall came down to the bench and right up to Ray. Marshall said, 'You've got to get so-and-so into the game if you want to win.' Ray looked at him and said, 'Mr. Marshall, if you want me to coach, get back up in the seats. If you want to coach, take over right now and I'll go back home.' Marshall never challenged Ray again."

Marshall also never forgot, which eventually would be a factor in the team's late-1940s decline. But in 1937 the Redskins were the toast of Washington, and Marshall had the sense not to spoil something good by firing Flaherty, as he would many other coaches. A rarely deflated Marshall returned to his seat and kept an unusual silence. The experience burned him. He was, after all, Mr. Somebody, with one of his desks in the Redskins office in front of the large window on 9th Street, so people could look in, past the wooden cigar-store Indian he had placed out front, and see him at "work." He fancied himself a showman, and being on display was part of his showmanship.

Marshall had, in fact, tried to pursue a theater career, starting in New York in 1914, but he hadn't gotten very far. He nonetheless loved being on the public stage and talking incessantly, which made him a target for newspapermen's zingers. Rodger H. Pippen of the *Baltimore News-Post*, who knew an egotist when he saw one, called Marshall "always his own best pal." Another wrote Marshall up as "a man of a few words — a few thousand."

His hair parted in the middle and slicked back, Marshall cut a figure in elegant double-breasted suits with a triangle of handkerchief jutting from his breast pocket. He dressed like an owner of something important. In Washington he was, but in Boston he hadn't been. He and three others had bought an available franchise in 1932, moved into Braves Field and named their football team the Boston Braves after the baseball team. The next year Marshall moved the team a few blocks to Fenway and thought up the name Redskins.

His performance at the NFL's owners' meeting of 1932 wasn't worthy of Broadway, but it was an attention-getter. The moguls, meeting in Atlantic City, were about to disband from a hotel ballroom when a newcomer among their ranks got to his feet. "Gentlemen. I have some proposals to make concerning changes in the rules," he said, as one magazine reported. The NFL owners weren't accustomed to changing rules. But he anticipated their initial thought: What does a laundry man know about football rules?

"I realize that you men know your football inside and out. I know football only from the spectator's point of view. But that's why I'm speaking to you. From the spectator's point of view, the kind of football you play makes a lousy show. It's dull, uninteresting, boring. The way I look at it, we're in show business. And when a show becomes boring to the public you throw it out and put a more interesting one in its place. That's why I want to change the rules. I want to give the public the kind of show they want." He wanted goal posts on the goal line to make field goals more important and other alterations. The next year, the NFL created a rules committee, and his proposals were adopted.

Boston was frustrating in one way or another. The story goes that Marshall trooped over to Harvard Yard to meet with the school's president. Marshall wanted to hire Eddie Casey, the football coach, and launched his plea without any indication of the sport he was talking about. "Casey? Casey?" Harvard President A. Lawrence Lowell said finally. "Doesn't he have something to do with one of our minor sports?

Champs: The Washington Post of December 13, 1937 reports the Redskins' championship victory in their first Washington season.

In Boston Marshall couldn't give away tickets and couldn't coax newspapermen to write about his team. He took this as a personal setback, because he had prided himself on his sales ability since his boyhood. He was born October 13, 1897 in Grafton, West Virginia, and at the age of 9 placed an ad for his pet rabbit in his father's newspaper. Young Marshall received no response. So he tried again, this time hyping the rabbit: "Fine Jacksonville hare for sale." He had three offers and sold to the highest bidder.

Marshall had done all he could to make a success in Boston. In 1936 he had stopped in New York to hire a football player for his team. That night Marshall was to join his new wife on the train from Washington, and together they would continue on to Boston. Marshall got on the train thinking football. Not so his bride.

"It was to be our first railroad trip together," she wrote. "Around one in the morning

Continued on Page 25

George Preston Marshall

No Boredom or Blacks Allowed

By Shirley Povich

The man who brought the Redskins to Washington in 1937 was an uncommon laundry chain owner with a bent for show business. He was widely considered (1) one of pro football's greatest innovators and (2) its leading bigot.

George Preston Marshall was a dashing fellow whose love of show business manifested itself in many ways. It was evident in his own failed fling at acting, in his first marriage to a former Ziegfeld Follies girl and in his second to silent screen goddess Corinne Griffith. It was apparent in his invention of halftime extravaganzas worthy of Hollywood and in his ground-breaking radio and TV broadcasts of football games. It was what mainly drove the NFL rules changes he engineered — to make sure nobody got bored with a gridiron performance.

Marshall liked to live the part. One of his trademarks during football season was his full-length raccoon coat. Another was his always-at-the-ready chauffeured limousine. (He never acquired a driver's license, hated to fly and loved riding railroads.)

Marshall also produced a few theatrical shows in Washington, including a musical called "Getting Gertie's Garter." This was in addition to running the Palace Laundry inherited from his father. In fact, he built the laundry from two stores into a 57-outlet chain before selling out in 1948, making the "Long Live Linen" slogan emblazoned on its trucks a byword in Washington.

The year he brought the Redskins to Washington, he even did a stint as publisher of Hearst's *Washington Times*. That was on the heels of another year in which the mercurial Marshall accepted a $100,000 salary to be director of the Great Texas and Pan-American Exposition in Dallas. All the while, he managed to superintend his football team, with the tight-fisted Marshall watching every penny.

For the 24 years when he was identified as the leading racist in the NFL, he simply stared down the criticism of his refusal to sign a black player. It was the only subject on which the voluble Marshall never expressed a public opinion, never resorted to a quip. But he bristled when this columnist reminded him in print that "the Redskins colors are burgundy, gold and Caucasian."

He caved in, finally, when Interior Secretary Stewart Udall issued an ultimatum: Sign a black player or be denied use of the new 54,000-seat D.C. Stadium (later renamed RFK) that the government had paid for, and to hell with the 30-year lease Marshall had signed. Marshall's chief response

THE WASHINGTON STAR

was to make Ernie Davis, Syracuse's all-American running back, his No.1 draft choice for 1962. Ernie Davis's response was: "I won't play for that S.O.B." He demanded to be traded and was, to Cleveland, for all-pro Bobby Mitchell. The Ernie Davis tale had a sad denouement; he developed cancer and died in 1963, never playing a down for Cleveland.

Some argued that Marshall's anti-black policy was grounded more in commerce than in prejudice. Marshall had brought his football team to Washington with a plan to make the Redskins "the South's team." To that end, he established a network of radio stations in Southern cities and towns to carry the games, and he directed his coaches to draft players mostly from Georgia, North Carolina, Virginia and Texas colleges. They did, and the team became the Confederates of the NFL. One original line in the Redskins' fight song went, "Fight for Old Dixie," before it was revised to "Fight for Old D.C."

To this day, many season ticket holders make the trip north on Sunday from South and North Carolina, Richmond and the Tidewater areas of Virginia.

Commercial concerns, however, couldn't explain away the provision in Marshall's will seeking to forbid funds that he had provided for child welfare programs from going to anyone with integrationist notions. That intent was foiled after his death in 1969.

To Marshall the NFL meant entertainment. He was, for example, the first owner to form a volunteer team marching band. In 1937, when 10,000 wild-eyed Washington fans boarded special trains to New York to watch the Redskins beat the Giants for the division title, sports writer Bill Corum of the *New York Journal-American* wrote: "George Preston Marshall slipped unobtrusively into New York today at the head of a 100-piece band."

He also would argue furiously with referees from his box or the field, never more so than after the infamous final-game loss to the Giants two years later when Bill Halloran ruled that Bo Russell's last-minute field goal kick was wide. Marshall positively erupted and wanted Halloran banned from officiating at NFL games. Halloran never did referee again, though it was not clear whether that was because of Marshall's fury.

What was clear was that not all of the angry Redskins fans at the Polo Grounds that day were sober. Of the scores of irate letters I received about Russell's kick, one was particularly memorable. "I was sitting on the 50-yard line," the fan wrote. "I saw two balls and two sets of goal posts, and I know damn well one of those balls went through one set of those posts."

Redskin fans had no complaints with Marshall in those early years. He delivered five title appearances in the Redskins' first nine years in Washington, winning two championships. He spent generously on halftime shows that had no equal in other cities. He even had surprise halftime arrivals of Santa Claus at final home games, with fans wondering each year whether Santa would make his entrance by helicopter, space ship, reindeer or motorcycle. One year Santa never made it into the stadium: Arriving by parachute, he drifted over Griffith Stadium's right field wall.

Marshall's coaches, though, were not always so pleased with him. When it came to inteferring with them, he was the expert, often calling plays from his box or on the field and sometimes even making his own substitutions. When it came to dispensing with coaches, he had an itchy trigger finger. Six head coaches passed through his revolving door in the team's first 14 years in Washington.

One of his more notable moments of meddling occurred when his team was still in Boston and his head coach was Lone Star Dietz. One day before the kickoff, he told Dietz: "If we win the toss, I want you to kick off."

On the way to the press box where Marshall took up his usual station, outfitted with earphones and a phone to the bench, Marshall heard: "Redskins win toss." When he arrived in the box, he had difficulty adjusting the headphones, which were in a tangle. When he finally fixed them, he was astonished to look out on the field and see the Redskins in kick-receiving formation. He called Dietz and fumed, "Dammit, Dietz, I thought I told you to kick off, not receive."

And Dietz said, "Where have you been, George? We did kick off, and they ran it back for a touchdown."

Marshall won the admiration of other NFL owners, who swept Marshall into the Pro Football Hall of Fame as a charter member. This was not only because they followed his lead with halftime shows, marching bands, radio networks or the TV broadcasts he began in 1950, important as all those were. The owners had cause to honor Marshall for contributing much to the game.

He had succeeded, for example, in ending a rule that hampered quarterbacks by forbidding them to launch a pass within five yards of a line of scrimmage. He eliminated plays so near the sideline that they crimped signal calling; Marshall asked for and won a new rule saying the ball could be moved to new hashmarks 10 yards from out-of-bounds. His most important innovation, though, was his proposal to separate the league into two divisions. That kept more teams alive in the title races, with a corresponding increase in fan interest. "The game was getting too dull," said Marshall, ever the entertainer.

To pull off his plans for the Redskins in Washington, Marshall had sought to enlist the help of sportswriters. "I need the support of you guys," he said. "I'm paying Sammy Baugh $8,000, and I need to put 12,000 people in the park [Griffith Stadium] to break even." In 1937 the Redskins sold 958 season tickets. By 1947, with the help of Marshall's promotional flair, all of the stadium's 31,440 regular seats were selling out.

Marshall had bought into pro-football on the cheap, a partner with three others in the purchase, for $1,500, of an idle franchise in 1932. Three years later he bought out his partners, for another $1,500.

But he was unhappy in Boston, where he couldn't get many people to games. In 1936, when the Boston Redskins were to host Green Bay in the league title game in Finley Park, Marshall abruptly moved the game to New York, outraging Boston fans. He could be like that. "There were times on game day," he explained, "when the Boston papers played the Radcliffe girls' field hockey team above the Redskins game."

Marshall would get angry with coverage in other ways as well. In 1942 Marshall told *The Washington Post* that this writer was denied access to the press box in the Redskins Club House for sins like making light of Marshall's coaching experience with observations like, "He learned his football in a raccoon coat." He even sought to get me fired for my columns. An indignant *Washington Post* managing editor, Casey Jones, told Marshall: "You run your goddamn Redskins and I'll run *The Washington Post*."

The next year Marshall sued this writer and *Post* publisher Eugene Meyer for $200,000, charging libel and defamation of character for a report that the Redskins had taken a check for $13,000 out of an Army relief charity game. Marshall charged that he had been called unpatriotic, a swindler and a defrauder of widows and orphans. The jury ruled that Marshall had not been defamed.

Nobody, though, could doubt his business or negotiating skills. Jack Kent Cooke paid $350,000 in 1961 for 25 percent of the team Marshall had established for $1,500 in 1932. To a friend Marshall once described that transaction:

Marshall: "Let me tell you what you're buying. The Redskins make $100,000 a year. That's my salary."

Cooke: "No problem."

Marshall: "You buy the Redskins and you'll be getting your name in the paper."

Cooke: "No problem."

Marshall: "You're also buying my house in Georgetown."

Cooke: "No problem."

Marshall: "And my apartment in town."

Cooke: "No problem."

Marshall: "My chauffeur and car are on the Redskins payroll and go with the deal."

Cooke: "No problem."

Marshall: "Welcome, partner."

■

Shows and yells: Marshall was ever promoting the team or screaming at referees and players. From top, counterclockwise: posing with local twins who jointly were named Miss Redskins of 1954; a halftime arrival of Santa Clause by helicopter, and Marshall shouting from his box at Griffith Stadium.

PHOTOS BY THE WASHINGTON STAR

the train pulled into New York and George came aboard, triumphantly reporting that he had got his gridman. I stepped into the washroom to put on a lacy negligee, and then stuck my head out for a moment to ask some unimportant question. George was already sound asleep, and in the lower berth at that.

"I was still fuming, and George was still snoring, when I got myself down from the upper the next morning. George must be punished, I decided. I would make him think I had left. I dressed, slipped out into the car, and took a seat where he would be unable to see me from the room.

"In due time he appeared in the doorway and anxiously peered this way and that. Finally, in obvious agitation, he started calling for the porter. I began to feel ashamed of my little scheme. George had been dead tired from his talent hunting, and I was just being feminine and unreasonable.

"The porter came running up. 'Porter!' said George excitedly. 'Have you seen anything of that big football player I brought on the train last night? I went to a lot of trouble to sign him.' "

The Marshalls were divorced in 1957. Marshall's marriage to Boston was briefer. He closed the show after attracting only a few more to the last 1935 home game than his Redskins would draw to their first practice in Washington.

In Washington large crowds kept coming to Griffith Stadium, and the Redskins more often than not won. In 1937 they won eight games and lost three, finishing the regular season with a 14-6 victory over the defending champion Packers and a 49-14 drubbing of the Giants, in which Baugh completed 11 of 15 passes and future Hall of Famer Cliff Battles got off touchdown runs of 75 and 76 yards. An estimated 10,000 Washington fans invaded New York for that game, marching up Broadway behind the band. As Eastern Division champions for the second straight year, they would take on the Bears at Wrigley Field in Chicago.

The Redskins-Bears rivalry can be compared in Redskins' history only to the more recent one with the Dallas Cowboys. Redskins-Bears meant everything that pro football could offer: giants who trod the earth playing 60 minutes, usually on bitter-cold days, always with the most brutal combat the game allowed.

When Baugh and Battles led the Redskins into Wrigley Field, it was into freezing weather. The field was slick with ice. Both teams wore sneakers. Three thousand

Washington fans had made it all the way to the Midwest to join 12,000 Bears fans. Robert Ruark, later renowned as the author of the novel *Something of Value* and other works, wrote in his *Washington Daily News* piece: "It was colder than nine miles in an iceberg, slippery as a Vaselined eel, and wetter than a duck's spats."

When Baugh knocked the Bears' Dick Plasman out of bounds in front of the Redskins bench, a football war broke out. Ruark: "The team arose as one Indian, and systematically commenced to separate Mr. Plasman from his hair, hide and tallow." Officials pulled apart a pile of players only to find the Washington trainer, Roy Baker, atop Plasman. "He had fastened himself to Plasman's pelt," wrote Ruark, "and apparently was trying to bite his initials into Dick's ear. In between bites he was belaboring Plasman's puss with both knotty little fists, and a luscious, iridescent mouse even then had appeared on Plasman's peeper."

The score? Washington 28, Chicago 21.

The lead kept changing. The Redskins scored first, Battles running in on a short-yardage reverse. But the Bears scored two straight touchdowns, the second one after Baugh threw an interception. Baugh also banged up his knee and sat out the end of the first half and the early minutes of the second half. Little wonder Baugh was hurt. When he was playing defensive back, Bronko Nagurski kept running right at him. "He'd just run straight up and try to knock me down and step on me," Baugh recalled. "I couldn't understand why nobody ever tried to block me out of the plays until [Bears tackle] Joe Stydahar told me after the game that they had orders not to waste a blocker on me. They didn't think it was necessary when Nagurski had the ball. If I was fool enough to try to tackle him, they figured that was my own fault."

But early in the third period Baugh limped onto the field when it became apparent that he was needed. And the first time he touched the ball he threw a 55-yard touchdown pass to Millner.

The Bears plugged away and made it 21-14. But Baugh retaliated again — and one can only imagine TCU coach Dutch Meyer listening on radio, wondering whatever happened to the short pass, as Baugh slung another scoring pass to Millner on a play that covered 77 yards. Millner, a big-game player from Notre Dame, was having one of his greatest days since catching a last-minute pass from Bill (The Bard) Shakespeare to give the Irish an 18-13 victory over Ohio State in 1935, a game for the ages. With the

Redskins and Bears tied at 21, Baugh threw a 35-yard touchdown pass to Ed Justice. That gave Baugh three scoring passes in 10 minutes, and he would finish with 335 yards passing. The defense did the rest. An interception by Riley Smith clinched it.

The Redskins' play of 1937 suggested a dynasty. Baugh won the league's passing title, the first of six he would garner, and he signed a three-year contract at $10,000 a year. Battles retired prematurely when Marshall refused to raise his salary from $2,800 to $4,000. But Flaherty engineered a trade with Pittsburgh for Frank Filchock, demonstrating again Pittsburgh's knack for letting good throwers get away and giving the Redskins an unusual bounty of two excellent passers. With his No. 1 draft pick, Flaherty got Andy Farkas, from the University of Detroit; Farkas would become the running-back replacement for Battles and the Redskins' famous number 44 before John Riggins. He was 5 feet, 10 ° inches and 190 pounds.

"He had short legs, and that was how he was able to run. He ran with his head down and his eyes up, blue eyes up. A lot of times he played without his helmet," said Ellen Farkas, Andy's wife of 58 years. "He played eight years, 60 minutes a game."

But the Redskins fell just short of championships in 1938 and 1939. Baugh was injured off and on during both years, although he played hurt, and a 36-0 defeat at New York ended the Redskins' 1938 season and their title hopes. Flaherty suggested taking the team west for training camp the following summer, to his hometown of Spokane. That began the Redskins' tradition of training in the West, which for years was highlighted by a charity exhibition game against the Rams in the Los Angeles Coliseum.

In 1939, Flaherty set up camp at Cheney Normal School, 18 miles outside of Spokane. The clear air buoyed the spirits. More importantly, Baugh stayed a bit healthier that season, and the team went 8-2-1. The "1" was a scoreless tie with the Giants in the second game of the season, the only scoreless game in Redskins history. In a victory over Pittsburgh, Filchock flipped a pass from his own end zone to Farkas, who went 99 yards for a touchdown — a Redskins distinction to be duplicated in years to come by George Izo and Bobby Mitchell and then Sonny Jurgensen and Gerry Allen. Redskins title hopes for 1939 hinged, as they often did, on the final regular-season game with the Giants. Played before 50,000 at the Polo Grounds, that game proved as controversial as any the Redskins would ever play.

The Giants took a 9-0 lead into the fourth quarter with three field goals. But the Redskins' Wee Willie Wilkin, a mammoth tackle, blocked a punt, and Filchock threw a touchdown pass to Bob Masterson, who kicked the point after. It was 9-7.

With less than two minutes to play, the Redskins drove to the Giants' 7-yard line. Then, with seven seconds to go, Bo Russell put his foot to a field goal attempt that would win the East. He had not missed all season. Nor did the Redskins believe he missed that one. They celebrated as the ball soared high into the air, and several Giants, heads down, walked away. But referee Bill Halloran ruled that the ball went wide of the right upright. Flaherty was incensed, charging up to the referee as the Giants scurried from the field with the title. Marshall, some people thought, would tear his own hair out. Halloran never officiated another game, although it was never clear whether the few thousand words of venom Marshall uttered over the next weeks were decisive.

A 9-2 Redskins team had been denied, and hearts were heavy among the thousands of Washington rooters who had journeyed to New York and among all those back home.

Fan interest continued to surge. For 1940, temporary bleachers would be added along one sideline at Griffith Stadium. Six home games sold for $9. The team moved to a new training facility, still in Washington State but at Flaherty's alma mater, Gonzaga. There, the Redskins lived like the champions they had been and the champions they felt confident of becoming again.

Vincent X. Flaherty, the *Washington Times-Herald* sports columnist, called the facility "the most ultramodern" he'd seen, "with its rigging of nickeled heat lamps, violet ray contraptions, lily-white cots and rubbing tables which would make a Hollywood masseur blink in admiration."

Going into the 1940 season, Flaherty and his players were upbeat; they sensed a repeat of 1937. Nevertheless, some days Marshall would go around grumbling — even complaining about Baugh, of all people. There was a reason, of course: Baugh's three-year contract would be up after the season, and Marshall already was planning to pay him as little as he could while trying to goad him to further greatness, as if Sammy needed inspiration. "I think he will get out of football if he bumps into another spotty season," Marshall told a reporter. "I think he will make a good coach. It's unfortunately true that the last two of Sammy's seasons here have been spotty." He said that Baugh would never be as good as he was in 1937.

Another day Marshall predicted that Wendell Willkie would win the presidency from

More for Moore: A 1943 run by Wilbur Moore, whose early return from surgery helped win the Eastern title that year.

FDR and that the Redskins would win the championship. Marshall loved seeing his name in print; it fed his ego and helped keep the turnstiles spinning.

The Redskins of 1940 were, in the current vernacular, "awesome." They won their first seven games. And yet before kicking off at Griffith Stadium, they had traveled 7,229 miles by train, getting to and from camp and making exhibition-game stops. In Boston, where the Redskins' departure now was rued, 25,000 showed up to watch them beat a team of College All-Stars. Washington knew what it had, and the excitement was palpable when the likes of the Giants came to town in the season's second game. These were the Giants who, in Washingtonians' minds, had "stolen" the Eastern Division title the previous December.

This time the Redskins won, 21-7, before 34,713 at a packed Griffith Stadium as Dick Todd ran back a punt 78 yards for one Washington touchdown. Flaherty had assembled such depth that he was able to insert Todd into his backfield after Farkas had been sidelined by knee surgery during the exhibition season. Todd played so well in several games that Baugh, rarely euphoric, was moved to remark, "Dick Todd is the greatest running back I've ever seen in my life — and I'm not excepting Cliff Battles. Get Dick into the open field and nobody will catch him."

After a 16-14 loss to the Brooklyn Dodgers, the Redskins took on the hated Bears at home in the season's ninth game. Since their 1937 title game, they had played only once, but it had been an embarrassment for the Redskins: The Bears had crushed them, 31-7, in Chicago in 1938. An enraged Marshall ran down on the field once during that game, though he stayed away from Flaherty. George Halas, the Bears' owner-coach, chortled after the game in the presence of an attentive scribe: "That's too bad, girlies. I'm awfully sorry my boys were a little rough. What say we all go down to the corner for a double banana split and a fistful of chocolate eclairs? And get this, Gertrude — one more squeak out of you pantywaists and I'll lick the lot of you myself, and that goes for your boss, too."

Neither team would bend in the 1940 game, a late-season defensive struggle. Baugh twice punted more than 70 yards. The difference was an 18-yard touchdown pass from Filchock to Todd — that and an ankle tackle by Todd that stopped the Bears at the Redskins' 1-yard line. The final score was 7-3. Marshall acted as if the score had been 70-3 or something. "The Bears are a team that folds under pressure in the second half against a good team," he said. "If they come here to play us in the championship game, they'll have to win by a big score or they won't win at all."

When the rematch was set for the championship, Marshall continued his tirades. Baugh wished Marshall would shut up. "I never played against a poor Bears team," Baugh recalled. "I always thought they had the toughest damn defense in the league. Day in and day out, they were the best team when I was up there. We never had any game with them that was easy. Any time we went up against them we got two or three boys hurt.

"We're getting ready to play the championship game, and Mr. Marshall called them crybabies. That's the way to get a team ready for you; you don't want to say things like that. A lot of the boys hated that. They hated what Mr. Marshall was putting out."

Marshall didn't have to say anything anymore to fill the stadium. As Flaherty noted before the 1940 title game, "We could sell 100,000 tickets." So it wasn't hype that Marshall was spewing — it was malice. To know fully the kind of man he was, people would have to wait until after his death in 1969. It was well known that he was the last in the NFL to integrate his team, and he did so only because he no longer had any choice. His will further documented his meanness. It called for funds from his estate to go for child welfare programs, but attached this stipulation: "Said corporation shall never use, contribute or apply its money or property for any purpose which supports or employs the principle of racial integration in any form . . .'"

In 1940, Marshall's tirades infuriated the Bears. Washington fans were on edge. *The Washington Post*, giving unique advance notice, advertised that the game account would appear Monday on the front page. Who could have imagined how bad the news would be? A crowd of 36,034 squeezed into Griffith Stadium. And then: The Bears scored 11 touchdowns.

Unbelievable, but true: 73-0.

The Post did not print the game account on the front page.

If the turning point of that game wasn't the dawning of day itself, some placed it early in the first period when the Redskins suffered a mishap. The Bears had taken a 7-0 lead in the first minute as Chicago's (Bullet) Bill Osmanski swept around left end and raced down the sideline 68 yards. Halas would say later, "When I saw the type of blocking we were getting on that play, I knew it was only a question of the final score."

Still, when the Redskins got the ball back, it looked to be a game. Max Krause, the first player Flaherty obtained by trade, returned the kickoff 56 yards to the Bears' 40-yard line. From there Baugh calmly continued the attack. At the Chicago 26-yard-line, he threw to Charley Malone for what appeared a certain touchdown. But Malone dropped the pass. What followed was the Redskins' Waterloo.

An irate Marshall stormed into the dressing room afterward. Reporters surrounded him. "They quit," Marshall screamed. "Some of our players were yellow. There were too many high-paid players on our club trying to get by on their reputation. There'll be plenty of new faces next year."

Marshall also blamed Filchock for not using Todd and the recovered Farkas to run the ball. Filchock, when informed of this, suggested that the score was 21-0 when he first got to play and that passes were in order.

A reporter asked Baugh what he thought would have happened had Malone caught the pass. "The score would have been 73-7," Baugh replied.

Tackle Jim Barber recalled: "My locker was close and I thought, 'Damn good answer, Sam.' We stunk it up pretty bad. But then everybody in town had an excuse for us. Walking downtown, nobody said, 'Hey, you bums.' They were all for us. 'You just had a bad day.'"

Jock Sutherland, Brooklyn's coach, saw it all and summed it up. "The Bears," he said, "were just the greatest team I ever saw."

Flaherty went home to Spokane to solitude. His wife Jackie, whom he married in 1946, recalled that Marshall had given Flaherty a dog, "a championship dog, a boxer, a great big boxer. I hated to hear about the 73-0. Ray said the dog was the only one who loved him."

It took the Redskins some time to get over the shock. Baugh, of course, never considered retiring, and Marshall wouldn't have let him. Still, the 1941 Redskins turned in the poorest record in Flaherty's regime, 6-5. They salvaged a winning season with a 20-14 victory over Philadelphia at Griffith Stadium, but no one celebrated that night — it was December 7, and all anyone could think of was Pearl Harbor and war.

Flaherty, like so many others, knew that his days as a civilian were numbered, and he was eager to serve. He would have one more season with the Redskins — and he would make the best of it. "He had a brilliant football mind," Barber said. "He developed the screen pass. He could handle players. He knew when to kick you in the fanny and pat you on the back. Everyone respected him. Sammy had eight coaches with the Redskins, but Ray was the best by far."

The 1942 Redskins went 10-1. Their only loss was 14-7 to the Giants in the second game of the season, a score they reversed against the Giants amid a nine-game winning streak. The Redskins allowed only 13 points in their last four games. Once more, their title-game foe would be the Bears. The Bears, who had won 18 straight games, were favored.

Flaherty was feisty. "If the Bears want to get tough in the clinches," he told reporters, "we'll get tough, too. You can look at the pictures and see how they use their hands and get away with other stuff that should be called by the officials. This time we're going along with them and play their way. If there's some rough stuff, we're going to be in on it."

Flaherty took his one assistant coach, former tackle Turk Edwards, with him to scout the Bears in Chicago in their last game of the season, against the Chicago Cardinals. They left Baugh and Wee Willie Wilkin to run practice. For his reading displeasure Flaherty found this in a Chicago newspaper: "The Bears say that Sammy Baugh is the most overrated passer in football. They point to the records which show that Sid Luckman [of the Bears] and Cecil Isbell [of the Packers] do more damage with one pass than Baugh does with five. Baugh gets his team to the 50-yard line with five short passes and Luckman and Isbell get their teams over the goal line with one."

ASSOCIATED PRESS

*Backs in front:
The Redskins'1942
backfield of, from left,
Wilbur Moore, Cecil
Hare, Sammy Baugh
and Andy Farkas*

More importantly, Flaherty and Edwards returned from Chicago with film from the Bears' 21-7 victory over the Cardinals. *The Washington Post* reported that Flaherty would prepare his Redskins with lighter physical training than usual and more through "the medium of lectures and motion pictures."

Baugh, having learned a lot from Marshall's behavior before the 1940 championship game, all but conferred sainthood on the Bears, even though everyone knew how rough they were. "Ah wouldn't say they're meaner than any other team," Baugh said. "The Bears just play harder. That's what they're supposed to do, after all. They make it look rougher because four or five of 'em hit a ball carrier at the same time. A lot of 'em get the same idea at the same time about making a tackle, and you can't condemn 'em for that."

NFL commissioner Elmer Layden ordered "a clean game." Halas, a lieutenant commander in the Navy, flew in from duty in Oklahoma and watched in uniform from the Bears' bench as Heartley (Hunk) Anderson did the coaching, as he would until Halas returned after the war. What Halas saw was the Redskins upsetting Chicago, 14-6, and winning the championship on Baugh's all-round play.

Behind 6-0 as time was running out in the first period, Baugh quick-kicked because he had the wind with him. The ball went 85 yards. Baugh explained later, "If I waited until the second quarter I would've had to kick into the wind."

Shortly afterward, Baugh threw a touchdown pass to Wilbur Moore, who caught the ball over his shoulder. The play followed a Moore interception. The Redskins had three interceptions in all, one by Baugh in the Redskins' end zone to hold off the Bears. The Redskins outgained the Bears on interception-return yardage, 114-0. Luckman did not have a good day. He ended up with two yards net passing. The Redskins put away the game on a 1-yard plunge by Farkas. Afterward, the subdued victors, knowing they were about to lose their coach, posed for a team photo; Flaherty sat in front, his boxer at his knee. He was bound for the Navy in two days, never to coach another game for the Redskins.

In his six seasons in Washington Flaherty won two NFL championships and three Eastern division titles (and he was 2-1 against the Bears in title games). His 49-17-3 record gave him a winning percentage of more than 73.5, the best of any coach in Redskins history.

George Marshall started spinning his revolving door for coaches. Arthur (Dutch) Bergman was up first, and the 1943 Redskins were off fast with four straight victories. Farkas, who led the team in rushing for four seasons, returned the opening kickoff 84 yards against the Cardinals. In a 48-10 victory at Brooklyn, Baugh played 60 minutes and threw six touchdown passes. Later in the season against Detroit, he intercepted Heisman Trophy winner Frankie Sinkwich four times as the Redskins won, 42-20. If Baugh wasn't the Babe Ruth of football, no one was. Like Ruth, who pitched before he became a home run hitter, Baugh excelled at every phase of his game. In 1943 he led the league in passing and interceptions, with 11 takeaways. His career punting average of 45.1 yards is an NFL record that still stands.

The 1943 Redskins again appeared to have everything necessary, even a distinguished water boy. He was none other than Max Krause. By then in the Navy, he was stationed at Anacostia, and at every opportunity he did chores for the team. Vincent X. Flaherty wrote that Krause wanted "nothing more than the chance to imparadise himself in the environment." In games, Krause rushed the water bucket onto the field. During a timeout in one game, he warned the players, hunched down taking their breather, that the Giants were cross-firing on their rushes to try to block Baugh's punts. No one listened to the water boy. And when the Giants did, in fact, block a punt, that was the ball game.

Wilbur Moore was injured in that game and had to be hospitalized for surgery. Krause gave blood for the transfusion Moore needed. The Redskins lost once more to the Giants the following week, to set up yet a third straight Redskins-Giants game, this one for the Eastern title. The Redskins won the most important of the three consecutive meetings: Moore returned faster than expected, adding inspiration to Baugh's 16-for-21 handiwork in a 28-0 victory. Moore's effort moved line coach Turk Edwards to remark, "That was Max running the ball out there on Wilbur Moore's legs. You couldn't lick a combination like that, with Krause's blood on top of the Moore's courage."

And so for the world championship one more time . . . the Chicago Bears.

Baugh and Luckman would duel in the wind — at least that was the prospect in Chicago. But Baugh was kicked in the head while making a tackle on Luckman on a punt return, and he had to be helped from the field. He suffered a mild concussion, missing two-thirds of the game, and the Bears won easily, 41-21. Luckman had a good day — five touchdown passes. Bundled in blankets against the cold, Baugh wept on the Redskins bench as teammates leaned close to him, trying to console him.

"What's going on out there? Why won't they let me play?" Baugh reportedly cried.

"What's the matter, Baugh, lost your guts?" a Bear is said to have shouted at him.

One more time, too, Marshall took to the field, showing up close to the Chicago bench near the end of the first half. Ralph Brizzolara, the Bears' president, yelled at him, "You're trying to listen in on our strategy talks. You're trying to steal our plays."

"Like hell I am," Marshall responded. "I came down here to see you and Halas at the half, and I got here too early. I'm just standing here waiting for the half to end."

Police and ushers had to escort Marshall away. He repaired to the Redskins' locker room, where he futilely ordered them to win.

The Bears victory left an impression of another kind on Marshall. Luckman had switched successfully to the T-formation, and now Marshall thought it time for Baugh to do the same. So in 1944, with Bergman retired to broadcasting and Dudley DeGroot in as the next head coach, it was T time in Washington. "We didn't have a boy on the team who had played the T," Baugh recalled.

But Baugh's bigger challenge was war-related. His cattle-raising had been important in providing beef for the military, and that fact had gotten him a "rancher's exemption" from the draft. By 1944 he had to oversee the cattle-raising himself. He pitched in with the work, making certain that the government got its beef shipments on time. He missed the first two games of the season and afterward could fly to Washington only on weekends to lead the team.

Filchock, back from the Coast Guard, had to do the weekday chores in practice. Clark Shaughnessy, T-formation guru who was coaching at the University of Maryland, instructed Filchock, who responded by leading the league in passing. But it was not to be Washington's year. The Redskins wore down late in the season, losing three of their last four games.

Going into 1945, Redskins fans had no way of knowing two things: that this would be another great season, and that it would be the end of an era of greatness. After 1945, Baugh would never again play in a championship game; he would retire after the 1952 season. And the Redskins, a power on the Potomac through the 1945 season, would manage only three winning seasons until Vince Lombardi's arrival as coach in the distant future.

The turning point of the 1945 season came in the third game against a tough Philadelphia team. The Redskins won in a 24-14 upset; they then won six straight and finished by shutting out Pittsburgh and the Giants. As Eastern Division champions, the Redskins earned a trip to play the Cleveland Rams in the title game. It would be Baugh versus Bob Waterfield. It also would be cold — six degrees at Municipal Stadium. The Redskins band could scarcely blow a note. On the bench, Redskins wore parkas and kept their legs warm by covering them with blankets and, of all things, hay.

The footing was treacherous because of an icy field. But the Redskins came prepared — they had brought tennis shoes from home. The home team, inexplicably, had no tennis shoes. Before the game, Cleveland's coach, Adam Walsh, pleaded with DeGroot not to let the Redskins wear sneakers. "I'd appreciate it if we could play this game on even terms," he said. In a gesture of sportsmanship, Dud DeGroot agreed. With that, everyone began skidding around the field.

If 73-0 was the game Redskins' fans wish could be stricken from the books, a play that always would haunt the team occurred in the first period of that 1945 championship game in Cleveland. Passing from his own end zone toward a wide-open Millner, Baugh

Passers and receivers: At left, Harry Gilmer (62) with legendary quarterback Sammy Baugh. Above, the younger Hal Crisler (55) gets a few tips from seasoned Redskins end Hugh (Bones) Taylor.

hit the goal post. "Wayne would have gone the rest of the distance, no question," said Al Demao, then a rookie. As it happened, the ball fell back into the end zone. It was an automatic safety, according to the rules then (Marshall would get that rule changed for 1946). The score was 2-0, Cleveland.

At the half, Marshall showed up in the Redskins locker room, demanding to know why the team wasn't wearing sneakers. DeGroot revealed his "gentleman's agreement." "What do you mean, gentleman's agreement?" Demao remembered Marshall roaring. Demao: "DeGroot finished the game, but actually he was fired on the spot," making way for yet another head coach, Turk Edwards.

The final score of that loss to Cleveland was 15-14. Baugh always would hold himself accountable. "If I hadn't done that," he recalled, remorse in his Texas drawl, "we would have won the game."

Thus began the long decline of the Redskins.

Marshall made no effort to bring back Flaherty after the war. It was evident why. "Ray didn't let anybody dominate him, which was difficult when he was working for Marshall," recalled his wife.

Flaherty signed on in 1946 as head coach of the New York Yankees of the new All-American Football Conference. Flaherty's Yankees were impressive: 10-3-1 in 1946 and 11-2-1 in 1947 before he had a falling-out with owner Dan Topping after four games in 1948. In 1949 Flaherty accepted the impossible task of trying to make the AAFC's Chicago Hornets respectable. He then retired to Hayden Lake, Idaho, and was inducted into the Pro Football Hall of Fame in 1976. He died in 1994 at the age of 90.

As the AAFC went after big-name players and coaches from the NFL, salaries went up a bit, but Marshall failed to keep pace. "Mr. Marshall started getting rid of some of the boys," Baugh said. "Only one guy I ever told Mr. Marshall to keep. I said, 'Don't ever get rid of Filchock. He's a hell of a good quarterback.' Two years later, he traded him to the Giants."

The Redskins were aging, Marshall let players go, and Marshall never again found a coach to match Flaherty. The best the Redskins could offer, for a long time beginning in the late 1940s, were individual standouts. Mostly, though, there were dreary defeats.

The Post's Shirley Povich put this bottom line to one of the Redskins' particularly harsh losses in 1947, a 56-20 thrashing by the Bears: "They are suffering from Halas-tosis." In the lean late-1940s — and for years to come — they suffered a form of it against every other team, too.

Slingin' Sammy Baugh

The Magic of Number 33

By Shirley Povich

An event occurred in Washington in 1937. A skinny young Texan named Sammy Baugh arrived that year, and pro football would never be the same. Baugh became the biggest name in the game and took the Redskins to four NFL titles in the next seven years. His special magic was the forward pass, as it had never been thrown before.

Rookie Baugh scoffed at pro-football's view that the forward pass was a no-no on first down, that it was to be used as the basic third-down desperation play. He startled the league by passing from any spot, on any down, and he immediately led the league in passing. Ultimately, he collected more passing — and punting — records than any man who ever played the game.

In the 1937 title game, when his golden arm was the undoing of the monster Chicago Bears, Baugh confounded the Bears on the first play from scrimmage. From behind his own goal line, he suggested a pass to signal-caller Riley Smith and launched the ball to Cliff Battles for 42 yards, a daring move at the time.

For 16 years his accuracy shredded defenses. "The only place I had trouble was in Cleveland," he said. "Out there they pumped up the ball to make it round and hard to throw. The league didn't have a regulation ball when I broke in."

The Sammy Baugh story with the Redskins began when the team sweated out the first round of the 1937 college draft. After Baugh hadn't been picked by other teams, the Redskins grabbed as fast as they could for the tailback who had been an All American for two years at Texas Christian University.

Redskins owner George Preston Marshall, a man who rarely bumped into a promotional gimmick he didn't like, immediately sought to exploit the Texas angle. He wanted to introduce Baugh as an exciting, rootin', tootin', 6-foot, 3-inch cowboy type — despite the fact that city-boy Sammy at that time had never seen a cow except from the other side of the fence.

"Get a Stetson," Marshall said on the phone.

"What size do you wear?" Baugh asked.

"It's for you, not me," said Marshall, "and get yourself a cowboy outfit, a fancy one."

When Baugh deplaned in Washington for his contract-signing ceremonies, he was outfitted in a flaring Stetson, a checkered shirt, whip-cord pants and, worse luck, those high-heeled boots, the complete cowboy except that he didn't know which side of a horse to mount.

Those narrow Texas boots were his undoing. "Mah feet hurt," said Sammy as he literally limped to the Occidental Hotel for his welcome-to-Washington luncheon. But Marshall had given him a $500 bonus for signing, atop an $8,000 contract, and Sammy said, "Ah guess I've got to dress to suit him, not me."

The irony was that in years to come, Tenderfoot Baugh, of the literally tender feet, whose cowboy career started out as a gag, would become as genuine a cowpoke as any wild-riding sonofagun on the range. With football earnings that reached $15,000 a year, tops, and other income from Hollywood, he would acquire the 35,000-acre cattle ranch in Rotan, Texas, a passion for horses and enough ability with a rope to get him into some rodeos.

The defining anecdote about Baugh through the years has been the story of how, when he first reported to the Redskins, he was told by coach Ray Flaherty, "Sammy you're with the pros now, and they want the football where they can catch it. Hit 'em in the eye."

Whereupon rookie Baugh said, "Which eye?"

Of course, the tale was widely taken as a bit of hyperbole, a way to underline Baugh's passing perfection. But, whaddayaknow, it turns out to be true. Sammy confirmed it 60 years later on the phone from Texas. "Yep, ah said it," he acknowledged. "First and last time in my life ah was cocky."

Despite his reputation as the great Hall of Fame quarterback, Baugh didn't get to play quarterback for the Redskins until his fifth season. Signal calling was handled mostly by Smith, the wingback in the Redskins' single-wing and double-wing forma-

Sidelined: "Why won't they let me play?" Baugh asked after suffering a concussion in the 1943 championship game.

tions. Sammy was the tailback, throwing passes and doing the punting. He also did some running for the first three seasons — until his passing became so valuable that Baugh's runs were verboten.

When the Redskins put in the T-formation in 1940, with Baugh taking the snaps close up, Sammy continued his string of years in which he led the league in passing: 1937-40-43-45-47-49. He often was the leader in punting as well, most often resorting to his favorite, 70-yard quick kick when he saw his receivers covered.

The quick pass was one of Baugh's strategies as well as the quick kick. He got the pass away with speed because the center, on signal, would snap the ball to him in the vicinity of his right ear, where it would be in instant throwing position.

In one season, Baugh completed a record 70.3 percent of his passes, and one day he had an 85.7 completion rate. In his best season his kicking average was 50.7 yards a kick. The NFL archives are laden with his records.

Never was there a more popular football hero in Washington. His Number 33 was so famed that when my 12-year-old son suggested that I watch his neighborhood football team play one day, he said, "I'll be wearing Number 33." When I arrived at the field I noted that jersey Number 33 was also the choice of both tackles, the center, the quarterback and the fullback.

Truth to tell, Baugh originally was endowed with the name of "Slingin' Sammy" because of his great arm as a baseball player, not as a passing quarterback.

And it was on a baseball scholarship that he went to TCU, not a football scholarship. He played shortstop for TCU, was scouted and signed by the St. Louis Cardinals upon graduation. He was in training camp with the Cardinals and played in their minor league system. But the curve ball was his enemy, and he saw the futility of continuing as a Cardinal shortstop hope when Marty Marion suddenly appeared on the Cardinal scene as their prize rookie.

So it was to football that he would devote his career, starting in the era before the platoons. Sammy played both ways for the Redskins, as a tailback and defensive back. His interception of four passes in a single game broke a league record. Actually, the first time he laid hands on a football as a Redskin it was to make a 30-yard runback of the opening kickoff in his first game, against the Giants in Griffith Stadium.

Baugh started barking his signals in 1941 when the Redskins switched to the T, and he was in complete charge of the game. Now he was the quarterback, beholden only to general instructions from head coach Flaherty. He called almost all his shots, in contrast to the modern system in which plays generally are sent in from the sideline.

Redskin fans went wild for Baugh. In his tenth season here, "Sammy Baugh Day" was celebrated, with the fans giving him a maroon station wagon. Usually, athletes flop when they are given a "day." In baseball they go 0 for 5 as a rule. Not Baugh. That day he gave the 35,361 celebrant fans six touchdown passes. This was against the Chicago Cardinals, then the best defensive team in the NFL.

When Baugh retired from the Redskins in 1952, after his 16th season, *The Washington Post* editorial page stated: "Washington, especially in the autumn months, will be a duller and sadder place." One is tempted today to borrow Thomas Jefferson's memorable tribute to a departed friend: "He will have successors, but he will not be replaced."

HARRY GOODWIN, THE WASHINGTON POST

Still on the mark: A Baugh pass to Harry Gilmer in 1952, Slingin' Sammy's last season.

TRIVIA QUIZ 1

1. Which franchise in the young NFL did George Preston Marshall acquire to start his football team in Boston?

a) Duluth, Minnesota
b) Newark, New Jersey
c) Pottsville, Pennsylvania
d) Boston

2. Who was the only Redskin ever to wear the numbers 00?

ASSOCIATED PRESS

3. Which star tackle's playing career ended when he injured his knee running back from a coin toss?

4. Six members of the 1937 Redskins are in the Pro Football Hall of Fame. Name them.

5. In the infamous 73-0 drubbing of the Redskins by the Bears in 1940, in which one of the following statistics did the Redskins outdo Chicago?

a) Fumbles
b) First downs
c) Passes intercepted
d) None of the above

6. In which 1940s game did the Redskins give up the most penalty yards in team history?

7. Redskins owner George Preston Marshall had a history of involvement in two other sports. They were:

a) Auto racing
b) Basketball
c) Baseball
d) Hockey

8. The Redskins drafted the same UCLA back No. 1 in 1946 and again in 1947. Who was he?

9. Which head coach had the shortest career with the Redskins?

10. Name the Hollywood film series in which Redskins quarterback Sammy Baugh starred.

ANSWERS ON PAGE 269

CHAPTER 2
The 1950s and 1960s

Trying to Kick the Losing Habit

By Ken Denlinger

Bobby Mitchell of the Cleveland Browns may have been among the last people to know. He was stationed at Maryland's Fort Meade, one of several NFL players summoned into military service during the 1961 Berlin crisis. After reveille on a fall morning, he was chatting with Redskins defensive end John Paluck, who also had been called up.

"He kept saying, 'Boy, the greatest thing in the world has happened. It's gonna blow everybody's mind,' " Mitchell recalled, adding, "I kept saying to myself: 'What the hell is Paluck talking about?' "

What he was talking about was the most significant moment of the 1950s and 1960s for the Washington Redskins, one that became official on December 14, 1961. That was when Redskins owner George Preston Marshall finally ended his segregationist policies, the last NFL owner to do so. That was when he announced his stunning trade with Cleveland for Mitchell, the remarkable runner/receiver who later would enter the Pro Football Hall of Fame.

Marshall, of course, didn't make the move out of the goodness of his heart. As previously noted, he did it because the federal government had threatened to block his team from playing in the new stadium it had financed. But whatever the reason, the team never would be the same again. At last, Washington no longer would have to draw players solely from the limited pool of white talent, a restriction that long had hamstrung the Redskins.

The Mitchell acquisition was by no means the only watershed of those decades. The Redskins, for example, were the first team in the NFL to have all of their games televised — and Marshall used that 1950 coup to increase his cultivation of Southern fans. In addition to "Hail to the Redskins," the team band played "Dixie" before home games.

Redskins fans also welcomed and bade farewell to many other pivotal men besides Mitchell in those years. Baugh played his final game for the Redskins in 1952. Sonny Jurgensen played his first game for the Redskins in 1964. So did Charley Taylor. Jack Kent Cooke bought 25 percent of the team, for $350,000, in 1961. On February 7, 1969, Vince Lombardi was hired as head coach. Larry Brown arrived as a Redskins rookie that year. On August 9, 1969, Marshall died.

Marshall's near-unique flair as a showman also may have reached its zenith in the period, on October 10, 1954, when the halftime performance included the entire National Symphony Orchestra. This may have helped Redskins ticket sales, but it didn't do much for the team's prospects on the field: The Redskins lost that day, 51-21, to the New York Giants. That was no surprise to Redskins fans at the time or to anyone who has looked back at the team's frightful records of the 1950s and 1960s.

Of Redskins players and coaches now in the Hall of Fame, most — 10 of them — were active in those two decades. There were coaches Earl (Curly) Lambeau, Otto Graham and Vince Lombardi. There was linebacker Sam Huff, running back Bill Dudley and defensive tackle Stan Jones. There were quarterbacks Baugh and Jurgensen and wide receivers Mitchell and Taylor.

Granted, many of these men either had made their marks with other teams or were near the end of their careers in those Washington years. Still, the Redskins could manage just three winning seasons — in 1953, 1955 and 1969 — out of 20.

This doesn't mean that there were no exciting or funny moments in those decades. There were, sometimes in the same game. Running back Dick James scored four touchdowns during a 34-24 victory over the Dallas Cowboys on December 17, 1961. He could have scored five, James said, had rookie quarterback Norm Snead been more attentive. According to James, he came into the huddle with the Redskins less than two yards from the goal line and said: "Let's take it in." Snead thought James said: "Sneak it in." So Snead did.

Marshall's continued meddling also provided some comic relief. Through most of the 1950s, he had a direct phone line from his box to the bench during games and barked orders with regularity. Frustrated players and coaches did their best to ignore him. "We had those big capes for cold weather," said running back Jim Podoley, "and sometimes we'd hang one over the phone at the bench, to muffle the sound. When Marshall saw what was happening, he'd send his chauffeur down to take the cape off the phone."

During one of his frequent halftime visits to the clubhouse, Marshall directed his anger at linebacker/ defensive back Pete Stout, who had been beaten badly in pass coverage. Stout told Marshall that he was playing hurt and giving it his best. At one point, according to lineman Joe Tereshinski, Stout grabbed Marshall — and nobody moved to stop him. Stout quickly let go. Marshall gathered himself, got up on a stool and shouted: "Now that's the kind of fight I want."

CASAMENTO — THE WASHINGTON POST

Bobby Mitchell in 1962: Finally, the team tapped the large pool of black talent.

He was not eager for any fight, though, when it came to players' pay. The salaries were not exactly munificent: several hundred dollars a game. Payments were weekly and in cash, usually in a brown envelope, and 25 percent was withheld each week and given in a lump sum after the year's last game. That way, players had enough money to get home at the end of the season. When the NFL became prosperous and players whose careers ended before 1959 were included in the pension plan, the yearly retirement money for many was more than they had earned during their highest-paid seasons as players.

Everybody, of course, had off-season jobs. Most also had part-time jobs during the season. "We'd work out from about 9 to 11:30 each morning, then go back down to the stadium for meetings Tuesday, Thursday and Saturday nights," said former center Al Demao. "That gave me all afternoon free. Some of the fellas chose to play golf; some of them decided to play cards in their rooms all afternoon. I wanted to work, and an hour after practice ended I'd be on the street" for liquor distributor Milton S. Kronheim & Co. "The only time I'd miss was when we were in training camp out in California. I'd just send my customers a little postal card — and many of them were happier than if I'd made the regular call."

Before the 1952 season, the Redskins heard that a few teams, the Chicago Bears and Detroit Lions among them, actually were paying players for preseason games. Anywhere from $30 to $50 a game. Marshall was scheduling up to six exhibitions a year and wasn't shelling out a penny for them. Demao and Baugh were part of a committee formed to broach the idea of exhibition pay to Marshall. But Marshall would have none of it. At practice later that day, Demao said, Marshall emphasized his decision to the entire squad. He even pointed to a gate and told the players they were free to go if they disagreed with his policy. Nobody left.

Despite such varied and memorable moments, however, the Redskins' defining characteristic in those two decades was a seeming determination to lose, with periodic lapses into victory along the way.

Early in the 1950s and at the end of the 1960s, the Redskins tried the same maneuver to kick-start team performances: They hired legendary coaches who had made their marks with the Green Bay Packers. The first was Lambeau, in 1952.

Herman Ball had been retained as coach for the start of the 1951 season, even though his record the previous two years had been a sorry 4-12. After three straight losses — by a combined 115-31 points — he was replaced by former running back Dick Todd. The team responded, winning five of the remaining nine games in Baugh's final season as the regular quarterback.

Impatient after two preseason losses, though, Marshall fired Todd the next year and brought in Lambeau. Lambeau had helped found the Packers in 1919 and had led them to six NFL championships in 31 years as their coach. He was part of the first class in the Hall of Fame. Lambeau left the Packers after the 1949 season over a financial dispute and had coached the Chicago Cardinals, though to no great effect. He had 5-7 and 3-9 records the previous two seasons.

Lambeau's results with the Redskins were mixed. The team went 4-8 in his first year, 1952. That also was the first season for one of the Redskins' most endearing players, 5-foot, 7-inch quarterback Eddie LeBaron. LeBaron had been a Korean War hero, wounded twice and decorated for what his Marine commendation called "complete disregard for his own safety to rescue members of his own platoon . . . while his platoon was under persistent artillery and mortar barrage."

LeBaron threw nine of his 14 touchdown passes that 1952 season in the final three games. But friction developed between him and Lambeau — and increased the next season, when LeBaron was forced to share quarterback duties with first-round draft choice Jack Scarbath. Even though the Redskins finished 6-5-1 in 1953, LeBaron bolted to the Canadian Football League.

"I really didn't want to play for him anymore," LeBaron said in the book *Redskin Country: From Baugh to the Super Bowl*, "and I'm sure he didn't want me around either . . . I told Marshall I'd go to Canada or, if he stood in my way, I'd go into private business. He put up a fuss, but he knew people were unhappy. It wound up that [lineman] Gene Brito and I both went to Calgary. I guess he thought Curly was right and we were wrong."

Other players considered Lambeau good but unlucky. "The big problem with Curly was injuries," said Gene Pepper, who played guard on offense and tackle on defense from 1950 through 1953. "The blockers and runners were hurt just enough so we couldn't turn the damn corner on running plays." But Demao and some other Redskins thought Lambeau stressed defense too much. "Hardly ever gave any time to the offense," Demao said.

As matters developed, Lambeau was gone before the 1954 season began. After an exhibition game in California, Marshall's wife, Corrine, saw some players carrying beer to their rooms and told Marshall. There was a rule against drinking in the club-house or the team hotel, but Lambeau backed the players because the game they had played was an exhibition. There was a loud argument and some shoving between Marshall and Lambeau — and Lambeau soon was fired.

Joe Kuharich replaced Lambeau, and that was fine with LeBaron. He and Brito returned for the 1955 season, after the team in 1954 had kept up its obsession with losing, accumulating a 3-9 record. But the 1955 season was the Redskins' best of the

1950s and 1960s. Their 8-4 mark for once put them solidly in second place in the NFL's Eastern Conference, behind the mighty Cleveland Browns. The only post-season game back then was between the conference winners, and the Browns beat the Los Angeles Rams, 38-14, for the NFL title.

Washington actually had defeated the Browns that season, 27-17, in the 1955 opener. Their 31-30 victory over the Eagles a week later in Philadelphia was even better. When Alan Beall selected the 50 greatest games in Redskins history for his 1988 book *Braves on the Warpath*, that was one of them.

LeBaron was back at quarterback for that game. The crowd of 31,891 that Saturday evening in Philadelphia included a large number of Washingtonians, each of whom had gotten tickets to the game and round-trip rail fare for a total of $10. What they saw for the first three quarters was depressing, if familiar: LeBaron fumbling the ball, later having to punt from his own end zone, and the Eagles racing to a 16-0 lead.

But Washington's defense provided the first break when middle linebacker Chuck Drazenovich belted Eagles halfback Jerry Norton and caused a fumble. Brito recovered on the Philadelphia 32. After moving the ball to the 19, LeBaron threw a short pass that Vic Janowicz turned into a touchdown. Janowicz also added the extra point, cutting the deficit to 16-7.

Norb Hecker kicked off — and the Redskins got a huge break when Norton assumed that the ball would roll out of bounds near the end zone and failed to field it. To Norton's horror, the ball took a crazy hop and stayed in bounds. The Redskins' Ralph Thomas recovered it at the Eagles' three and immediately rolled into the end zone for a touchdown. It was Philadelphia 16, Washington 14.

On the first play after the next kickoff, Norton fumbled again, and defensive lineman LaVern (Torgy) Torgeson recovered it for Washington on the Philadelphia 13. LeBaron and Janowicz combined on a pass for the first nine yards, and Janowicz soon scored from the one and kicked another extra point. In 2 minutes and 17 seconds of play, the Redskins had gone from trailing by 16 points to leading by five.

The Eagles, however, charged back. A combination of runs and passes moved the ball to the Redskins 36, and Norton redeemed himself by grabbing a Bobby Thomason pass in the end zone. Philadelphia was ahead again, 23-21. But LeBaron went to work on the next drive, combining with running back Bert Zagers on a 57-yard pass play and later sneaking the ball in from the one on the last play of the quarter. It was now Redskins 28, Eagles 23.

Kuharich was using a defensive alignment unlike any other in the NFL that season, one with four down linemen and three linebackers. To accomplish that, he moved the middle guard from the traditional five-man line and dropped him between the two outside linebackers. Within a few years, the 4-3 would become the standard NFL defense. It had been more than adequate the week before against the Browns. Now it finally stopped the Eagles early in the fourth quarter, and the Redskins took over at their 40. Runners Leo Elter, Dale Atkeson and Zagers bulled for four first downs, and Janowicz kicked a 20-yard field goal that increased the Redskins' advantage to 31-23.

Hometown hero: Quarterback Eddie LeBaron, a 5-foot, 7-inch Korean War hero, was a favorite of Redskins fans in the 1950s. Here he stands beside 6-foot, 8-inch tackle Bob Hendren.

The Eagles still were not about to cave. They drove nearly the length of the field, and with a five-yard touchdown pass by Thomason to Bill Stribling and Bobby Walston's extra point, they whittled the lead to one point. But the Redskins controlled the ball the final 3 minutes and 20 seconds of the game, and Redskins fans were treated to another unaccustomed victory.

That season the Redskins defense allowed 222 points, or about half of what it had surrendered the year before. Kuharich was chosen 1955 coach of the year in the NFL, and Redskins general manager Dick McCann said that he had done "the greatest reconstruction job since the Civil War."

The Redskins and their fans actually had reason for optimism as the 1956 season approached, but the fates were not on their side. On August 17, 1956, after an exhibition victory over the Rams in the Los Angeles Coliseum, halfback Janowicz was returning to training camp at nearby Occidental College when the car in which he was riding crashed into a telephone pole. Janowicz, whose 88 points were second only to Doak Walker of the Detroit Lions among NFL scorers in 1955, was in a coma for several days and never resumed his NFL career.

Quarterback Al Dorow was injured in another car wreck that same week and was sidelined for a month. With LeBaron wrenching his left knee in a preseason game, the Redskins opened the season with a rookie, Fred Wyatt, at quarterback. With Wyatt and a recuperated Dorow, Washington lost its first three games in 1956. The Redskins righted themselves against a Browns team that would have a rare off year, then beat the Cardinals before playing another game considered among the 50 best in Redskins history.

That was on November 11 in Griffith Stadium against a Detroit Lions team that included four future Hall of Famers: quarterback Bobby Layne, middle linebacker Joe Schmidt and defensive backs Yale Lary and Jack Christiansen. The Lions had won the NFL championship in 1952 and 1953. In 1956, they entered the Redskins game with a 6-0 record.

Even though LeBaron was healthy, Kuharich stayed with Dorow at quarterback. Dick James was a rookie that year, but he had shown big-play potential by returning the opening kickoff of the season 83 yards. Halfback Billy Wells, the team's most valuable player in 1954, had returned after two years in the service. The defense had been spotty the five previous games, allowing 30 or more points twice but holding opponents to 14 or fewer points the other three times.

The Redskins took a 3-0 lead on a field goal by the man who replaced Janowicz as the placekicker, the colorful Sam Baker. (During training camp, Baker had taken one of roommate Drazenovich's fancy suits and run it up a flag pole near the dining hall.)

Defensive backs Hecker and Joe (Scooter) Scudero both intercepted Layne — and James increased the lead to 10-0 late in the first quarter with a 59-yard, nothing's-gonna-stop-

Period poses: Quarterback Al Dorow leaps over tackle Don Boll in 1956, while members of the 1957 backfield — from left, Eddie LeBaron, Dick James, Leo Elter and Tom Runnels — dash across the field.

me run. He took a lateral from Dorow, slipped three tackles, and got a block from one of his guards. At the 10-yard-line, 230-pound linebacker Bob Long collared the 175-pound James. But James twisted out of Long's grasp, out of his own helmet even, and ran into the end zone.

After the Lions cut the lead to 10-3, LeBaron replaced the ineffective Dorow at quarterback. But LeBaron fumbled on his first handoff, and, after James returned a punt to midfield one minute before halftime, LeBaron reinjured his left knee. Back came Dorow, who threw close to a perfect pass — which Steve Melinger proceeded to drop at the goal line. Washington nonetheless moved the ball down the field, and a field goal by Baker sent the Redskins into halftime with a 13-3 lead.

The Lions mustered a touchdown early in the second half after a call that angered Redskins fans. On fourth down and one from the Washington three, Lions fullback Gene Gedman seemed to be stopped shy of the first down. That's what one official signaled. He was overruled, however, and Gedman soon wedged into the end zone.

Washington then charged back 75 yards, mostly on the ground, and had fourth-and-three from the Detroit five. But Kuharich opted not to go for an almost certain field goal, and Wells was thrown for a 1-yard loss.

Late in the game, the Lions made several mistakes. Layne was intercepted again — and Lary twice cost the Lions valuable yardage by fielding punts inside his 10-yard line. On the second of those mistakes, Lary was nailed at his 1-yard line, and, after three Layne incompletions, Lions coach Buddy Parker surprised nearly everyone by inexplicably ordering an intentional safety. The Redskins lead widened to 15-10.

Wells returned Lary's free kick to midfield, and the Redskins quickly moved to the Detroit 29. But Baker missed, from 36 yards. With just under two minutes left, the Redskins upped the lead to a seemingly insurmountable 18-10 on a 31-yard field goal by Baker.

But Layne could rally a team as few quarterbacks in NFL history. With just two passes, he proceeded to take the Lions 80 yards and into the end zone. With one minute remaining on the clock, the Lions trailed by 18-17. Jim Martin squibbed an onsides kick, and the Redskins' Ralph Thomas recovered it to assure another surprise victory.

In addition to defeating the Lions, the 1956 Redskins beat the Browns twice and split with a Giants team that would win the NFL title. But after a 6-6 record that year, the Redskins suffered through a victory drought that would yield only two seasons of .500 or better records until the end of the 1960s. The five-year slide from 1957 through 1961 was the worst of the 20-year period: from a 5-6-1 record to 4-7-1 to 3-9 to 1-9-2 to 1-12-1.

Still, LeBaron finished second in the NFL in passing in 1957 and was first a year later. After throwing for more than 1,000 yards in 1959, he retired, but only briefly. The expansion Dallas Cowboys traded No. 1 and No. 6 draft choices and tackle Ray Krouse to get him.

There were several other fine players during those seasons — among them runners Ed Sutton, Podoley and Don Bosseler — but not nearly enough of them. Marshall never emphasized scouting even in the best of times, and he seemed even less interested during this period.

"They used to say the Redskins' scouting budget was 50 cents, the cost of *Street and Smith* and another football magazine," LeBaron told author Paul Attner. "It was the joke around the league on draft day, when all the teams would meet in New York and Marshall would walk around the table, trying to see who other people thought were good. Teams would deliberately expose names of guys they didn't want or who weren't any good, and he would draft them.

ASSOCIATED PRESS

Yes, they beat the Giants: Five Redskins scorers in a 1957 upset — from left, Bert Zagers, who ran a punt back 76 yards, back Ed Sutton, kicker Sam Baker, end John Carson and back Don Bosseler — enjoy a rare opportunity for a victory celebration.

"Marshall was a showman first of all. He wanted entertainment. That's how he looked at his draft picks. We never had very good defensive teams when I was there, but we kept drafting offensive players. [From 1951 through 1960, the Redskins took six quarterbacks — Larry Isbell, Scarbath, Ralph Guglielmi, Don Allard, Richie Lucas and Norm Snead — on the first round.] He wanted big names, people who would draw fans and bring excitement. It was like treading water."

The team also was seriously hurt by Marshall's whites-only policy, which was coming under increasing attack from several quarters, including the press. *Washington Post* columnist Shirley Povich not only wrote that the Redskins' colors were "burgundy, gold and Caucasian" but that Cleveland runners Jim Brown and Mitchell had "integrated" the Washington end zone. The players knew that Marshall's bigotry was hurting them, but they did not speak out at the time.

Podoley: "There were only so many good players anyway — and when you eliminate half of them, it was tough. Very tough."

Tereshinski: "No doubt in my mind that was a very important reason we did not reach ultimate success."

One factor that did distinguish many of those 1957-1961 Redskins teams was the number of players who later became NFL head coaches: cornerback Don Shula (Baltimore Colts and Miami Dolphins), end Joe Walton (New York Jets), Hecker (Atlanta Falcons) and defensive lineman Ed Khayat (Philadelphia Eagles). In addition, guard Dick Stanfel and defensive lineman Torgeson went on to become longtime NFL assistants. Torgeson spent nearly 20 years of his coaching career working with Redskins' defensive linemen.

But the Redskins coaches they played under in the 1950s and 1960s rarely had distinguished records. After their 4-7-1 season in 1958, the Redskins lost Kuharich to his alma mater, Notre Dame. He was replaced by Mike Nixon, who said at one luncheon: "The fans don't ask for much in this city." Despite an occasional aberration (as with the Redskins' 27-24 upset of the powerful Baltimore Colts in November of 1959), he helped see to it that the fans' low expectations were met. His were the teams that went 3-9 and 1-9-2.

Nixon was replaced before the 1961 season by Bill McPeak, who was elevated from assistant coach. The Redskins moved into their new stadium that year — and in typical fashion. In the home opener, after losses to the San Francisco 49ers and the Eagles, they initially rolled up a 21-0 lead over the Giants. They then blew the game, 24-21.

The only success during that 1-12-1 year was against the Cowboys, then in their second season. The Redskins had tied the Cowboys on the road and, in the final game of the season, won at home. Not surprisingly, the only team the Redskins could beat in 26 games during the 1960 and 1961 seasons was Dallas.

In the fall of 1961, "I was leaving military duty every weekend and starting for the Browns," said Bobby Mitchell, who was to become assistant general manager of the Redskins. "I'd get there Saturday morning, find out what the game plan was and play the game the next day."

He added: "I came home, with two games to go, and Jim Brown came up to me and said: 'All this stuff you been hearing, I had nothing to do with.' What had happened was they had in the papers that Jim had gone up to Syracuse to talk with Ernie Davis about playing with the Browns. I guess he thought I'd already heard about it. I hadn't."

Coaching gallery: Otto Graham with Bobby Mitchell, Joe Kuharich, top, and Mike Nixon.

But he soon learned that he would be the first African American to play for the Redskins.

"I never thought of Washington as a Southern city," he said. "To me [he was raised in Arkansas], Washington was North." Reality hit Mitchell shortly after the Redskins returned from training camp in 1962. "I began to go places, and people kinda got uptight," he said. "All of a sudden I thought, 'Holy hell.' Because I hadn't experienced that.

"There were restaurants I couldn't go in . . . Ted Marchibroda [then a Redskin assistant coach] and I came out of the offices [on 9th Street, NW] to a place across the street where the coaches used to eat all the time. He invited me in. We walk up to the door and all of a sudden the guy doesn't know him. I was so embarrassed for Ted, because I caught on pretty quick. So I said: 'There's another place where I've been wanting to eat.' I didn't even know the name of the damn place. I just pointed to the first joint I saw." Mitchell also remembered being in Duke Zeibert's restaurant once and having a man walk by and spit on his shoe.

"I'd been through being a first before," Mitchell said. "At Illinois, I was selected to integrate a dorm. And with a white student, not an athlete."

Many of his teammates didn't exactly welcome him, either. "They were used to playing mediocre football and still being in the paper," he said. "All of a sudden, I'm raising a little hell on the field, so I was getting in the paper. It was a little tough on 'em. And they got the rumors, too, that maybe I'm making more money than some of 'em." In fact, because of his remarkable record with the Browns, Mitchell had arrived as the highest-paid Redskins player.

"I always had something going on" during his seven seasons playing for the Redskins, Mitchell said. "Some of the whites didn't want me there, and the blacks got mad if I'd drop the ball. To the blacks, I had to be perfect. But Norm Snead was great. He just wanted to throw the ball to a guy who would go get it. And Dickie James was a helluva guy. [Guard] Vince Promuto, of course, didn't give a damn what color you were. So there were some guys, Vinnie, [tackle] Frannie O'Brien. Super people."

Mitchell's arrival was the first of a series of dramatic Redskins changes from 1962, when he took the field for the first time, through the end of the decade. Mitchell himself was switched from running back to flanker, making him even more effective. There were three different coaches in the period — McPeak, Graham and Lombardi — and two of the biggest trades in team history — for Jurgensen and Huff.

All of that came during the most important change, the transition in decision-making from Marshall to Edward Bennett Williams, the brilliant Washington attorney who first made a name for himself by defending such high-profile figures as Teamsters boss Jimmy Hoffa, mob boss Frank Costello and red-baiting Wisconsin Senator Joseph McCarthy. Williams had a lifelong passion for sports, especially boxing and baseball, and had, in fact, sought unsuccessfully to acquire a baseball franchise for Washington.

He also had cultivated a relationship with Marshall, starting in the 1950s. According to Robert Pack's 1983 biography, *Edward Bennett Williams for the Defense*, Williams nearly bought the 25 percent interest in the team that later was sold to Cooke, stock that had been owned by Redskins broadcaster Harry Wismer. Williams' private arguments urging Marshall to integrate the Redskins cooled their relationship for a time. But on March 28, 1962 — after the trade for Bobby Mitchell — Marshall let Williams buy 38 shares of stock, or 3.8 percent of the team, for $58,463. Later that year, he bought 12 more shares, raising his stake to 5 percent.

THE WASHINGTON STAR

Shakeup: Coach Bill McPeak stunned the town with trades for Sam Huff, kneeling left, and Sonny Jurgensen, right. Behind them at their first training camp are, from left, Tommy Neck, Jim Carr, Angelo Coia, Fred Williams and Dick Drummond.

Marshall still owned 52 percent of the stock. But by the end of 1963 he was suffering from a damaged heart, an aneurysm in his abdomen, diabetes and emphysema. His mental state, according to a petition for temporary conservatorship by minority owners Leo DeOrsey, Williams and Milton King, left him "unable properly to care for his property and his interests."

In August 1964, DeOrsey, Williams and King were named permanent conservators of Marshall's estate — which mainly meant his Redskins stock. Then, in April 1965, DeOrsey died. Williams, despite his small stake in the team, became president of the Redskins. It was a role he relished, with friends from the media, politics, the Catholic church and Washington society regularly in his box as he cheered or fumed at the games.

Jack Kent Cooke, who was still quietly in the background with his larger 25 percent holding of Redskins stock, was not unhappy with these developments. The people who were dismayed were Marshall's two estranged children, who challenged the conservators' control of Marshall's stock in court as a conflict of interest. Their argument wasn't without merit, as time would prove.

After Marshall's death in 1969, Williams, the conservator, dealt with Williams, the Redskins president, on selling Marshall's 52 percent holding back to the team. (The proceeds, from a bank loan, went in part to settle with the Marshall children, who had been cut out of their father's will, and in part to the child-welfare foundation established by the will, with its anti-integration provision now skirted.) As another Williams biographer, Evan Thomas, noted in *The Man to See:* "By voting to sell Marshall's stock back to the Redskins, he was giving himself more control over the team and increasing the value of his own investment."

Indeed. The Redskins retired Marshall's 52 percent holding, leaving just 48 percent of the original stock outstanding — which meant that the proportion and value of the remaining owners' shares more than doubled. That's how Jack Kent Cooke first became majority owner of Redskins stock. Because he also owned basketball's Los Angeles Lakers and hockey's Kings, however, he was prevented by NFL cross-ownership rules from active involvement in Redskins management. Williams voted his shares.

If Williams could have arranged for the team to do as well on the playing field, they would have been unqualified winners. But in the 1962-1964 seasons, Washington wasn't sure what to make of the Redskins. The team had shown considerable improvement in 1962, going from a 1-12-1 record to 5-7-2. That season Mitchell led the NFL in receiving, with 72 catches, and scored 11 touchdowns.

In his first game, Mitchell returned a kickoff 92 yards for a touchdown, scored two more touchdowns on passes of 81 yards and 6 yards from Snead, and set up two other touchdowns with long receptions. Still, the Redskins could manage nothing more than a 35-35 tie with the Cowboys that day. Mitchell also sparked the Redskins during a 17-16 upset of his former team, the Browns, with an electrifying 50-yard run, following a short pass from Snead, for the winning touchdown.

But the optimism of 1962 faded with a 3-11 record in 1963. That caused McPeak to shake up the team — and the town — during a nine-day stretch in April of 1964. The first move was trading Snead and defensive back Claude Crabb to the Eagles for Jurgensen and linebacker Jimmie Carr. No one was more stunned by the trade

RICHARD DARCEY — THE WASHINGTON POST

The bomb: Jurgensen drops back into his end zone to throw a 1968 pass that gained 99 yards, matching a team record first set in 1939.

than Jurgensen, who heard the news on April 1 from someone who burst into the Philadelphia deli where he was having lunch.

Initially, he thought it was an April Fool's joke, because he had just come from a two-hour meeting with the new Eagles coach, Kuharich. "We talked about what needed to be done," Jurgensen said of an Eagles team that had had an even sorrier 1963 record — 2-10-2 — than the Redskins. "It was a very positive meeting. A trade was the furthest thing from my mind. I had no clue."

In three years as the regular Eagles quarterback, Jurgensen had amassed impressive numbers. His 3,723 yards passing in 1961 set a league record. He threw 32 touchdown passes that first season. Under pressure once, he flipped the ball behind his back and completed the throw. He and the team were much less effective the next two seasons — and when the won-lost record plummeted, the Philadelphia boo-birds went after him in full fury.

"One of my friends told me that he started to defend me once," Jurgensen said, "but I was so bad he joined in, too. Said it was fun."

Redskins fans, however, were impressed with Jurgensen. His Eagles had beaten the Redskins four of the six times they had met during his three years as a starter, and one of his performances in 1961 was as splendid as anyone could recall at the time.

The Redskins in that game had a 24-20 lead, with just 40 seconds left. To hand the Redskins yet another last-minute defeat, Jurgensen needed only 35 of those seconds. What he did, against a formation with seven defensive backs, was drive the team 81 yards in three plays. An instant before being sacked, Jurgensen threw a typically beautiful spiral that Tommy McDonald caught 22 yards downfield and ran 20 more yards for the winning touchdown. In all, Jurgensen had completed 27 of 41 passes for 413 yards and three touchdowns that day.

Jurgensen's early reaction to the trade was self-doubt: "Why did they think I wasn't doing my job that they needed to let me go?" After his first trip to Washington, though, he was excited. "I really liked McPeak," he said. "Plus it was a chance to start over, with a new team. And, being from North Carolina, everybody back home could follow me."

The town barely had time to digest the Snead-for-Jurgensen trade when, on April 9, McPeak sent the hugely popular James and defensive tackle Andy Stynchula to the New York Giants for Huff. Like Jurgensen, Huff was flabbergasted. Unlike Jurgensen, Huff was a hero of the team and the city he was leaving. He had made the cover of *Time* magazine in 1959 and, a year later, was featured in the CBS documentary *The Violent World of Sam Huff.*

Few of the hits Huff had taken had more impact on him than that trade. "It was 7 o'clock," he said. "I even remember exactly where I was: Ed (Big Mo) Modzelewski's restaurant in Cleveland. A brick couldn't have hit me any harder." Huff said Giants coach Allie Sherman called him with the news and said Huff should be "proud" because the team got two players for him. Huff was livid.

"That really tore me up," he said. "I really carried a grudge. Not against the Giants. I couldn't carry a grudge against the Giants. But I carried a grudge against Sherman for many, many, many years."

THE WASHINGTON STAR

ELLSWORTH DAVIS — THE WASHINGTON POST

Mr. Linebacker: Sam Huff taught younger players when he joined the team (inset) and was still plugging away in 1969, here running back an interception for a touchdown against the Philadelphia Eagles that November. He retired as a player at the end of that season.

McPeak was not finished. To an offense that included Mitchell and Jurgensen, he added what he hoped would be a ground game by choosing Arizona State's Charley Taylor with the first pick in the 1964 draft. To the defense came another fine rookie, safety Paul Krause.

The team began having some exciting days in 1964 and 1965, when Jurgensen passed for a total of 5,301 yards and 39 touchdowns. Mitchell caught 60 passes each season. Krause led the league in interceptions in 1964, with 12. And the game against the Dallas Cowboys on November 28, 1965, was one of the most thrilling in Redskins history, another rightly picked by Beall as an all-time favorite.

Jurgensen started horribly, throwing two interceptions and fumbling the ball away in the first eight minutes. Taylor, the NFL's rookie of the year in 1964, fumbled twice in his first three carries. The Cowboys converted Jurgensen's fumble and one of Taylor's into a 14-0 lead. Matters worsened when Dallas safety Mike Gaechter blocked a Redskins field goal attempt, recovered the ball and ran 60 yards for a third touchdown.

After the Cowboys' Danny Villanueva missed a 25-yard field goal, Jurgensen led an 80-yard drive that ended with a 26-yard pass to Taylor in the end zone. The extra point was blocked, however, and Dallas took a 21-6 lead into halftime.

The second half brought more misery. The Redskins fumbled two more times, Dallas quarterback Don Meredith escaped a seemingly certain sack and completed a 19-yard pass, and Villanueva kicked a 29-yard field goal that lifted Dallas to a 24-6 lead midway through the third quarter. But Jurgensen produced an 82-yard scoring drive near the end of the quarter, sneaking in himself from the one. Then reserve halfback Danny Lewis capped a surge at the start of the fourth period with a two-yard dive that narrowed the Dallas lead to 24-20.

Dallas quickly increased that to 31-20 after an interception by Cowboys linebacker Dave Edwards. Receiver Frank Clarke took a short Meredith pass near midfield and raced into the end zone. Fewer than six minutes remained.

On the Redskins' next possession, Jurgensen was aided by Angelo Coia's acrobatic catch of a 39-yard pass at the Dallas 10. One play later, Jurgensen hit Mitchell in the end zone. Huff and the defense held — and Jurgensen got the ball on the Redskins 20. Left on the clock: 1:41.

Jurgensen promptly fumbled, then just as promptly picked the ball up and scrambled for a nine-yard gain. Pass interference provided another nine yards. Jurgensen next hit rookie tight end Jerry Smith for 22 more yards. From the Cowboys' 40, Jurgensen lofted a pass that Mitchell grabbed at the five an instant before being belted by Dallas defensive back Cornell Green. On the clock: 1:14. Washington called time.

On the next play, Coia faked a block inside and then cut outside. Backpeddling, Jurgensen floated a pass over the Dallas defenders and into his arms. From the 21-0 hole, the Redskins had climbed into a 34-31 lead.

Dallas, however, had a minute to rally. Meredith quickly completed a 20-yard pass to Pete Gent and later hit Hayes with a 35-yarder to the Washington 37. With only seven seconds left, Villaneuva tried a 45-yard field goal. But Huff and Fred Williams pushed the Cowboys interior linemen back — and Lonnie Sanders burst through to block the kick and preserve the Redskins victory.

Despite that kind of excitement, however, the Redskins finished 6-8 in both 1964 and 1965. Impatient, Williams fired McPeak. Star-struck, he hired Otto Graham as head coach and general manager.

As a quarterback, Graham had led the Browns to NFL titles in 1950, 1954 and 1955 and to the championship game his other three years in the league. Coaching at the Coast Guard Academy at the time, Graham claimed not to be interested in the NFL. But a five-year contract valued at half a million dollars apparently was an offer he couldn't refuse.

In his first year of training camp at Dickinson College in Carlisle, Pennsylvania — the Redskins had moved there three years earlier — Graham made a profound position change — switching Taylor from running back to wide receiver. Taylor was as shocked as anyone. His dream had been "to be the next Jimmy Brown."

Even before the move, Taylor had been uncomfortable with Graham. That was because of a 1964 incident when Graham was head coach of the College All-Star team. He had said publicly of Taylor: "He's a great athlete, but he is very lazy. He could have a great future or he could fall flat on his face. He comes late to practice and is the first to leave. He even misses practice. And it has happened too often for him to be the victim of circumstances. He seems to have no interest."

When Graham signed on with the Redskins, according to Taylor, "he said he had misjudged me, that I was a very hard worker and a great player. I believe he meant those compliments."

Graham saw several things in Taylor. One was his productivity in his two seasons at running back: He had averaged 3.8 yards on 199 carries the first year and 2.8 yards on 145 carries the second. Another was Taylor's ability in the open field: He had caught 53 passes out of the backfield as a rookie, a league record for running backs. Taylor's running skills would be ideal for turning short passes into long gains. At 6 feet, 3 inches and 215 pounds, moreover, he was unafraid to go over the middle as a receiver and as a blocker. It was too much to ignore the possibilities from combining Taylor with Mitchell and tight end Jerry Smith.

"When he first talked to me about moving," Taylor said, "I didn't want any part of it. I didn't know anything about running pass patterns. We had our words about it. I don't think I ever said no, but he understood I was unhappy . . . He was the head coach, and I didn't have a choice. I didn't brood about it. I respect authority. Maybe you didn't like the guy, but you respect the position."

Taylor was so gifted that NFL scouts thought he could have made the Hall of Fame on defense. By leading the league with 72 catches and turning them into 1,119 yards and 12 touchdowns, Taylor in 1966 immediately showed the talent that would get him there as a wide receiver.

In fact, the entire Redskins passing attack was potent almost beyond belief. Taylor led the league in receiving in 1966 and 1967. Smith was second in 1967 and Mitchell fourth. Jurgensen set NFL records in 1967 for pass attempts (508), completions (288) and yards (3,747). His 31 touchdown passes set a Redskins record. That sort of excitement — plus rookie place-kicker Charlie Gogolak scoring a Redskins-record 105 points in 1966 — triggered a string of stadium sellouts that never seemed to end.

Atop this were high-scoring 1966 duels with the Cowboys that set the tone for a rivalry that became as fierce as any in the NFL. The Cowboys won the first game, 31-30, at D.C. Stadium. The Redskins then won in Dallas, 34-31. In between, at home against the Giants on November 27, the Redskins put on a scoring binge unlike any other in the NFL — one that was pure heaven to Huff.

"I knew the Giants were awful," Huff said of his former team, "and what a great feeling it was. Getting Sherman fired had been my goal. I lived and breathed for the day he got fired. That's how much I hated the guy . . . So I looked at the films [before the game] and, man, they were terrible. I thought we'd score 60 points against 'em with Sonny. I even told him that before the game."

The points came quickly and in bunches. By the time the Redskins were leading 49-41, an embarrassed Huff met Jurgensen as the Redskins defense was going back on the field. "How many points do I have to score?" Jurgensen yelled. Replied Huff: "Don't let up, don't let up."

Jurgensen didn't. With 20 seconds left, the Redskins were on the New York 20 and ahead 69-41. Jurgensen was prepared to drop to his knee on the next play and let the clock run out. On the Washington sideline, however, someone yelled: "Field goal team."

Gogolak and the others followed orders — and his field goal gave the Redskins 72

MATTHEW LEWIS — THE WASHINGTON POST

Reluctant receiver: Running back Charley Taylor, who dreamed of being "the next Jimmy Brown," wasn't happy about being switched to wide receiver.

points, two more than the Los Angeles Rams had scored in setting the previous record 16 years earlier against the Baltimore Colts.

Who had ordered this pound of salt to be ground into so open a wound? "I sent 'em in," Huff said. "Poor Otto was the one who got all the heat. But I was the one who sent 'em in. That was my day of reckoning. And I called it before the game. I really did."

Although the 1966 team finished with only a 7-7 year, it was the best Redskins record in a decade. Jurgensen and the offense had scored more points, 351, than any Washington team ever. Unfortunately, the defense also had given up 355 points. That pattern continued for two more years. In 1967 the team scored 347 points, surrendered 353 and finished with a 5-6-3 record. A year later, during a 5-9 season when Jurgensen often was hurt and Huff had retired, the offense produced just 249 points while the defense was down to its usual standard, allowing 358.

Amid all those years of defeat were other memorable moments. During practice, for example, Graham had a habit of pounding his clipboard when something pleased him. So the players got up a pool one day before leaving the clubhouse for the work-out: How many times would Graham tap his clipboard? Running back Steve Thurlow, nursing a hamstring injury at the time, was the official counter.

Each player kept a tally in his head — and as practice was winding down, an offensive linemen, fearing that he was about to lose by one tap, shouted the rarest request in football: "Coach, can we run just one more play?" The innocent Graham would call that practice one of the most spirited he had seen.

Then there were the escapades of Jurgensen, who was notorious for bolting training camp after bed check. At the start of one of his escapes, a ball boy was outside the dorm and accepted Jurgensen's invitation to join him. According to Jurgensen, the entertainment was nothing more than shuffleboard at a nearby tavern. Around 3 a.m., there was a call at the tavern. Coaches had checked the beds a second time — and Jurgensen was told to report to Graham's room.

A sleepy Graham opened the door and proceeded to scold the quarterback. Graham asked if anyone had joined Jurgensen. The door happened to get pushed back at that moment and there, looking sheepish, was Graham's own son, Dewey.

"He kicked Dewey out of camp for a while," Jurgensen said. "Dewey also got us started calling Graham 'Toot.' That's Otto inside out."

It would not be too long, however, before it was the senior Graham's turn to be kicked out. The players, the fans and team president Williams all had grown disenchanted with him. They questioned his dedication and recalled one of his early quotes: "Instead of winning games 3-0, I'd rather risk losing some games by, say, 35-28, and have the fans up off their seats with excitement."

Williams had not helped Graham. Often, he had spoken to the team with neither Graham nor his assistants present. Williams also initiated a 1968 trade of a first-round draft pick to the Los Angeles Rams for former Heisman Trophy winner Gary Beban, who never worked out. And Williams was the major reason the Redskins in 1966 acquired one of pro football's all-time characters, running back Joe Don Looney.

Looney was an immense talent, the first-round choice of the Giants in 1964. That's why so many teams took a chance on him. As a college player at Oklahoma, he had punched an assistant coach. Before coming to the Redskins, Looney had played briefly with the Colts and Lions. When Lions head coach Harry Gilmer ordered Looney to carry a play from the sideline to the quarterback, Looney refused, saying, "If you want a messenger boy, call Western Union."

Graham consulted with Jurgensen and Huff before Looney was acquired. The team even gave Huff a $1,000

I'll take it: Cornerback Pat Fischer leaps to make one of two interceptions in an October 1969 game against his former team, the St. Louis Cardinals.

bonus to room with Looney. That stopped, however, during the second year, when Looney and Huff got into a fight during practice. Not long after that, Looney was gone.

Despite all of the unhappiness with Graham, some NFL veterans look back on those Redskins teams and credit Graham for being ahead of his time offensively. That's the view of Mike McCormack, Graham's offensive line coach at the time and later a head coach with three NFL teams and a prime builder of the expansion Carolina Panthers in the mid-1990s. "That West Coast offense everybody talks about [that started with coach Bill Walsh and the San Francisco 49ers] — Otto was running it in the late '60s," McCormack said.

Before Williams hired Graham in 1966, he had tried to lure Vince Lombardi. But Lombardi wanted something Williams could not provide then — equity in the team. So Lombardi went on to win two more NFL titles, and the first two Super Bowls, before retiring as Packer coach in February of 1968.

Lombardi remained general manager of the Packers. Less than nine months later, however, during a breakfast meeting with Williams before a Redskins-Packers game in RFK Stadium, Lombardi admitted that he missed coaching. This time, Williams was armed with what Lombardi wanted — and Lombardi was interested. The two men subsequently met several times, sometimes in New York, sometimes in Florida, but always in secret because premature disclosure might complicate the negotiations.

What Williams had available was Redskins stock formerly held by DeOrsey's widow. He had persuaded her to sell her 130 shares to the other owners for $10,000 a share. Eighty shares had been retired — and the other 50 shares were made available to Lombardi. So the package was that he would own 5 percent of the team and become executive vice president and coach at a salary of about $110,000.

However, two potential deal-breakers had to be overcome. Lombardi's arrangement with the Packers barred him from coaching another team during the life of his contract, which did not expire until January 31, 1974. Also, Williams apparently had violated the NFL rule requiring a team to ask permission before commencing negotiations with someone else's employee. Williams argued that Lombardi, after all, was the Packers' chief executive officer. The Packers executive committee, however, thought Williams should have requested its permission

NFL commissioner Pete Rozelle intervened. He told the Packers executive committee that if it did not recommend Lombardi's release, he would not approve the Redskins deal. The delay caused Williams to cancel an introductory press conference in Washington for Lombardi. "I was never more humiliated," he said later.

MATTHEW LEWIS — THE WASHINGTON POST

Any way you can: Linebacker Chris Hanburger grabs Gale Sayers' jersey to bring him down in the 1968 opener at Chicago.

On February 4, 1969, Lombardi spoke with reporters in New York, after he had been honored at a Catholic Youth Organization dinner at the Waldorf-Astoria, and said: "Like anyone else, you always hope to own something . . . People say you're crazy to put your great reputation on the line. I say reputation, swepulation, the hell with it. I've found out the challenge in something is not maintaining it, but attaining it."

The next evening, in the room of a Green Bay hotel named in Lombardi's honor just six months earlier, Packers directors met for two hours and voted "with deep regret" to release Lombardi from his contract. They did not demand compensation. "I would not cheapen this deal by measuring his worth to us in dollars or a couple of players," said team president Dominic Olejniczak.

Lombardi arrived in Washington early on Thursday, February 6, attended a congressional prayer breakfast on Capitol Hill and then met with the Redskins staff. After lunch at Duke Zeibert's, Lombardi held a press conference in the Chandelier Room of the Sheraton-Carlton Hotel. He was both serious and jovial, insisting: "It is not true that I can walk across the Potomac, even when it is frozen . . . I will demand a commitment to excellence and to victory. That is what life is all about."

What role would Williams play? "I've just asked Vince if I could have my same season tickets," he said.

Lombardi then went to work. Decades later, former players could see and hear Lombardi preaching and teaching. Jurgensen quoted him explaining how to execute what had been the staple of the Green Bay offense, the power sweep:

" 'Tight end, split three feet. All you do at the snap of the ball is stand up. That linebacker opposite you will react. He has to, because the play's coming toward him. All you do is stand up — and wherever he wants to go, you take him. If he wants to go inside, you block him inside. If he wants to go outside, take him outside.' "

As for the pulling guards and the ball carrier: " 'The only thing you look for is the tight end. If you see his helmet, go outside. If you see his ass, go inside.' "

Lombardi's training-camp practices were shorter than Graham's, rarely more than 90 minutes, but they were more organized. Instead of calisthenics, he sometimes called for what he referred to as "rooster fights," players hopping on one leg and trying to knock each other off balance. His conditioning drills, according to guard Promuto, were "the worst thing I've ever been through."

He cut some veteran players in a hurry, among them the team's first-round draft choice in 1966, running back Ray McDonald. He then coaxed Sam Huff, with whom he had worked when both were with the Giants in the late 1950s, to return as a player-coach.

Almost daily after practice, Lombardi would hold a "happy hour." Mostly, that amounted to drinking a few beers and poring over the league-wide cut list. Sometimes, he would relax and tell stories.

Lombardi once insisted, for example, that he could talk to a group of equally oversized players he had never seen before and, within minutes, separate the offensive linemen from the defensive linemen. The blockers, he said, would ask questions such as: "What are the meeting and practice routines? Does the team provide benefits?" The defensive linemen would talk only about payday and which opponents to hit.

Arrival of a legend: "It's not true that I can walk across the Potomac, even when it's frozen," Vince Lombardi said after Edward Bennett Williams, left, introduced him as the new Redskins coach at a Sheraton-Carlton news conference on February 6, 1969.

The great coach's instincts for spotting talent were not limited to blockers and tacklers. Jurgensen recalled: "He told me after the first practice, 'See that [rookie] over there in the overalls? When the rest of these guys are gone, he'll still be here.' " Lombardi was looking at Larry Brown.

73

To others at the time, Brown was no more than an undersized (5 feet, 11 inches and 195 pounds) running back, an eighth-round draft choice who had impressed Redskins scouts with his toughness as a blocker at Kansas State. After performances that included catching about a dozen passes during an exhibition game, however, Brown seemed an emerging star.

"I knew the next issue was going to be to tone Larry down," Brown recalled years later. "One day in camp, I ran a particular play and just laid the ball down very quickly. Lombardi ran over and shouted: 'Mister, you don't fumble in our camp!' I made a real big mistake right then: I talked back to him. In front of the entire team, I told him I hadn't fumbled.

"In a way, that's when my feeling [about being successful with the Redskins] got good. You get to be such a perfectionist that management begins to seek means to show any little fault. That's when you get to realize that now you're starting to control them. Before, they had control over you, in terms of not knowing what to expect, not knowing whether you're going to make the team or not. I felt that change then. When he jumped on me that time, I said to myself, 'Hah, I got you.' "

To underline his point about fumbling, Lombardi "made me carry a football [everywhere but to bed] for an entire week," Brown said. "It was an embarrassing situation . . .What made me feel good was that he'd literally chewed me out in front of the entire team. Still, I didn't speak to him for a week. I was young; I was uptight. I'd just look at him. Stare at him. I knew that quietly it was becoming a concern of his.

"One day he walked up to me and said: 'Larry, you're a great athlete. You've got potential and are a hard worker. But don't talk back to me in front of my team. You can call me anything, but do it under your breath.' I felt he was actually saying: 'Relax, let's get over this hurdle. You have nothing to worry about.' I think it takes one hell of a man to say something like that."

When the Redskins jumped to a 4-1-1 record in their first six games, fans began to consider the possibility of a miracle — a division championship. Lombardi was more realistic, mixing pronouns and saying: "We're a team that's playing in spurts . . . They're playing with everything they got and once in a while they put it all together for a long drive . . . But obviously we can be outclassed. We can be overpowered."

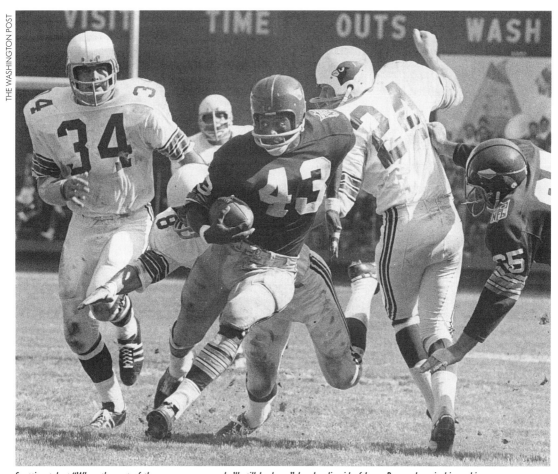

Spotting talent:"When the rest of these guys are gone, he'll still be here," Lombardi said of Larry Brown, here in his rookie year.

Sometimes they were. They lost to the Colts, 41-17, to the eventual division-champion Cowboys, 41-28, to the Rams, 24-13. Like Graham's teams, the Redskins under Lombardi that year allowed more points than they scored. But they finished with the first winning season in 14 years, 7-5-2. Jurgensen completed 62 percent of his passes, for 3,102 yards and 22 touchdowns. Brown gained 888 yards rushing and was runner-up to the Cowboys' Calvin Hill in rookie-of-the-year voting.

One of those disheartened about his own performance was Huff, who announced his retirement as a player after the season. "I'd been struggling to get to the cutoff spot," he said, referring to the place where a runner makes his move back upfield during a sweep.

I could still make the tackle. But even they weren't crisp. You see this on film. You see yourself struggling, still making the play but really having a tough time.

"So we coaches are watching films — and Lombardi never knew anybody's name. All of a sudden he says, 'Who in the hell is that No. 70? We gotta get rid of him next year.' I said: 'Hey, wait a minute. That's me.' "

Williams was euphoric about the team's progress and said of Lombardi: "He may have done his greatest coaching job . . . If there were some way to measure what one can do with the material at hand, I think we could demonstrate he did his greatest job here."

Lombardi talked about how much more was needed. "Once you win a team's heart," he said, "they'll follow you anywhere. They'll do anything for you. I haven't won this team's heart yet, maybe. But it's not for lack of trying. And I'll keep trying."

TRIVIA QUIZ 2

1. When the Redskins became the first NFL team to televise their games in 1950, what company was the sponsor?

2. Which coach had the poorest career record in Redskins history?

3. Name the only Redskins player ever to wear the number 0.

4. Which Redskin holds the record for most receiving yards in a season?

5. In the 1957 offseason, which Redskins defensive back was shot to death in the San Francisco bar he owned?

6. Which player who joined the team in 1965 ended up making the most Pro Bowl appearances of any Redskin?

7. In 1950, a Redskins record was set for the longest punt return in team history. Who ran back that kick?

8. In November 1966, the Redskins routed the Giants in a game with the most points scored of any in the NFL. The points total was:

a) 123
b) 101
c) 113
d) 166

9. In 1959 and 1960, the Redskins drafted top college quarterbacks with their No. 1 picks, but neither signed with Washington. Who were they?

10. Who set the record for the longest Redskins run from scrimmage?

ANSWERS ON PAGE 269

Sonny Jurgensen

Breaking Records and Conventions

By Anthony Cotton

Although he already was a record-setting quarterback in 1964, Christian Adolph Jurgensen III didn't become the legendary Sonny Jurgensen until he joined the Washington Redskins that year in a trade with the Philadelphia Eagles. Over the next 11 seasons, Jurgensen would break both records and conventions and leave behind a host of memories.

One was as a pinpoint passer who completed 1,831 throws for 22,585 yards and 179 touchdowns. He found receivers with footballs thrown from assorted angles — overhead, sidearm or even behind his back.

"He could change speeds on the ball like a baseball pitcher — even throw a screwball," said former teammate Sam Huff. "He was just so wonderful to watch — some quarterbacks could throw a great short pass, some were good with the long ball, but very few could do both — Sonny could."

Each pass was delivered from a body that one teammate said was better suited for the pro bowlers tour than for the NFL.

"My problem was I didn't have a good enough tailor — I picked my uniforms out off the rack," Jurgensen said. "Vince Lombardi was the only coach I had who didn't mention my weight; every other one did. They'd ask me how much I weighed, and if I said 215, they'd say they wanted me to play at 210. If I said I weighed 210, they'd say they wanted me to play at 205. I never understood why it was so important to look good in your uniform — you don't throw the ball with your stomach, you throw it with your arm."

When weight-lifting started to become the rage, the only use Jurgensen had for the training room was as an impromptu lunch counter, leaving mustard stains on the bars for teammates to clean up before they could pump their iron.

But Jurgensen had a mind as sharp as any suit cut along Saville Row. That was part of another persona — the cigar-chomping raconteur who used his head not only to read opposing defenses but also to find ways to indulge his love of a good time. One enduring story holds that Jurgensen used to bundle a wooden Indian under his covers to meet training camp bed checks while he slipped off to tip a few with his many friends in town.

"His lifestyle . . . Sonny was cool," said Huff. "Back then it was cool for a quarterback to drink a lot, and Sonny did his share."

"He was at the tail end of that era when quarterbacks did whatever they wanted to — they were the kings who didn't have to do what everyone else did," added Bobby Mitchell. "He'd hang out and make the younger players buy him drinks . . . That was just the start of it. I wasn't out there — I'd just hear things from some of the guys — but they were wild stories."

Jurgensen's flair on the field had surfaced as early as 1962 with Philadelphia. The season before, he had thrown for a then-NFL-record 3,723 yards, completing 57 percent of his passes, with 32 touchdowns — all on a salary of $14,000. When Jurgensen asked for a raise during training camp, the Eagles balked. Nonplussed, Jurgensen gathered backup quarterback King Hill and left.

"It may have been one of the NFL's first holdouts . . . but I couldn't get the general manager's attention. He was the kind of guy who wouldn't speak to you if you were standing next to him on an elevator," Jurgensen said. "So one day, King and I left Hershey, Pennsylvania, where we were having camp, and we went off to play golf. King was a fantastic golfer.

"The team couldn't even practice that day. After a while, [teammate] Tom Brookshire and [journalist] Jack Whittaker found us on the 12th green — King was putting and I was on the fringe. They ran up to me and asked me what I was thinking about, and I told them that my main concern was getting the ball down [in the hole] in two shots. I had a meeting with the team the next morning, and my salary went up to $19,000."

Two years later, Jurgensen found out, to his great surprise, that he had been traded to Washington. Although he had made a mark in Philly, in Mitchell's opinion Jurgensen still "needed to make a team his own."

His first season in Washington, Jurgensen began to take possession, passing for 2,934 yards and 24 touchdowns. In 1966, those numbers increased to 3,209 yards and 28 scores. Even that stellar performance was topped a year later, when Jurgensen completed 57 percent of his passes for a then-NFL record 3,747 yards and 31 touchdowns. He also set league records for attempts (508) and completions (288) in a single season.

"Sonny could hit a gnat from 50 yards away," said Mitchell. "I hated to lose Norm Snead [who went to Philadelphia in the Jurgensen trade], because I was getting a ton of balls from him — Sonny spread it out more — but you knew Sonny had a better game. I never saw anyone handle a team like Sonny. I used to rate [Baltimore Colts quarterback] Johnny Unitas as the best field general I ever saw, but I might change that to Sonny — there was definitely no comparison between them in throwing the football."

Although his Redskins teams scored points with regularity, Jurgensen never got the chance to play on the stage where every football fan could witness his gifts — the Super Bowl. In his 18 years, Jurgensen said, he played for nine different head coaches. Although there were some legends like Norm Van Brocklin and George Allen among them, it wasn't until 1969 that Jurgensen realized what he had been missing.

That was the year Vince Lombardi joined the Redskins. With his two Super Bowls and three other NFL championships with the Green Bay Packers on his resume,

Lombardi commanded respect, even from Jurgensen, who curtailed his carousing and dedicated himself completely to football.

"I finally had a coach who I really respected, a man who worked hard and wanted to win," Jurgensen said. "Sure, a little bit of it was me maturing, but it was more. Here's a guy who's won —— if we do what he says we'll have a legitimate chance to win. "

That season, Jurgensen threw for 3,102 yards and 22 touchdowns, completing 62 percent of his passes as the Redskins improved from 5-9 to 7-5-2, their first winning record in 13 seasons.

"My career wasn't like someone like [Dallas quarterback] Roger Staubach's, who played for the same guy [Tom Landry] the whole time," Jurgensen said. "I was always changing every other year it seemed — changing systems, changing keys. Lombardi had the simplest system and by far the best. There's no telling what I would have done had I played for him my entire career."

But Lombardi's tenure in Washington was cut tragically short by his death, and Jurgensen's was curtailed by injuries. In 1970 he threw for 2,354 yards and 23 touchdowns but injured his left shoulder in an exhibition game the following year and missed the first eight regular games. In 1972, after leading the Redskins to three straight wins after recovering from the shoulder injury, Jurgensen ruptured his Achilles tendon.

Still fighting injuries, Jurgensen threw a total of 312 passes in the 1973 and 1974 seasons. He retired on May 1, 1975 as the NFL's all-time leading passer and holder of the league's single-season records for pass attempts, completions and yardage.

As for what he values most from his Redskins days, Jurgensen goes back to his season with Lombardi. That year, former Packer stars Paul Hornung and Max McGee came to Washington to visit their former coach during a Redskins practice. At one point in their conversation, Lombardi reportedly looked at Jurgensen and told the duo, "If we'd had him, we'd have never lost a game." This from a man who had coached Bart Starr, one of the NFL's legendary field generals.

"I also heard that Lombardi once said I could perhaps be the best who ever played," Jurgensen said. "For him to say things like that . . . when I look back at my career, those are the words I cherish the most."

CHAPTER 3
The 1970s

Heading Down the Glory Road

By Leonard Shapiro

Vince Lombardi watched as a number of his veteran players worked out before the 1970 training camp, using the practice field at Georgetown University. A work stoppage mandated by the players' fledgling union was imminent that summer, and Lombardi wanted the Redskins to be prepared for anything once it ended.

He rarely ceased being concerned about the team — though he had more important things to think about. Lombardi was looking down on the workouts through his window at Georgetown University Hospital, where he was recuperating from surgery. He had been given a room with a view of the field so that he could watch, and several players made it a point to visit him each day after practice.

"I remember him telling me that everyone had to stick together, and if anyone broke the rules, I was going to be in trouble," said safety Brig Owens, the players' union representative. "Even before he was put in the hospital, he came over to Georgetown and told all the guys that he didn't agree with what we were doing, but that he understood it. I went to the hospital to see him with Jerry Smith. He had that bed by the window so he could see who was working out and who wasn't, and he kept telling me to hold everything together. He told us that a team was like a wheel and that if one spoke on the wheel was loose but the rest of them were tight, the wheel would still work the way it was supposed to.

"I'll never forget that. When we left, Jerry said to me, 'What do you think he meant?' But I think we both knew and we didn't want to admit it."

Sonny Jurgensen also visited Lombardi regularly. The 1969 season had been the most memorable of the veteran quarterback's career, and he couldn't wait to get going under a coach who brought out the best in him. "One day he asked me who was leading the team when we did laps," Jurgensen said. "I told him it was me. He looked at me with that big grin and said, 'Don't you lie to me, Jurgensen,' and we both started laughing. I was so much looking forward to playing for him again. That '69 season was the highlight of my career. It was so special, and now the next year we knew we were going to win and get better. He'd put it all in order to make it happen."

Lombardi had indeed put it all in order. He had turned the tide the previous year. He had begun to instill a fierce commitment to excellence. He had started the rebuilding of the team. He had, in short, pointed the way to the glory days ahead.

The 1970 college draft had helped, even if the Redskins previously had traded away their first-round and third-round choices. With his first choice in the second round, Lombardi had taken Bill Brundige, a brainy defensive tackle from Colorado, then added Paul Laaveg, a somewhat undersized offensive lineman from Iowa, Manny Sistrunk, another defensive tackle from obscure Arkansas AM&N, and Mack Alston, a tight end from Maryland State. All four would make significant contributions to the Redskins over the next few years.

But Lombardi would not see that or the results of everything else he had done.

That June, unable to shake what he thought was a stubborn case of the flu, he had visited team physician George Resta, who immediately sent him to Georgetown University Hospital for tests. It was announced initially that Lombardi was suffering from a stomach virus and would undergo a complete physical work-up. But on June 27, doctors performed exploratory surgery that uncovered what was first described as a benign tumor in his colon. Surgeons removed a section of the colon as a precautionary measure, and Lombardi remained in the hospital.

He did get out long enough to see his team play one more time. Still weak from the surgery, he was driven to Baltimore to watch a rookie scrimmage against the Colts in Memorial Stadium. Huff, who had agreed to stay on as an assistant coach, recalled Lombardi coming into the team's locker room before the scrimmage started.

"He looked very bad," Huff said. "He'd lost about 40 pounds, and you could barely hear him talk. But he gathered the team around him, and he directed his remarks at the

RICHARD DARCEY — THE WASHINGTON POST

Breaking records: With a hearing aid to help him hear signals, Larry Brown became the first Redskin to rush for over 1,000 yards.

players he drafted that spring. 'You're my people, I've selected you,' he told them. 'You're going to wear this uniform with pride. You're now a member of the Washington Redskins, and there's a lot of responsibility that goes along with that. Don't you ever forget it.' It was the last time I ever saw him alive."

A few days later, on July 27, Lombardi returned to the hospital for more surgery after it was determined that the original diagnosis had been incorrect. The tumor was malignant, and this particularly virulent strain of cancer had spread. Though his family ordered a news blackout on his condition, the team and his loved ones knew that the illness was terminal. At 7:12 on the morning of September 3, the man many consider the greatest coach in the history of the game died at age 57, two weeks before the start of the 1970 season.

President Richard Nixon interrupted a state dinner for the president of Mexico in San Diego to speak about Lombardi. The entire football team flew to New York to be among 3,000 mourners at the funeral at St. Patrick's Cathedral. Williams eulogized Lombardi, saying that "he had a covenant with greatness. He was committed to excellence in everything he attempted. Our country has lost one of its great men. The world of sports has lost its first citizen. The Redskins have lost their leader. I personally have lost a friend."

There was a sorrowful irony in Lombardi's death. He was a man who Huff said "probably knew more about his players' physical condition than any coach who ever lived." Yet Lombardi detested physicals for himself, especially the proctology exam to check for colon cancer. He had never had one done, and there still are people in the organization who believe that he would have lived to coach for many a day if only he had taken better care of himself, if only he had had what's now considered a routine exam.

Instead, the Redskins went into their first season of the 1970s with an interim head coach, Bill Austin, hand-picked by Lombardi to run the team when he entered the hospital the second time. Austin was considered one of the game's better offensive line coaches, a gruff, no-nonsense type who had had a brief fling as a head coach with the Pittsburgh Steelers from 1966 to 1968, compiling a dreadful 11-28-3 record. Lombardi's death so close to the start of the season precluded hiring another big-name coach, and Williams announced that Austin would focus on offense while running the team, with Harland Svare, another holdover, commanding the defense.

Lombardi's death had a devastating impact on the players. Jurgensen took it particularly hard.

"No one could follow Lombardi," Jurgensen said. "You were missing the one ingredient that was going to make it so special. He's the guy who made it happen, he's the guy who was able to get the best out of everyone on that team. To lose that just when you're starting to see the light at the end of the tunnel really was tough to swallow."

Though the Redskins won their last five preseason games, they lost three of their first five in the regular season, then soon afterward had a disastrous five-game losing streak on the way to a dismal 6-8 season. The highlight of an otherwise thoroughly forgettable year was the play of Larry Brown, whom Lombardi had taken under his wing the year before. Among other things, Lombardi had discovered that Brown had a previously undetected hearing problem, making him a step slow at the snap of the ball. He cured that by installing a hearing aid in Brown's helmet, allowing him to hear the signals better and get off the line with perfect timing. In 1970, Brown became the first running back in team history to gain more than 1,000 yards rushing. He ran for 1,125, averaging 4.7 yards a carry, and racked up six games of 100 yards or better, also a club record at the time.

The offense, as usual, was a high-powered unit, but the defense remained a disaster zone despite the infusion of younger talent in the off-season. The Redskins still had no dominant pass rusher. The linebackers, with the exception of perennial All-Pro Chris Hanburger, were adequate at best. And the secondary was no match for quarterbacks who had all day to stand in the pocket and let their receivers get open.

"It got to the point where Austin would come into our defensive meeting rooms and snidely ask the coaches, 'Well, how are you guys gonna screw up this week?' " Huff recalled. "One time, Austin got on us and I'd had it. We were about to play the Cowboys and we knew it was a lost cause, but you have to try something. At one point I said to Austin, 'You were a jerk in high school, you were a jerk in college, you were a jerk when we played together in New York, and you'll be a jerk all your life. So let's see how great a coach you are. Why don't we switch this week. Let us coach your offense and you coach the defense, and we'll see how damned great you are."

That never happened. What did happen, as expected, was that the Redskins lost big to the Cowboys, 34-0.

The Redskins managed to win their last two games that season, but everyone knew that Austin and his staff had little chance of coming back in 1971. Not with Williams in charge. Not after the Redskins president had seen the sort of magic a big-time coach could work on his team. Williams was accustomed to winning in the courtroom, and with a little help from Jack Kent Cooke, he did not wait long to make his move.

Even before he had hired Lombardi, Williams had been intrigued by George Allen, the intense head coach of the Los Angeles Rams. Their paths had first crossed in 1966 at a league meeting after Allen's first season with the Rams. They spoke for more than three hours, and Williams was impressed by Allen's single-minded focus on football as well as by his history. A brilliant young defensive mind as an assistant with the Chicago Bears under George Halas, Allen had been carried off the field by his players when the Bears upset the heavily favored New York Giants in the 1963 title game.

When Rams owner Dan Reeves wanted to hire Allen after the 1965 season, Halas was unwilling to let his assistant coach out of the two years remaining on his contract. Ultimately, the issue went to court, with a judge ruling that Allen had signed a valid contract and was required to stay with the Bears. Moments after the judge announced his decision, however, Halas stood up in court and said that he would allow Allen to leave, that Allen was a minor issue. The man known as Papa Bear told the court that he was far more concerned about upholding the sanctity of a contract. So Allen went west.

In Los Angeles, however, Reeves and Allen did not exactly have a meeting of the minds. In fact, they butted head for several years, particularly over Allen's penchant for wheeling and dealing. Finally, on the morning after Christmas in 1968, Reeves announced that he was firing Allen. That very day, Cooke, then living in Los Angeles, contacted Allen to express the Redskins' interest in him.

"I got a hand-delivered message from Jack," Allen once told an interviewer, "saying that it was urgent that I call him. He had tried to call me, but the phone was so busy he couldn't get through. Two days later, Ed Williams flew out to Jack's home in Bel Air, and we met for about three hours. I told them then that I was interested in the Redskins job but I wanted to finish my job in Los Angeles. I thought we had a chance to win the championship. I still had two years left on my contract, and I wanted to complete the job.

"I remember Jack made the statement at that time: 'It's 10,000-to-1 that you'll get the job back.' And I said, 'Well, I'd like to take that one shot.' We had built a home and had made so much progress with the team. I felt that once you start a job, you should finish it."

Allen's players in Los Angeles apparently felt the same way. They threatened a boycott if Reeves did not take Allen back, and the owner reluctantly agreed to honor Allen's contract. At that point, the Redskins decided to turn to Lombardi, but Williams had come away from his 1968 discussions with Allen convinced that if he ever needed another head coach, he had found his man.

That opportunity presented itself two years later, after the 1970 season. Reeves announced then that he would not renew Allen's contract, despite the Rams' 49-17-4 record and two playoff appearances over Allen's five-year tenure. Still embroiled in a major personality clash with Allen, Reeves had had enough. This time, so had Allen.

"I operated in an atmosphere of hatred," Allen once said of his relationship with Reeves, who would die of cancer a year later. "Our whole team did. Reeves hated me. Hating me, he hated the team. He sought to split us so we'd come apart. Somehow, I held the pieces together."

Over those five LA years, Allen had engineered 51 trades, including the one for Gary Beban that had victimized the Redskins. In 1968, Allen had convinced Williams to give up the Redskins' No. 1 choice the next year in the trade for the UCLA star quarterback. Allen had drafted Beban on the second round, but the Rams had not been willing to meet Beban's contract demands. It was not only Williams who jumped at the opportunity to get such a high-profile player. He was seconded by Cooke, who was convinced

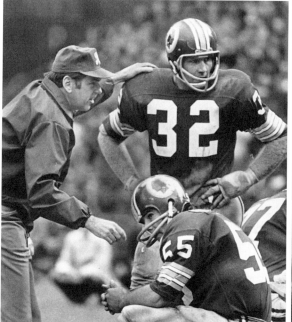

Allen for the defense: The intense George Allen liked to have a safety-first offense and leave the rest to players like linebackers Jack Pardee (32) and Chris Hanburger (55).

BILL SNEAD — THE WASHINGTON POST

that Beban would be the Redskins quarterback of the future after an apprenticeship under Jurgensen.

Williams compounded his error by negotiating a guaranteed, three-year, $350,000 deal for Beban. Despite the promise the rookie had shown, though, Beban failed in attempts at both quarterback and defensive back. "Poor Gary," Williams once said. "He just couldn't cut it. I don't know why. George doesn't talk about it. He probably doesn't want to embarrass me."

All of that was forgotten on January 6, 1971, when Williams introduced Allen as the Redskins' next head coach, "the best football coach in the world" and "the last coach I ever hire." Williams had paid a high price — including ceding to Allen complete control of the football operation, with the last word on trades, the college draft, even player contracts.

Allen became the highest paid coach at that point in NFL history. His seven-year contract called for a salary of $125,000 a year, with a $25,000 bonus for signing and up to $150,000 toward the home of his choice, plus interest payments on the mortgage. He also would receive incentive bonuses for making it into post-season games: $5,000 for the playoffs, $10,000 more for the conference championship, $15,000 more for the Super

Bowl. Nor was that all. Allen got a limousine and chauffeur, a virtually unlimited expense account, permission to keep all revenue from his TV and radio shows, and expenses for visiting his family in California until they could move east and for dental trips to the West Coast.

Shortly afterward, Allen even convinced Williams and the team's directors to invest nearly $1 million in a new practice facility in the Virginia suburbs, not far from Dulles International Airport. It was a state-of-the-art operation, with two practice fields, one with artificial turf so the team could work out even in bad weather. It was surrounded on three sides by dense woods, the better to prevent opponents from spying on his team (as Allen himself had been accused of doing before his Rams teams played the Dallas Cowboys). The new Redskin Park came with a complete workout area, basketball and racquetball courts, a carpeted locker room, the finest training room in the league, and a complex that included classrooms and offices for the coaching staff and players — as well as a massive office overlooking the practice field for the head coach.

Not long after construction began on the project, Williams acknowledged that "when Coach Allen came to Washington, we agreed we had an unlimited budget. He's already exceeded it."

Allen wasted little time reshaping his team. Less than three weeks after taking the job, he sent fourth-round and eighth-round draft choices and linebacker Tom Roussel to the New Orleans Saints. In return he got veteran quarterback Billy Kilmer, who was to back up Jurgensen. Though Kilmer's teams never had beaten the Rams, they had always played well, and Kilmer had a knack for moving his offense against Allen's complex defensive schemes. But Kilmer had become expendable in New Orleans after the Saints made it known that they would use their No. 1 choice in the 1971 draft to pick quarterback Archie Manning, the Heisman Trophy winner from Ole Miss.

"Three teams were interested in me," Kilmer said, "and I wanted to go to Lou Saban in Denver. That seemed the best chance to play right away. I was at Hialeah watching a friend of mine's horse run when I got two phone messages, from Dave Brady [who covered the Redskins for *The Washington Post*] and J.D. Roberts [the Saints' new head coach]. Right then I knew I'd been traded. I figured I'd never play there, that I'd never beat out Jurgy . . ."

On draft day the following week, Kilmer phoned Allen and told him that he thought he still could be a starting quarterback somewhere in the league. He asked Allen to trade him. But Allen had no such intention — though he was very much in his wheeler-dealer mode that memorable day.

Over the next 24 hours, Allen pulled off one of the most stunning deals in the annals of the NFL. He traded seven draft choices, as well as Redskins linebacker Marlin McKeever, to Los Angeles. In exchange, LA sent back six of Allen's favorite Rams, including an entire unit of linebackers. Allen gave up his first-round and third-round picks and four choices in the 1972 draft to obtain linebackers Jack Pardee, Mo Pottios and Maxie Baughan, defensive tackle Diron Talbert, guard John Wilbur and special teams standout Jeff Jordan. The Rams also had given him a fifth-round choice, but he traded that pick later in the day to the Green Bay Packers for tight end Boyd Dowler. Dowler had already joined Allen's staff as an assistant coach, but the trade was needed to make another experienced body available at tight end just in case.

"This is great, terrific for the Redskins," Allen said. "We've upgraded our defense at least 25 percent. It's worth at least two victories. Our goal now is nine or 10 wins."

That was only the beginning. Before the start of training camp in 1971, Allen continued to send picks all over the league (including one he didn't own, which cost him a $5,000 fine from the league office). From the New York Jets he got defensive ends Verlon Biggs and Jimmie Jones. From the Buffalo Bills came defensive end Ron McDole. From the San Diego Chargers he acquired return man Leslie (Speedy) Duncan. From the Rams he added strong safety Richie Petitbon, running back Tommy Mason and center George Burman.

Even after the Redskins had assembled in Carlisle for training camp, he was still making moves. Unhappy with his second-round draft choice, Texas receiver Cotton Speyrer, Allen sent the swift rookie up the road to Baltimore, along with two medium-round draft choices, in return for receiver Roy Jefferson. Within six months, Allen essentially had transformed the Redskins in his own image. His new team inevitably was being called the "Ramskins," though Allen and his players much preferred "The Over-the-Hill Gang."

Either way, the team was heavy with the veterans Allen preferred. Never mind that Baughan barely could walk on a bad foot that would sideline him for the season. He knew Allen's defense better than anyone and could teach it to the younger players. It didn't matter that Jack Pardee had survived a cancer operation and was 35 years old when he reported to his new team. He clearly was a coach on the field, a leader who reported to camp in what he later said was the best physical shape of his life. Who cared that McDole, the "Dancing Bear," had one of the worst bodies in football? He had a remarkable knack for penetrating offensive line schemes to block field goals and extra points, and he still could rush the passer effectively. So what if Kilmer's passes often wobbled instead of hitting receivers with the classic spirals launched by Jurgensen? He picked up the offense almost immediately.

Kilmer also picked up the starting position he never thought he would get when, in the next-to-last preseason game, Jurgensen busted his shoulder trying to tackle Miami defensive back Dick Anderson on an interception return.

In truth, Allen had always preferred Kilmer. His coaching philosophy was simple enough. He wanted his offense to score a few touchdowns the safest way imaginable and leave the rest to his defense. With Larry Brown and hard-blocking fullback Charley Harraway around, the Redskins would be a running team. The days of Jurgensen throwing 40 and 50 times a game downfield were over. Kilmer, already being called "Whiskey" by his teammates for obvious reasons, was perfect for the safety-first offense directed by offensive coordinator Ted Marchibroda. His passes weren't pretty, but they didn't have to be with receivers like Charley Taylor, Jefferson and tight end Jerry Smith. Harraway and Brown also could catch the ball out of the backfield, and Kilmer had no qualms about checking off from his primary receivers to dump the ball off to his backs.

The fans, of course, weren't so sure about the quarterback choice. Jurgensen was one of the most popular players in the history of the franchise, and any time he was healthy, fans clearly were split. Soon bumper stickers sprouted, proclaiming either "I Like Sonny" or "I Like Billy." It was not a bitter quarterback controversy, however, because the two men never let it become one. In fact, they became close friends and often went out on the town together (far more than Allen would have preferred).

"I'm the first to say Sonny Jurgensen might be the best [passer] ever to play the game," Kilmer said. "I was there to win. He and I never had any problems, and I had no ego problems. All I wanted was for us to win it all."

The Redskins certainly started the 1971 season as if that were possible. With Kilmer at quarterback, they took the opener, 24-17, against the favored Cardinals as the defense came up with seven turnovers. "It's pretty hard to lose when the defense takes the ball away seven times," Allen said. The next week yielded a 30-3 victory over the Giants that included a late-game melee when three Redskins were thrown out for fighting. And in Game 3 on the road against the powerful Dallas Cowboys, the one team Allen

RICHARD DARCEY — THE WASHINGTON POST

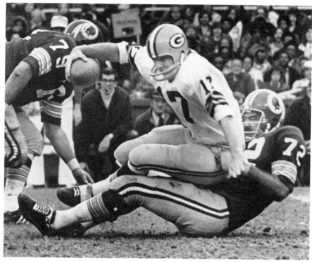

In with the old: The original Over-the-Hill Gang — from left, Mo Pottios, Ron McDole, Richie Petitbon, Diron Talbert and Jack Pardee — was central to Allen's teams, making key defensive plays like Talbert's sack of Green Bay's Jerry Tagge.

always loved to hate, the Redskins demonstrated that they definitely belonged among playoff contenders.

With Harraway running 57 yards for a touchdown and Kilmer throwing 50 yards for another, the Redskins prevailed, 20-16. "This was the first time we were a team, really a team," veteran guard Ray Schoenke, a holdover from the awful 1960s and a former Cowboy himself, exulted in the locker room. "This was the football we always wanted to play. There was a closeness, a magnificent, sustained effort with everyone pulling together."

When the team returned to Dulles International Airport later that night, more than 5,000 fans were there to greet them. Two more wins followed, giving the Redskins a 5-0 start. Allen and his players were becoming the toast of the town. When the coach walked in the door at Duke Zeibert's old L Street restaurant the night after beating the Cardinals a second time, 20-0, Allen got a standing ovation. Even after the Redskins had been dealt their first loss, a 27-20 defeat by the Kansas City Chiefs in Game 6, more than 20,000 fans were at Dulles to welcome home their team.

"This team had a different personality than what people in Washington were used to," Pardee said. "It used to be Sonny Jurgensen and the bomb. With us, it was scrap, cling, hold on, battle. It was like the old Green Bay teams. We'd wait patiently and then some-body — it could come from anybody on the offense, defense or special teams — would make the big play."

By mid-season, however, the Redskins began to wilt, especially after Taylor, their star receiver, had gone down with a broken leg against the Chiefs. Other injuries followed, and Brown and Harraway were feeling the effects of the poundings they were taking. Jurgensen made his first start against the Eagles in Game 11 — but he lasted only until the second quarter, re-injuring his shoulder when he was tackled scrambling away from defenders. He would be lost for the year. Kilmer came on in relief and led the team to a 20-13 victory, their first triumph in a month.

Kilmer was in the headlines again the day after leading the team to a 24-7 victory over the New York Giants in Game 12. Following a night of celebration, Kilmer and a female companion went into a short-order restaurant — The Toddle House in Arlington, Virginia — at 2 a.m. He tried to pay for his bacon and eggs with a $100 bill. When he got into an animated discussion with the waitress, who said she couldn't break the $100, an off-duty policeman at the other end of the counter thought Kilmer was being too boisterous. He advised him to walk outside to his car to calm down. When Kilmer declined, telling the cop, "If you think I'm wrong, put me in jail," he was arrested and subsequently charged with drunk and disorderly conduct. He spent only a few hours in the pokey and was released after posting $15 collateral (paid for with another $100 bill).

The story was front-page news in Washington. It wasn't exactly the way Allen had wanted to start the week before his team would be traveling back to Los Angeles to play the Rams. But Allen, who had fined Kilmer and Jurgensen $500 each for breaking curfew before a preseason game in Denver, this time took a different approach. "I'm not going to make a big thing out of it," he said. "My only concern is getting ready for the Rams."

Six days later, The Toddle House Affair was mostly forgotten. In one of the sweetest victories of his head coaching career, Allen took his team to Los Angeles for a Monday night game witnessed by 66 million TV viewers and left town with a 38-24 triumph — clinching the Redskins' first playoff berth since the 1945 season. Kilmer was worth a stack of C-notes that day, completing 14 of 19 passes for 246 yards and three touchdowns.

There was sheer joy in the Redskins locker room that night. "This is a great, great victory," Allen told his players. "It's the best win of our lives. Men, let's just go on from here."

On the plane ride home, Allen allowed his players to sip from nine magnums of champagne. The next day, his post-game news conference at Redskins Park brought more of the same. The only folks Allen disliked more than rookie starters were reporters, those pesky people who always peppered him with questions he didn't want to answer. But on this day, two bottles of champagne were popped for the media — the label read "Chateau de George" — and Allen offered up comment after comment.

"Imagine playing that game on TV," he gushed. "Pete Rozelle came up to me before the game. He was just thrilled about this being the final Monday night game, and I told him, 'Even Cecil B. DeMille couldn't upstage you on this one.' Imagine, the 13th game on December 13, and both teams having to win it."

His cheerfulness, however, was short-lived. After losing a meaningless regular-season

RICHARD DARCEY — THE WASHINGTON POST

Toward a title game again: Charley Harraway breaks away for a 57-yard touchdown run to help defeat Dallas 20-16 on October 3, 1971, on the way to the Washington Redskins' first playoff berth since 1945.

finale to Cleveland, the Redskins went through a week of controversy as they prepared to face San Francisco in the opening round of the playoffs.

The turmoil began early in the week when Allen complained bitterly that none of his defensive players had made the Pro Bowl team. During the week, a reporter also drew Allen's ire when he wondered why the Redskins had been able to score 180 points in the first half of their regular-season games but only 96 in the second half. Was that a sign that this gang really was over the hill? "That has nothing to do with it," Allen snapped. "Anyone who says that does not know what he's talking about."

The largest controversy, however, came when former Rams punter Bruce Gossett, now a member of the 49ers, sounded off against his former coach. "There isn't anything good I can say about Allen," Gossett told the *Oakland Tribune.* "I just don't think he's a first-class guy. He lies to you, and he's out for himself. There's no question about it . . . Allen is just dishonest with people when there is no need to be. He told me face to face, in front of my wife, that I would be with the Rams as long as he was. A couple of weeks later, I was traded. What do you think of a guy who does that?"

Allen's response? "It will be a pleasure to play against Gossett and the 49ers . . . He can say what he wants."

In the end, though, it was no pleasure at all. On a day with strong winds and pelting rain, Washington was eliminated in a 24-20 defeat, the result of a series of mistakes — and some unsolicited help from the White House.

In the first half, the Redskins coach who was always so conservative on offense made a surprise decision. Faced with a fourth down and inches at the San Francisco 11, Allen decided to go for the first down instead of a short field goal. Kilmer called the play — a sweep to the left by Larry Brown that had worked for a key touchdown two weeks earlier against the Rams. But 49ers linebacker Frank Nunley came up and caught Brown for a two-yard loss, and San Francisco took over on downs.

Allen later would insist that his call had been right. "It was just inches," he said. "The percentages were in our favor to pick it up. It was just a few inches . . ."

Despite that play, Washington still was outscoring San Francisco. Late in the half, the Redskins were ahead 10-3 when Speedy Duncan returned a punt 47 yards to the San Francisco 12, with only 30 seconds left on the clock. Surely the Redskins would pad their lead and send a demoralized 49er team to the dressing room.

On the next play, Harraway gained four yards on a pass in the flat. But then Kilmer called an end-around to Roy Jefferson — and the 49ers were not fooled. On the contrary, Cedrick Hardman tackled Jefferson for a 13-yard loss. That may have caused some dismay in the White House. Bill Brundige later reported on TV that President Nixon, a huge Redskins fan, had called Allen the night before the game with a play-calling suggestion, adding: "President Nixon told Coach Allen, 'I'd like to see you run a flanker reverse with Roy Jefferson against the 49ers.' "

The Redskins next tried a field goal, but the snap was off target, and the 49ers blocked Curt Knight's kick. When the buzzer sounded, it was the Redskins who trudged into their locker room, morale sagging after a seemingly sure scoring opportunity had been wasted.

In the second half, the tide turned against the Redskins when San Francisco quarterback John Brodie threw one of his rare spirals, hitting receiver Gene Washington with a spectacular, 78-yard touchdown pass. The Redskins then helped the 49ers clinch their victory with two costly turnovers — an interception of a Kilmer pass and a bad punt snap by George Burman that San Francisco recovered in the end zone for a touchdown. Ironically, it was the defense and special teams — Allen's pride and joy — that had largely allowed the 49ers to send the Redskins packing.

Allen later would field another call from the White House, this one of consolation, and by the next afternoon he was already looking ahead to the 1972 season. After all, he had been named NFC coach of the year by UPI and was chosen NFL coach of the year by the Associated Press and *Pro Football Weekly* as well as by his coaching peers in a vote for *The Sporting News.*

"I'm glad we could give the Washington area a championship-caliber team," he said. "But I'd like to improve. You have to improve . . . Nobody knows what I went through, from the time I took the Redskins job up to today. The work, the agony, it hasn't been easy — it took so much energy and so many frustrations, and I beat myself up physically — I'll tell you what, I wouldn't go through this program again from the start to the finish for anything. I wouldn't go through it for $10 million."

In his first year, Allen had built a reputation as a workaholic who often slept on the couch in his Redskin Park office. It seemed that every game "was the biggest of our lives" and that, as he often put it, "losing was like death." He focused his entire being on the Redskins, with little patience for much else. He dined on ice cream, his wife Etty once said, because he didn't have to waste time chewing. His son Bruce once said that his father was so consumed with the team that even when he was working around the house he would tell his kids that "if I get this weed out in one piece, we'll beat the Cowboys."

He must have done a good job of weeding, because 1972 was to be the year when the ever more intense Washington-Dallas rivalry ended with the Redskins defeating the Cowboys for the NFC championship and going on to their first Super Bowl game.

In the lead-up to the 1972 season, massive team changes were no longer the order of the day. The Redskins added depth to their defensive backfield by acquiring one of Allen's old Chicago stalwarts, safety Roosevelt Taylor. He brought in two more veterans as well, running back George Nock from the Jets and offensive tackle Mitch Johnson from the Browns. Also on the roster that year was one of the most intriguing rookies in the league.

In the spring of 1971, Allen had held open tryouts for anyone who thought he was good enough to make the team. More than 300 young men of all shapes and sizes showed up on the Georgetown University practice field, and Allen signed a huge young defensive tackle, Otis Sistrunk, a distant cousin of the Redskins' Manny Sistrunk. Otis lasted a week in training camp before being cut, but he eventually would become a regular starter for the Oakland Raiders.

Undaunted and knowing a nice headline when he saw one, Allen held the free-agent tryouts again the next year. This time 385 hopefuls, not to mention scads of reporters and camera crews, reported to Georgetown while Allen and his staff recorded 40-yard dash times and put the mostly motley crew through drills to see if anyone had the right stuff. At the end of the session, Allen signed Herb Mul-Key, who had never attended college, to a free-agent contract. Mul-Key had run a 4.5-second, 40-yard dash on a muddy field, and eventually he would go on to make the team as a return specialist and back-up running back. In his three seasons with the Redskins, he averaged 27.8 yards per kickoff return, the second highest in team history.

All player injuries from 1971 had healed by the time the Redskins headed for Carlisle. Jurgensen, as well as Taylor and Brown, was back in good health, and there was a quarterback controversy almost from the start. "Bill Kilmer is our quarterback," Allen said the first week the veterans reported. "It's up to somebody to beat him out. He did an excellent job last year, and we won with him. But I'm pleased by the reports of Sonny. His weight is down, and that's a sign of self-discipline."

Kilmer opened the season as the starter, leading the Redskins to victories over the Vikings (24-21) and the Cardinals (24-10) before losing to the underdog New England

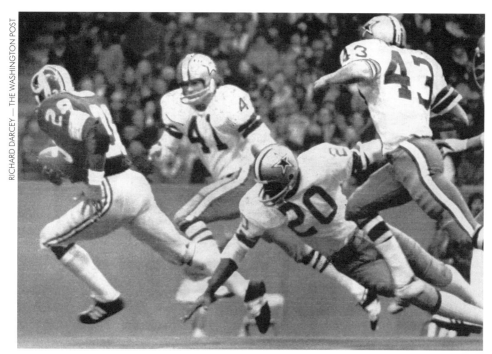

RICHARD DARCEY — THE WASHINGTON POST

One for the unknowns: Herb Mul-Key, picked from hundreds of would-be players in open-to-all tryouts, fires up the gut of the Dallas Doomsday Defense for 34 yards in a December 1972 game.

Patriots. Kilmer had played well in New England, and the Redskins felt that they had been robbed of a touchdown over a ball that they thought had been ruled recovered in the end zone. Instead, a safety had been awarded, and the Redskins ultimately lost by one point, 24-23.

The following week before the Eagles game at RFK Stadium, reporters covering practice noticed that Jurgensen was spending far more time with the first unit than he had all season. When *Washington Post* reporter George Solomon asked Allen whether he was planning to start Jurgensen, the coach snapped back, "That's my business. Personnel changes are strategy, and I refuse to have anyone writing about strategy at my practices. You're helping the enemy. The players and coaches are fed up with this. This is my team, and I say you can't write about our playing a new guard, or linebacker. It will help the other team."

The next day, Allen closed his practice to the press after *The Post* reported Jurgensen's increased load under a headline "Jurgensen Steps Up Drills, Speculation Irks Allen." After the workout, Allen told reporters, "If we lose Sunday, you can feel good because you'll be at fault."

Allen never did announce his quarterback choice, but when Jurgensen was introduced on game day, RFK shook to its foundation. It was not exactly a brilliant return — Jurgensen threw three interceptions that day — but with Allen's defense in fine form, the team won, 14-0.

By the time the Redskins went into their first game that year against the hated Cowboys, both were 4-1, and it was increasingly clear that they were the two best teams in the conference. In that first meeting of the year, the Redskins came away with a 24-20 victory, fueled by Brown's running and catching. The workhorse of the offense gained 95 yards rushing in 26 carries and added 100 more yards on seven receptions. Allen was so giddy over the victory that he awarded Jurgensen a game ball.

"In my 16 years here, I can't think of a more gratifying win than this one," Jurgensen said afterward. "We did what we started out to when we finally got around to getting it together. It's something we worked hard for."

Added Allen: "This was one of the finest games I've ever been associated with. It was a Super Bowl right there in RFK Stadium. Sticking together and playing as a team is the only way to beat the Cowboys. That's exactly what we did."

If that victory was a high point of Jurgensen's career, the following week's game against the Giants in New York clearly was the low point. Seven minutes into the first quarter, Jurgensen planted his foot to throw, as he had done for so many years, and the Achilles tendon in his left foot snapped. His season was over. A team physician told Jurgensen that it was the worst tear he had ever seen, and Jurgensen said, "My tendons looked like mashed potatoes."

Kilmer would come on in relief and help the Redskins win that game — and the next five straight. By then, they had beaten the Eagles for the ninth consecutive time, and their 11-1 mark for the season had clinched the NFC East title. That meant that they would host the Central Division champion in a home game at RFK on Christmas Eve.

First, though, would be a rematch with the Cowboys in Dallas. While the Redskins had the luxury of resting players with nagging injuries before that game, the Cowboys had to win to keep alive their wild card hopes — and they did exactly that with a 34-24 victory. The next day Allen complained bitterly that the Cowboys had used an illegal play to try to injure Jack Pardee with a "vicious and ugly" crackback block by receiver Lance (Bambi) Alworth. The Cowboys denied it, noting that Redskins receiver Charley Taylor also had cracked back and hit linebacker Chuck Howley, ending his season with a knee injury. But Dallas took the high road, saying that Taylor's block had been perfectly legal.

The controversy simmered for several weeks as the Redskins closed out the regular season with a dismal 24-17 loss to Buffalo, then prepared to play the Packers on Christmas Eve in the opening round of the playoffs. Allen closed his last two practices of the week to the media, and when the game began it became obvious why: He had decided to deploy a five-man defensive front against the Packers in an effort to stop running back John Brockington. It was the perfect tactic. Brockington gained only nine yards in 13 carries, and the Redskins, dominating the second half, advanced to the New Year's Eve NFC title game with a 16-3 victory.

Better yet, the opponent again would be the Cowboys, who looked like they would be coming to town with a new starting quarterback. In the team's playoff game in San Francisco, Roger Staubach had come off the bench to replace Craig Morton and had rallied his team from a 15-point deficit to a 30-28 victory.

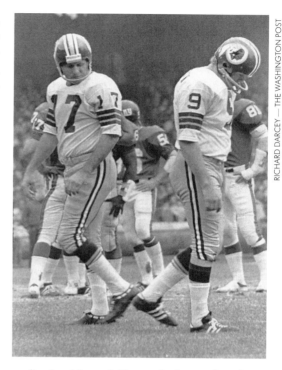

Changing of the guard: Kilmer watches Jurgensen limp off with a torn Achilles tendon that ended his 1972 season.

RICHARD DARCEY — THE WASHINGTON POST

Early in the week before the game, the crackback issue reared its ugly head. Alworth insisted that he had not gone for Pardee's knees, saying that the Redskins were upset only because the Cowboys had scored on the play. Alworth also charged that later in the game, Pardee had tried to knee him in the head. Pardee admitted that this was true, "but only after he went for my knees three times."

In Dallas, the Cowboys knew what Allen was doing. Coach Tom Landry said that "they were normal crackback blocks. I think George threw up an excellent smokescreen, and you [the writers] took the whole works. You took the bait, the hook and the sinker." Other Cowboys joined the verbal war. "The Redskins and their coach just can't say, 'We got whipped' and leave it at that," said Dallas center Dave Manders. "They've got to come up with an excuse, like Pardee bitching about a block. That's probably the reason I feel more emotion playing against the Redskins than I did when we used to play the Packers in championship games."

The Redskins were equally outspoken. "We hate the Cowboys," said Diron Talbert, whose big brother Don had once played for Landry. "It's been building up, and now we finally got a team that can whip 'em."

On Thursday before the game, Landry made it official. Though Morton had started all year, Staubach would be his man at RFK. "Craig got us into the playoffs, but Roger is the main reason we're in the finals," Landry said. For the Redskins there was no quarterback decision to be made. Jurgensen was still on crutches, his leg immobilized in a cast. Billy Kilmer would be in control, just as Allen wanted him to be.

Although the stadium rocked with jubilant fans, the game went scoreless until the second quarter — when a Curt Knight field goal put the Redskins on the boards with 3 points. Then came a Kilmer touchdown pass to Charley Taylor, with the extra point giving Washington a 10-0 lead. The Cowboys scored 3 points that quarter when their 35-yard field goal kick hit the left upright and fell in.

Early in the fourth quarter, the Redskins still were clinging to their 10-3 lead when Kilmer decided to go after third-year Cowboy cornerback Mark Washington, playing for the injured Charley Waters. Kilmer sent Taylor deep, and by the time the ball arrived in Taylor's hands, Washington was two steps behind and diving in a desperate attempt to break up the pass. But he couldn't do it, and Taylor's 48-yard scoring catch and Knight's extra point produced a 17-3 lead.

This time there was no miracle comeback from Staubach, only three more breathe-easy field goals down the stretch by Knight. That clinched a 26-3 victory, the first NFC title for the Redskins in 30 years. Thousands of fans streamed onto the field as Allen was hoisted to his players' shoulders in a raucous celebration of the new year and of the team's first trip to the Super Bowl, against the Miami Dolphins.

The Dolphins had lost the Super Bowl the previous year to the Cowboys and had vowed to return quickly. Under head coach Don Shula, the former Redskins defensive back whom many considered the finest mind in the game, they were now 16-0 and attempting to become the first team in league history to win every game played.

Like the Redskins, the Dolphins relied on a bruising running game, led by Larry Csonka, a 240-pound, smash-mouth fullback, and tailbacks Jim Kiick and Mercury Morris. They, too, had a thinking man's quarterback in Bob Griese, a future Hall of Famer, and their so-called "No Name" defense had excelled all year, even if the unit was slightly undersized compared to most.

RICHARD DARCEY — THE WASHINGTON POST

Too late: Backup Dallas cornerback Mark Washington makes a futile leap as Charley Taylor pulls in a touchdown pass in the 1972 Redskins playoff victory.

Allen wanted to begin preparations for Super Bowl VII immediately, considering it imperative that the team stay on the same schedule as always to keep its momentum going and to avoid distractions. Regular practices were called all week, long meetings were held upstairs in Redskins Park, and the coaching staff reviewed hours of Miami films, burning the midnight oil every night after the players had gone home.

The team flew to California on Sunday, and Allen clearly was nervous about what they would face. There would be adoring fans, plenty of diversions all over Southern California and the usual media mob.

The first problem of the week occurred on Tuesday night. Jim Snowden, a reserve tackle who was injured and not even eligible to play, was caught trying to slip out a window of the team's Newport Beach hotel after curfew. He was not alone — several other players also were missing in action that night — but Snowden was the only one caught. Allen was furious. He wanted to send him home the next day and fine him as well. But when it was learned that several starters were among the others who were AWOL, cooler heads prevailed and Snowden was allowed to stay.

On Wednesday, Allen made headlines when he told reporters at a news conference that, yes, he had indeed charted the sun in the Coliseum, the better to prepare his punt and kickoff returners to deal with rays in their eyes.

On Friday, in his last meeting with reporters, Allen complained that "yesterday, we had 31 players in interviews for one and a half hours, and we had our worst practice of the week." He whined that he was meeting with the media instead of his team and that "this is the first meeting I'm going to miss with the team in 23 years."

Three days later, his team gave perhaps its worst performance of the season. Of course, Shula and the Dolphins had a lot to do with it, but Kilmer was mostly ineffective. The Dolphins halted the Redskins ground attack at every turn, and when Miami opened a 14-0 lead at the half, Kilmer went to the air with little success.

Watching all of this from a coach's box high in the Coliseum was Jurgensen, still on crutches but unavailable to provide advice to his pal Kilmer on the sidelines. Allen had banished him to the booth. Jurgensen never figured out why, except for the animosity the two men felt for each other almost from the start.

Before the game, Jurgensen had been allowed to walk on the field, and at one point Shula came over to him, shook his hand and offered a few words of encouragement. "He told me he was sorry I couldn't participate and that it would be a better game if I was playing," Jurgensen said. "What a wonderful thing for him to say. My own coach wouldn't even let me on the damned field. I was stuck up in the box, by myself. It really hurt. I found out they also took two pictures of the Super Bowl team that year, one with me in the picture, and one with me out. That wasn't necessary. I'd played early, I'd contributed. But that was George. That tells you everything you have to know about the guy."

Watching upstairs, Jurgensen saw two of the more bizarre plays in Super Bowl history. Halfway through the last quarter, the Redskins finally began to mount a drive. On third down at the Miami six, Jerry Smith was wide open in the end zone, and Kilmer saw him — but his pass hit a goal post, bouncing incomplete. Kilmer's next throw was intercepted by safety Jake Scott, and the threat was over.

The Dolphins took over and moved all the way to a first down at the Washington 37. With 2:10 remaining, Shula ordered a field goal, but Bill Brundige blocked Garo Yepremian's kick. A former soccer player and native of Cyprus who was new to American football, Yepremian picked up the loose ball and struggled to throw it downfield. But Brundige tipped the pass, and it was intercepted by Redskins cornerback Mike

Bass and returned 49 yards for a touchdown. That cut the Miami lead to 14-7.

Allen elected not to try an onside kick, preferring to let his beloved defense get the ball back for one last try to tie the game and possibly send it to overtime. The Redskins did get the ball back, with 74 seconds remaining, but when Kilmer was sacked for a nine-yard loss on fourth down, the season and the dream of a Super Bowl championship ended.

"We just came out so flat," Owens said. "George was so paranoid about us being in LA, and he was afraid we wouldn't focus on the game. But that was crazy. This was such an unusual team. These guys were pros. They were used to practicing and playing on three hours' sleep. We'd done it all season. But we had more meetings, we practiced harder and longer than usual. It really hurt us. We were ready to play that game the Sunday before. Our performance against the Dolphins was not the Washington Redskins. We had to take responsibility for that, too. But we just didn't perform."

No, it's mine: Brig Owens intercepts a pass in the end zone intended for Miami's Marv Fleming in Super Bowl VII at the Los Angeles Coliseum.

RICHARD DARCEY — THE WASHINGTON POST

Some of the players never performed for the Redskins again. Pardee decided to retire, though he stayed on as an assistant coach. Richie Petitbon also turned to coaching, working with Houston Oilers defenses until 1978, when he became the Redskins' defensive secondary coach. Jim Snowden, Mitch Johnson, Rosey Taylor, George Nock, receiver Clifton McNeil and special teams ace Jon Jaqua, among others, soon would be gone as well, either released, traded or forced to quit because of injuries.

Allen soon was at it again with another spectacular trade. On May 15, 1973, he sent five players to the Houston Oilers — Snowden, McNeil, tight end Mack Alston, defensive back Jeff Severson and defensive end Mike Fanucci — for perennial All Pro strong safety Ken Houston. When Taylor broke his arm in training camp, Allen moved Brig Owens over to Taylor's spot, and Houston stepped right in as strong safety. He played there for the next eight years. Five years after he retired, with a reputation as the greatest strong safety in the history of the game, he was elected on the first ballot into the Hall of Fame.

Houston will long be remembered for one particular play, in a 1973 Monday night game against the Cowboys at RFK. Dallas was driving toward a last-minute touchdown. On fourth down, with 16 seconds left, Craig Morton tossed a short pass to running back Walt Garrison. As Garrison turned toward the goal line, Houston came up, hit him high and wrestled him to the ground a yard short of a touchdown. The play preserved a 14-7 Redskins victory.

"When it happened, I didn't think it was such a good play," Houston said. "I thought I was beaten on a pass. I went to intercept the ball, but I couldn't make the move, so I stopped and grabbed at him and tried to lift his body. I picked him up and pushed him back . . . It wasn't a smooth play, it was a desperation play. It was such an eerie feeling when it happened. There wasn't any noise in the stadium for maybe three seconds. I was screaming at Brig Owens to come and help, because I thought Garrison might want to lateral. All of a sudden, when everyone realized what had happened, the place went crazy. I had never seen anything like it."

Plays like that would help the Redskins make the playoffs again in 1973 and 1974. Both seasons, however, would end with losses in the initial round, first to the Minnesota Vikings and then to the Los Angeles Rams — a game that would mark the end of Sonny Jurgensen's career.

That 1974 season was also when Joe Theismann joined the franchise. The former Notre Dame quarterback had been a second-round choice of the Dolphins three years earlier, but he had opted to play right away for Toronto in the Canadian Football League rather than sit behind Bob Griese in Miami. Allen traded his second-round, 1976 choice to Miami for Theismann, envisioning him as the quarterback of the future. Jurgensen, after all, was 40 and Kilmer was 34.

Both veterans took a disliking to their new teammate, who had already written a book on how to play quarterback even though he had never seen a minute of NFL action. Theismann also crossed a picket line to get into training camp in a year that began with an ugly player's strike, another step that hardly endeared him to veteran players.

"He was a great athlete, but he was his own worst enemy," Jurgensen said. "He wanted to play, and I certainly could understand that. One day in the training room when he was getting his ankles taped, he said something like, 'I should be playing ahead of those two old guys.' We heard about it. We also heard he was telling people that the only reason he didn't win the Heisman Trophy was that Jim Plunkett got a sympathy vote because his parents were blind. What a terrible thing to say. That's where it all started. It was not a very good relationship. It got to the point where Billy and I had this understanding that we didn't care which one of us started, as long as it wasn't Theismann."

That was not a concern in 1974, when Theismann ran the scout team in practice and got most of his game action as a part-time punt returner. Kilmer started the first four games. But after going 2-2 and with the two-time defending Super Bowl champion Dolphins coming to town, Allen sat him down, using Kilmer's bruised leg as the rationale.

No you don't: Ken Houston wrestles down Dallas' Walt Garrison on the 1-yard line to preserve a 14-7 Redskins victory in the final seconds of a Monday night game in October of 1973.

Would he turn to Jurgensen? "George told me that most coaches wouldn't start a 40-year-old quarterback," Jurgensen said. "I told him if you want to win, you will."

He did, and that day Jurgensen rallied his team from an early 10-point deficit to a dramatic 20-17 victory. Trailing 17-13 with 1:44 remaining, Jurgensen drove the Redskins 60 yards to a touchdown, hitting fullback Larry Smith with a six-yard scoring pass for the winning points. He would finish that game with 26 completions in 39 attempts for 303 yards and two touchdowns — plus the satisfaction of helping the Redskins avenge their 1972 Super Bowl defeat.

Eventually, however, Allen would return Kilmer to his starting spot. Jurgensen, suffering from injuries, would play in only three more games, including a fourth-quarter relief appearance in the dreary playoff loss to the Rams to end the 1974 season.

One day in the off-season, Jurgensen was summoned to a meeting with Allen at the Dulles Airport Marriott. Kilmer also had been asked to go to the hotel for an earlier meeting with the coach, and the two quarterbacks had arranged to meet at a designated location after Kilmer had finished his session to discuss their situations.

"When I got to the hotel, George told me the plans were to go with Billy and Joe," Jurgensen said. "I already knew it. Billy had already told me about it when we met out on Route 28. They said I was too much of a luxury to have around, but there was a little catch. Billy told them he wanted to be traded. He was tired of the controversy, the fans had been on him, and he wanted out. They told me if Billy demanded to be traded, they wanted me back. I told them nah, I'm going to retire, and that was it. I'd had a lot of wonderful years, and I really wasn't ready to stop. It didn't end like I wanted it to. It ended on a real sour note."

Kilmer ultimately decided to stay, managing to keep his starting job in 1975.

Before the start of that season, Allen also had given away two No. 1 draft choices and a second-round pick to acquire defensive tackle Dave Butz from the St. Louis Cardinals. That became a controversial trade because the huge Butz — 6 feet, 8 inches and 325 pounds — hardly played that first season and often was teased unmercifully by team veterans. Ultimately Butz, nephew of U.S. Agriculture Secretary Earl Butz, would play a major defensive role in the team's 1980s success story. But that didn't help the Redskins in 1975.

Although the team began with six victories in the first eight games that year, it ended with an 8-6 record.

For the first time in Allen's tenure, the Redskins missed the playoffs in 1975, a season in which years of pounding finally took their toll on Larry Brown. He spent most games nursing injuries while rookie Mike Thomas gained 919 yards. If 1975 didn't close with a playoff berth, it did end with Charley Taylor catching the 634th pass of his career, shattering the NFL's all-time reception record then held by Don Maynard and long since broken again such players as the Redskins' Art Monk and San Francisco's Jerry Rice.

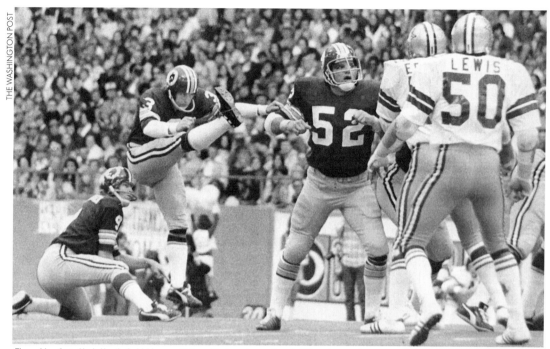

The golden foot: Mark Moseley's kicking would be critical on the road to Redskins glory again.

Halfway through the 1970s, the Redskins clearly were moving way beyond over the hill, and Allen had given away most of the team's draft choices. But because the league and its players' union still had not agreed to a new contract, there was an unusual window of opportunity after the 1975 season to acquire free-agent players whose contracts had expired. Allen took full advantage, signing New York Jets fullback John Riggins and adding two longtime Dallas nemeses — running back Calvin Hill and tight end Jean Fugett — to his 1976 roster.

Riggins saw most of his action that year as a blocking back, leading the way for Thomas to gain more than 1,000 yards. In addition, kicker Mark Moseley, signed as a free agent in 1974, led the league that year with 22 field goals, and Eddie Brown gain 646 yards returning punts, the second highest total in league history. The Redskins finished 10-4 with a wild-card spot, but they were crushed, 35-20, by the Vikings in the first round of the playoffs.

The 1977 season would be Allen's last hurrah in Washington. His contract was in its final year, and Allen and Williams were having difficulty reaching a new one. At a July

14 press conference, the two men had announced a tentative agreement allowing Allen to coach through the 1981 season at a salary of $250,000 a year. But Allen never signed it, saying that he wanted to exercise a disputed stock option in the team as part of the deal. Williams' dislike of Allen and his free-spending habits was well known around town, but the team president also knew that Allen still was one of the most savvy coaches in football, and he didn't want to risk the fans' wrath by letting him go.

So talks continued during a season in which Theismann was given increasing playing time ahead of Kilmer. Allen also made another little-noticed move that summer when he took on a young high school football coach as an unpaid intern. His name was Charley Casserly, and he would go on to become the team's general manager a dozen years later. The Redskins finished with a 9-5 record in 1977, but they were knocked out of the playoffs on the last weekend of the schedule when the Chicago Bears, by then being coached by Jack Pardee, rallied for a victory that clinched the wild-card berth.

Williams was still hoping to keep Allen as his coach, but a series of events intervened. In early January, Pardee broke off negotiations on a new contract with the Bears, the Rams fired head coach Chuck Knox, and Allen secretly visited Los Angeles to meet with Rams owner Carroll Rosenbloom. All of this led to Williams firing Allen on January 16.

"Our negotiations with George Allen have concluded," Williams said. "I gave George Allen unlimited patience, and he exhausted it."

Allen went on to sign with the Rams. By the time the Redskins reported for training camp in 1978, Williams had hired Pardee, a personal favorite, as his new head coach and Bobby Beathard, a personnel executive with the Miami Dolphins, as the team's new general manager. The George Allen era in Washington had ended, but he had left a legacy of winning football teams that would continue long after he had departed.

By now, however, the cupboard seemed bare. The Redskins were bereft of draft choices, and many of Allen's veterans were either gone or no longer especially effective. Taylor, center Len Hauss, cornerback Pat Fischer, tight end Jerry Smith and safety Brig Owens all retired by the time the regular season started. Pardee relegated Kilmer to the bench, finally handing over the job to Theismann and gearing his offense around the hard-running Riggins, who had been wasted as a blocking back the two previous seasons.

Meanwhile, back in Los Angeles, it did not take Allen long to wear out his welcome. Four weeks into training camp, Rosenbloom fired him after Allen became embroiled in a power struggle with other organization officials, including Rosenbloom's son Steve. Allen would never again coach in the NFL. He often claimed that he was being blackballed by league owners, a claim that he took to his grave when he died at age 72 on New Year's Eve of 1991, collapsing in the kitchen of his Palos Verdes, California, home after jogging around the neighborhood.

Remarkably, the Redskins began the 1978 season with six straight victories, but they then were jolted by back-to-back losses to the Eagles and the Giants. Though Riggins would gain 1,014 yards and Theismann would throw for more than 2,500 yards, the team staggered badly down the stretch, finishing 8-8 in what would be Kilmer's final season.

Beathard, a native Californian and dedicated marathon runner who still wore his blonde hair in surfer-boy style, did not have a pick in the first three rounds of the 1979 college draft. Still, showing a skill for finding diamonds in the rough in the later rounds, he added tight end Don Warren and linebackers Rich Milot, Neil Olkewicz and Mel Kaufman, all of whom would make major contributions both that season and in the future.

That year, the Redskins were 6-2 at midseason. Then, after winning four of five games going into the season finale, they were in a three-way tie for first place in the NFC East with the Eagles and Cowboys, their last-game opponent at Texas Stadium. A victory would assure a playoff spot and possibly the division title, and when the Redskins opened a 17-0 lead, both goals seemed within reach.

But Roger Staubach had other ideas. He rallied the Cowboys to two touchdowns that cut the lead to 17-14 before the half. The Redskins would open a 31-21 advantage on a 66-yard, fourth-quarter touchdown run by Riggins and were still leading, 34-28, when Staubach got his hands on the football one last time. He was at his own 25-yard line, with 1:46 left to play, and the master of the miracle comeback added another notch to his belt. He completed four straight passes to move his team to the Washington 8. Seconds later, he scrambled away from a fierce Redskins pass rush and spotted receiver Tony Hill in a corner of the end zone and somehow managed to throw him the ball for a touchdown. The ensuing extra point completed a stunning, 35-34 Dallas victory, keeping the Redskins out of the playoffs.

"One little point takes us from the division champs to the outhouse," Pardee said. It was little consolation that he would be named NFL coach of the year by the Associated Press or that he had taken a team many thought would be fortunate to finish .500 to a 10-6 record.

For the Redskins, it would be their eighth winning season in the 1970s and the team's first winning decade since the 1940s. The redskins had posted a 91-52-1 record over the ten years, made the playoffs five times and played in their first Super Bowl. Clearly, the tradition of excellence to which Vince Lombardi had pointed the way had become fully ingrained. But the best was still to come.

One little point: Theismann walks off the field after the 35-34 loss to Dallas that ended the Redskins' 1979 season.

Fans From Someplace Else

By Michael Wilbon

Every year, when thousands of transplants arrive in Washington, it's safe to assume that they don't come as Redskins fans. No other city in the NFL is so filled with people like me, people who grew up Someplace Else rooting passionately for their hometown teams, people who don't dispose of their roots in general like so much plastic. I grew up in Chicago, and after 17 years in Washington, the simple conversational question, "So, where are you from?" is one I still can't answer without hesitation.

I rooted for the Bears all my life, and that didn't stop when I took a flight to the nation's capital. Indeed, I suspect that there are more Cowboys fans in Washington than anyplace else outside Texas and more Giant fans than anywhere else beyond metropolitan New York. Yet, for the past 35 years no ticket has been more coveted in Washington than that to a Redskins home game. It's mystifying.

It becomes even harder to grasp when you are black and familiar with the racial baggage the Redskins carry. I tend to lose it when black Redskins fans talk about the Boston Celtics as "lily white." Washington was the last team in major league baseball, pro basketball or pro football to integrate its roster. Beginning in 1934, a decade after Paul Robeson and Fritz Pollard broke the NFL color line by playing with the Akron Pros, black players were in essence banned from the league for 12 years, until 1946. That's when Kenny Washington, who had been Jackie Robinson's roommate at UCLA, signed with the Los Angeles Rams.

The Redskins, who had what journalist Evan Thomas has called an "NAACP policy" — Never at Anytime Any Colored Players — took a lot longer, and then they acted only because the federal government in late 1961 forced George Preston Marshall to end his "whites only" policy. Since that was not so many years ago, there are plenty of blacks in Washington who have kept their vow never to root for the Redskins, and plenty more who have needed years for the scars to heal.

I didn't know about the team's racial baggage when I arrived in Washington. I simply hated the Redskins because I grew up in Chicago, as devoted a Bears fan as there is. I didn't hate the Redskins as much as I hated the Green Bay Packers, but enough. I tolerated Bobby Mitchell because he went to Illinois, but George Allen, Diron Talbert, Pat Fischer, Sonny Jurgensen, Roy Jefferson, Kenny Houston, Billy Kilmer, Larry Brown, Mike Bass, Len Hauss, Chris Hanburger — they and just about everybody else in a Redskins uniform were my longtime enemies. More than anything else, I think, I was infuriated by Redskins fans, who acted as if the moment a transplant came within 50 miles of the Potomac, he or she should discard a lifetime of allegiance to the Bears or Cowboys or Eagles.

I'd ask them, "If tomorrow morning you were relocated to Detroit, would you drop the Redskins like a rock and become a Lions fan?" Usually the response would be a blank stare, as if it had never crossed their minds that fan loyalty isn't so easily transferable.

This is, of course, part of the larger transplant problem: When exactly do you become a Washingtonian? When do Washingtonians stop becoming "them" and "you all" and become "us." Not having accepted that status 17 years into my tenure here, I suspect that it has something to do with the deepest way we plant roots: having children. At that point, I imagine, you get so entrenched you simply have to commit to being from and of one place.

But my problem, as a sportswriter, was unique to Redskins-hating. The systems analyst who comes to work for the federal government doesn't necessarily have to deal with, well, Redskins. I remember the first time I actually liked a Redskin. I was a summer intern at *The Washington Post* when I met Jean Fugett. He was young, Amherst-educated, a tight end, and had been a *Post* reporter. He was too smart and too engaging and too irresistible not to like.

Then I met Bobby Mitchell, the Hall of Famer who was the first black Redskin and who has been with the team for about 35 years. There has always been something regal about Mitchell, a greatness and dignity that, while most easily noticed in an athletic arena, probably have little to do with sports. I was too young at 21 to figure it out, but Mo Siegel wasn't. Siegel was the sports columnist for *The Washington Star* and one of the great storytellers. Most of Mo's stories began with him having lunch or dinner with somebody, and this one did, too.

The night before Bobby Mitchell's first game as a Redskin in 1962, he and Mitchell were having dinner in downtown Washington. Mitchell's arrival in town was a huge deal, the biggest imaginable for black Washington. So Mo was dining with Mitchell when a man walked by their table and said, "Excuse me, are you Bobby Mitchell, the new Redskin?" When Mitchell said yes, the white man picked up Mitchell's glass and spat in it.

It's an image that sticks to me like a nightmare. It's a story I can never bring myself to talk about with Mitchell. Just can't.

For me, identifying a man solely by the team he plays for stopped with that story. What bothered me for several years afterward, though, was how accepting and supportive black Washington had been of the Redskins. How could they have blindly supported a team whose owner thought they were subhuman?

Part of the answer is that many haven't supported the team. That's why more than a few black Washingtonians in their 50s and 60s — Mitchell's peers — root to this day for the Dallas Cowboys, a team that started with a clean slate in 1960 and was quick to draft players out of historically black colleges. The other part of the answer is that many still have conflicting feelings about the Redskins. It's another issue that only time can resolve. Intellectually, you know that Edward Bennett Williams and Jack Kent Cooke weren't in any way like George Preston Marshall. Williams, in fact, was a passionate civil rights advocate back in the 1950s. But emotionally, it's difficult to come to terms with an institution's history of bigotry.

Luckily for the Redskins, most people under 50 in this revolving-door town don't know of Marshall's racism. They have come to identify the Charley Taylors, George Starkes, Art Monks, Darrell Greens and others as the faces of the Redskins. It's a funny thing, inclusion. The great irony is that the first black quarterback to lead a team to a Super Bowl victory — Doug Williams — did it in a Redskins uniform.

In far less dramatic ways than the Mitchell saga, I started to become familiar with one Redskin or former Redskin after another. I should say one man after another who for a while wore a Redskins uniform, from Mark Murphy to Dexter Manley, Charles Mann to Mel Kaufman, Doug Williams to Darrell Green, Joe Theismann to Kelvin Bryant, Mark May to Jim Lachey, Sonny Jurgensen to John Riggins.

A few years ago I got up the nerve to tell Sonny how much I hated him when I was a kid. Sonny smiled, removed the cigar from his mouth and said, "Aah, doesn't matter 'cause you love me now, don't you?" There's also more than a little irony in the fact that 90 percent of whatever football I know — some would debate that I know any — I've learned from Jurgensen and Theismann. As different as they may be as people, they are as expert at explaining pro football to the uninitiated as they were at playing the game.

So on some level it's a little embarrassing that men I wanted to throw darts at as a teenager I now call on to help me professionally with everything from explaining complex schemes to weighing in on who's better with the game on the line, Emmitt Smith or Barry Sanders.

After covering pro football for 10 years, it's clear to me that the teams that won at the highest level in the 1980s and early 1990s — the 49ers, the Redskins, the Cowboys and, yes, the Bills — simply had more players and coaches who were smarter, more resourceful, more savvy and more dedicated. It's no coincidence that the same people keep winning. And while there's absolutely no need to turn your loyalties over to any team, there's no harm in taking a step back and appreciating those individuals who are undeniably worthy, regardless of where you call home. Even if you grew up hating them.

TRIVIA QUIZ 3

1. Which Redskins quarterback-hunter in 1975 had four sacks in one game?

2. In addition to George Allen, eight coaches and players on the 1972 Redskins became head coaches in the NFL. Can you name them?

3. In the early 1970s, when Larry Brown was making headlines, which blocking back who later jumped to the World Football League was central to Brown's success?

4. Defensive end Ron McDole's godfather was a Redskin. Name him.

5. In 1975, another Redskins wide receiver had more receiving yards and touchdowns than Charley Taylor. Who was he?

6. What quarterback spent three years with the Redskins without throwing a regular-season pass?

7. Only three Redskins have played in three different decades. Name them.

8. Who scored Washington's most career points?

9. Herb Mul-Key was one of a number of Redskins over the years who did not come from college. How many were there?

10. In 1983, Darrrell Green joined the team and became Washington's all-time interception leader. Which players were second and third in interceptions?

ANSWERS ON PAGE 269

CHAPTER 4
The 1980s

As Good as It Gets

By David Sell

Joe Gibbs was sitting in the cab of the 18-wheel trailer that carries his NASCAR team's cars and tools, remembering how it all happened. He talked about his first meeting more than 15 years before with Redskins owner Jack Kent Cooke and the "ridiculous" handshake deal they made. He spoke of his short-lived 1981 plan to trade away "that sucker" John Riggins. He stressed a point he likes to make in public speeches: "If you pick the right people, then you're going to be successful."

The Redskins of the 1980s certainly ended up with the right people, and they suc-ceeded magnificently, playing in three Super Bowls and winning two. Washingtonians were beside themselves with joy after the Redskins beat Miami in Super Bowl XVII on January 30, 1983. That was, after all, the franchise's first NFL championship since the 1942 season. Nobody could blame fans for going mad for awhile.

"You can get a smile on anybody's face in this organization, and really in this area, if you only ask about the '80s," said Bobby Mitchell. "Fans were excited. We were the talk of the league. Even teams that didn't like us couldn't help but say good things about us."

At the decade's outset, however, it was not so clear that the right people would be in place to create such golden years. Head coach Jack Pardee was in a power struggle with general manager Bobby Beathard. John Riggins walked out of training camp in 1980 over a contract dispute and didn't return that year, a season in which the team had a dreary 6-10 record. Gibbs was a little-known offensive coordinator for the San Diego Chargers who despaired of ever getting a head-coaching job at the college level, much less in the NFL.

So how did that struggling, uncertain team turn into the champions of the 1980s?

The Redskins did it in lots of ways, as many who were there will tell you. They did it with Gibbs, Beathard and Charley Casserly making shrewd picks for the team and for the strike replacement squad in 1987. They did it with Riggins' legs, Mark Moseley's foot, Joe Theismann's and Doug Williams' arms and tight-knit groups like The Hogs of the offensive line. They did it with players who kept going when they were injured and on painkillers and with plays with names like 50 Gut, Counter Trey and 70 Chip.

But perhaps above all they did it because Jack Kent Cooke got a divorce. The Redskins owner, who held more than 85 percent of the team's stock at the time, paid a then-record $42 million divorce settlement, sold his beloved Lakers and Kings and the Los Angeles Forum he had built for them, and in 1979 moved from California to Virginia. It was Cooke who made the ultimate decisions about the Redskins and the right people — picking Beathard's strategy over Pardee's, hiring Gibbs, agreeing to pay high prices for some of the right players, backing his people when times were not so great.

When Cooke came to Washington, he brought his intense competitive spirit with him. "Winning was his priority," said Lakers general manager Jerry West before Cooke's death in 1997. "Mr. Cooke is demanding. When you work for him, he wants the best, which is the way it should be."

Cooke's sale of the Lakers and Kings meant that Edward Bennett Williams no longer would be the man in the owner's seat at RFK. It removed the cross-ownership barrier that had prevented the Redskins' real and dominant owner from being just that.

"At first, it was a gradual transition," said son John Kent Cooke, former president of the Redskins. "But as Ed put it later on, we were operating under the golden rule, which was that whoever had the gold rules. And there was no question who was in charge."

Ultimately, Williams and Cooke would fight bitterly, especially over the Baltimore Orioles, the baseball team Williams had bought in mid-1979 with the help of a loan from the Redskins. In 1984 Cooke, citing a loose agreement with Williams, would demand half of the Orioles' profits and threaten a lawsuit — something Williams badly wanted to avoid. "He didn't want a high profile lawsuit with reporters digging into the past, examining how Cooke and Williams had come to gain control of all the Redskins stock from the George Preston Marshall estate," according to Williams biographer Evan Thomas. Williams, who would die of cancer in August 1988, ended up settling the dispute

The '80s chain: Jack Kent Cooke hired the little-known Joe Gibbs, who lured back the inimitable John Riggins, who scored the decisive touchdown reported here in Super Bowl XVII.

BILL O'LEARY — THE WASHINGTON POST

The Washington Post

Weather

Today—Mostly sunny and mild, high 50-55, continued fair and cold tonight, low 25-32. Tuesday—Morning sun, then increasing cloudiness and not as warm, high 45-50. Yesterday—Noon AQI: 50; temp. range: 50-35. Details, B12.

106th Year · · · · No. 57

MONDAY, JANUARY 31, 1983

Index

▼ 25¢

Redskins, Riggins Hog It All, 27-17

Don McNeal of Miami to score a 43-yard touchdown that put Redskins ahead for good, 20-17. *Game coverage begins on C1.*

Record Runs Bring Super Bowl Crown

By Dave Kindred
Washington Post Staff Writer

PASADENA, Calif., Jan. 30—Dreamy, so dreamy, floating in a rosy jewel of a bowl at the foot of mountains caressed by clouds and snow, the Washington Redskin today won the world championship they last held 40 years ago. The Hog who wears top hat and tails, John Riggins, made the earth tilt the Redskins' way as the chill of night and defeat settled on Miami's Dolphins, 27-17.

With an 18-wheeler load of Nagurski brutishness and a touch of Astaire's fanciful grace, Riggins broke every important running record (38 carries, 166 yards) in Super Bowl lore. He gave the Redskins their first lead at 20-17, running 43 yards on a fourth-and-inches play with 10:01 left in the game.

And then, at precisely 9:21 p.m. in Washington, with the Rose Bowl transformed by joy to RFK West, the Redskins called one last meeting of the Fun Bunch to celebrate Charlie Brown's confirming six-yard touchdown catch with less than two minutes to play.

Sing us no sad songs of the economy today, give us no dreary scoop on who's running or not running for president. Paint the White House a nicer color, a burgundy and gold, and get the confetti ready on Pennsylvania Avenue. These Redskins go on parade there Wednesday, the nicest thing that's happened to the nation's capital since we sprung the hostages from Iran.

The old offensive guard in the White House, Ronald Reagan, called his congratulations to Redskins Coach Joe Gibbs, saying, "It was just great." And Gibbs, standing next to his megabucks boss, Jack Kent Cooke, spoke of the Gipper's budget problems, "Mr. Cooke is used to dealing with a lot of money. He'll help you."

For his final play of the night, after the game had ended, Riggins, informed of Reagan's call,
See KINDRED, A8, Col. 1

...n Explodes In the Fourth Quarter

the area was afflicted last fan called a "Redskin seizure."

... game, the foggy night ... crackers, shotgun blasts, ... demented howls of sat-

... in the celebrations, po-... of Georgetown and a ...

along Wisconsin Avenue. Nearby, on M Street, a second bus with three passengers aboard was stalled helplessly as dozens in the madding crowd pounded on its sides. Others climbed to the tops of street lamps, window awnings, fire escapes—anything that wasn't moving, and some that were—to stick their index fingers into the sky and proclaim the Redskins "Number One."

by, Peter Hintze surveyed the bedlam and said: "Ya know what? Fifty percent of the town's work force will not be in tomorrow. And ya know what? The other 50 percent won't care."

Police fell easily into the manic spirit of the celebration, blasting their sirens and making no attempt to break up the carnival. District police Officer Mike Turner said authorities ...

Shells Pound East Beirut in New Violence

By Herbert H. Denton
Washington Post Foreign Service

BEIRUT, Jan. 30—Shells and rockets pounded commercial and residential neighborhoods of Chris-...

by selling Cooke his 14 percent-plus interest in the Redskins.

There certainly was no question about who was in charge of the Redskins, though what Jack Kent Cooke was in charge of in 1980 was a troubled team, and John Riggins didn't help matters then.

There were great and odd characters in Redskins history, but none quite like Riggins. Long before Dennis Rodman, Riggins was raising eyebrows with a Mohawk haircut. At a Washington Press Club Salute to Congress dinner, he was seated at a table with Supreme Court Justice Sandra Day O'Connor, to whom he reportedly said, "Come on, Sandy, baby, loosen up. You're too tight." But he played so hard and so well on the field that much of what he did off the field was forgiven, if not forgotten.

He also played hard in contract negotiations, and when he was unhappy with the way talks were going in the summer of 1980, he upped and went home. "It's a very simple situation," Riggins told *The Washington Post* in a 1980 interview from his house in Lawrence, Kansas. "Either we'll get together and work this out and I'll play, or we won't work it out and I won't play."

The answer was B: They didn't work it out and Riggins didn't play, dealing a blow to Pardee's defense-oriented strategy. That strategy required an offense that could run the ball, control the clock and avoid mistakes. Although the Redskins had missed the playoffs in 1979, Riggins had rushed for 1,153 yards. In 1980, with him gone, the running game broke down.

As the team's performance worsened that year, so did the simmering dispute between Beathard and Pardee. Beathard wanted younger players to get more action. Pardee wanted to stick with veterans. And each seemed to think he was in charge.

Cooke's frustration with the conflict and the team boiled briefly after a 35-21 loss to the Bears in Chicago in the season's 10th game. The Redskins record by then was 3-7, and Cooke knew that a key decision needed to be made.

"Not that anything I said made a difference, but Mr. Cooke did ask me what I thought one day, about a month before, and I had to give my honest assessment," Bobby Mitchell said. "And my honest assessment was that we needed Bobby Beathard. We were splintering pretty good, not that Mr. Cooke hadn't seen that."

So Cooke met with Beathard and Pardee, separately and together. Beathard was a good talker, which helped considerably with Cooke, while Pardee was not. "My father said that Jack was extremely quiet, almost recalcitrant, and it was very difficult for dad to communicate with him," John Cooke recalled. "The way we operate, it is crucial to have that ingredient for success, to have that open communication, where you can get mad if you want to, but we all have the same goal in mind and you don't hold that anger."

On January 5, 1981, Cooke fired Pardee, who had two years left on a contract that paid $125,000 a season. "I was hoping I could remain," Pardee told *The Washington Post's* Paul Attner. "But the owner has a right to do what he wants with his team."

Cooke now faced his second pivotal decision — picking a new head coach.

Numbered days: Coach Jack Pardee — at left with linebacker Brad Dusek and backfield coach Richie Petitbon and, right, during a November 1980 shutout at the hands of the Eagles — would lose a struggle with general manager Bobby Beathard and soon be gone.

A number of names were floated for the Redskins job, including an A list with people like John Madden and John Robinson. Then, among assistant coaches considered ready to move up, was Joe Gibbs.

Cooke associates told reporters that even before Pardee had been fired, George Allen had wanted his old job back. But that never would have worked. Allen, of course, also wanted total team control again. The idea that Allen and Cooke could co-exist was sheer fantasy.

Madden, who had been a teammate of Beathard's at Cal-Poly at San Luis Obispo, had retired in 1978 as head coach of the Raiders, and Robinson was head coach at USC. With his California connections, Cooke was familiar with both of them.

"At the time, both Madden and Robinson were mentioned, but Joe Gibbs' name was also mentioned at the very beginning," John Cooke said. "As I recall, Madden was asked, but he declined because he had had enough of coaching. We never met with Robinson, but dad was interested in Robinson." Robinson had accepted a USC contract extension, though two years later he would join the Los Angeles Rams.

The Redskins had to keep going down the list.

So who was this Joe Gibbs guy at the San Diego Chargers? Most fans had never heard of him, and Cooke certainly knew nothing of him until he spoke with Beathard. Actually, Ernie Zampese, the Chargers' wide-receivers coach, had recommended Gibbs to Beathard, just as he would recommend Norv Turner to Charley Casserly 13 years later.

"I had dreamed of being a head coach," Gibbs said while sitting in that cab of his NASCAR team's 18-wheeler. "But you've got to remember, I was 40 years old and couldn't get a college head-coaching job. I had two interviews — Missouri and Arizona — and they wouldn't hire me. But both were token things. I was 40 years old, and that's up there in coaching. I didn't know if it was going to happen."

Born November 25, 1940 in Mocksville, North Carolina, Gibbs was the son of a county sheriff. When he was 14, his family moved to Southern California, and Gibbs ended up at San Diego State. There he played tight end, guard and linebacker for Aztecs coach Don Coryell, a patriarch of the passing game. Then he spent three seasons as a graduate assistant to Coryell, working with the offensive line, followed by stints as an assistant coach at Florida State, USC and Arkansas.

In 1973, Gibbs joined Coryell's St. Louis Cardinals as running-backs coach. In five seasons the Cardinals won two NFC East titles, and Gibbs developed relationships there, as he would elsewhere, with men who would work for him years later: running back Terry Metcalf, who would play for the Redskins in 1981, and offensive line coach Jim Hanifan, who would work his magic with Gibbs' lines in Washington.

After the Cardinals fired Coryell, Gibbs became offensive coordinator at Tampa Bay, a team in need of a new quarterback. That's how Gibbs and Doug Williams first met. After trading their first overall draft pick in 1978, the Bucaneers made Williams — whose rifle arm had helped Grambling go 35-5 — the first African American quarterback chosen in the first round. The next year Williams led the Buccaneers to the NFC title game. Gibbs, however, wasn't there to enjoy it: After a 5-11 Bucaneers season in 1978, he had left in frustration.

"In Tampa, I was offensive coordinator, and it blew up in my face," Gibbs said. "We couldn't beat anybody. We won five games, and it was three more than they ever won, but it was still awful. I took the job in San Diego [with the Chargers' Coryell again], but it was going backward, to be a backfield coach, and I started to think I might not go any further.

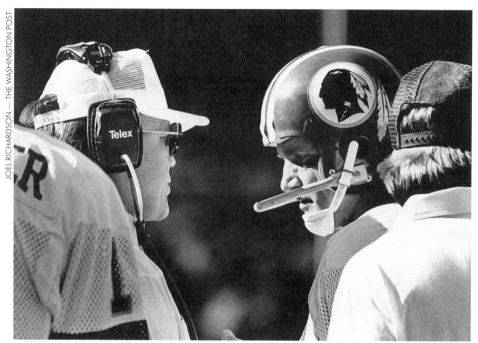

Close call: After his performance slipped in 1980, Joe Theismann, conferring here on the sideline with Joe Gibbs, nearly was traded in 1981 for the Detroit Lions' Gary Danielson.

"I remember sitting on a plane and saying to the Lord, 'You know what I want. I've been trying to do this on my own. I'm going to turn this over to you. If you want me to be a head coach, I'll put it in your hands.' Two weeks after that prayer, Ray Perkins, who had the offensive coordinator job in San Diego, went to the Giants. Don Coryell called me in the next day and said, 'Do you want to be the offensive coordinator here?' Two years later, I was the head coach of the Washington Redskins."

At the Chargers, Coryell and Gibbs made Air Coryell part of the football lexicon. With an 11-5 record in 1980, they went to the AFC title game, but they lost to Oakland. After that game, Gibbs, his wife Pat and their sons, J.D. and Coy, went out for a pizza. "When I got home, Bobby was on the phone, saying, 'Mr. Cooke wants to meet with you tomorrow night,' " Gibbs said.

It was no surprise. Pardee had been fired six days earlier, and Beathard had quickly flown to California. Beathard was not supposed to talk to Gibbs until the Chargers' season ended, but he didn't need a formal interview to get word to Gibbs. *The Washington Post* had interviewed Gibbs the week before the Oakland game and already had reported that he might be the next Redskins head coach.

So Gibbs and Beathard flew to New York, where Cooke had set up shop in a suite at the Waldorf-Astoria. When Gibbs arrived, Cooke was reading an article by Dave Kindred, a *Washington Post* columnist.

"I think he had floated my name out there to see what everybody was going to say: Would the Redskins be criticized for taking this guy, a nobody?" Gibbs said. "This article had talked about me being a genius, and I remember him dropping the paper and telling me, 'Do you know there have only been two geniuses in the world?'

"I had to agree with him that they weren't in football. I think he mentioned Michael-angelo and somebody else. But I'll tell you they weren't offensive coordinators. Then he corrected everything I said. He said, 'I don't think you meant what you said,' and I'm going, 'Geeezzz.'

"But that night, we hashed everything out. I had a legal tablet and I had everything listed on there. Who would be the film guy and a budget for that. Meals for the players — I didn't want them going out at lunch. I had eight assistant coaches listed. I had everything listed, from practice equipment to fields. He said, 'I'll get that.' 'We'll get that.' 'We'll get all the coaches.' I'm, like, there's no way. But we went and got all of them. We went through the whole list that night."

Although Cooke had decided to hire Gibbs, he refused to negotiate with Gibbs' attorney, Marvin Demoff. "The only lawyers Cooke liked were his own, and then only marginally," Demoff said in 1997.

In "negotiating" directly with Gibbs, Cooke told the coach that he wanted him to accept a three-year contract, at about $100,000 a season, with an option for Cooke to extend it for five more years. "It was the most ridiculous thing in the world," Gibbs said.

If Gibbs didn't work out after a couple of seasons, Cooke could fire him without owing him much money. If Gibbs turned out to be a great coach, Cooke could keep him under contract five more years at a relatively low NFL salary.

"It was the first time I ever got upset with him," Gibbs recalled. " I said, 'You want me to put my financial future and my family's financial future in your hands?' He said, 'That's right.' I said, 'I'm going to do it — but it's on you if this thing gets out of hand,'" alluding to the potential for a nasty disagreement if Gibbs were successful, deserved a big raise and didn't get one.

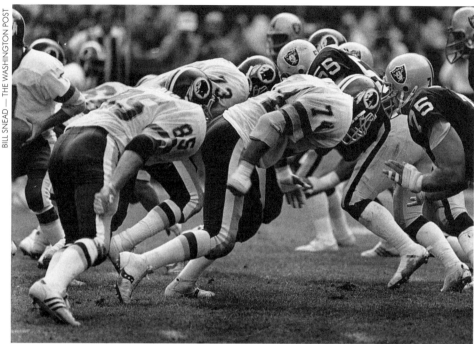

BILL SNEAD — THE WASHINGTON POST

Hogs as the slaughterers: Don Warren (85), Mark May (73) and George Starke (74) — key members of the close-knit Hogs of the offensive line — move in unison to bust open a hole in the Raiders' defense.

"I shook his hand, and it probably was the greatest thing I ever did, because I would never have guessed the numbers I ended up making," said Gibbs, who was earning more than $1 million a season when he retired. "Twice, on his own, [Cooke] said, 'I'm going to re-do your contract.' He was on the hook, and he remembered. But if I had done the eight-year contract and guessed at the numbers I wanted, I'd have done half" of what he ultimately earned.

On January 13, 1981, Joe Gibbs was introduced at a news conference as the 17th head coach of the Washington Redskins.

The cupboard wasn't bare when Gibbs took over. Beathard already had made one of his shrewdest draft picks by taking Syracuse's Art Monk in the first round in 1980. From the Canadian Football League, Beathard had imported punt returner Mike Nelms, who would make the next three Pro Bowls. Then there was Neil Olkewicz, a slow, undersized, middle linebacker from Maryland who had signed with the Redskins in 1979 and always seemed on the verge of being replaced — except that he stayed 11 seasons.

Jeff Bostic was an undrafted free agent from Clemson when he joined the team in 1980 as a long snapper. He became the starting center in 1981 and was that for most of the next 13 years. Dave Butz was still an anchor in the middle of the defensive line, and George Starke was the solid veteran at right offensive tackle.

Theismann was the quarterback. Although he had had an excellent season in 1979, he had slipped a bit in 1980 and nearly was traded in 1981 for Detroit's Gary Danielson, according to Casserly. Mark Moseley was still the kicker, but his poor 1980 season (18 of 33 field goal attempts) put him in danger of being cut as well.

The 1981 draft class was one of Beathard's best. It included offensive linemen Mark May and Russ Grimm, defensive end Dexter Manley, wide receiver Charlie Brown, guard Darryl Grant (who was switched to defensive tackle) and wide receiver Clint Didier (switched to tight end). Next, Beathard traded the team's second-round pick to Baltimore for running back Joe Washington, who had been to the 1979 Pro Bowl.

Finally, there was the case of Joe Jacoby. Casserly had seen the big offensive tackle at the University of Louisville in 1979. Like other scouts, he figured that Jacoby wasn't likely to be drafted but that he might get a contract as a free agent. When the draft ended, Jacoby still was unclaimed — and a Seattle scout was at Jacoby's house, hoping to sign him. But the Redskins called and wanted Jacoby to visit Washington. In a move that he surely regretted later, the Seattle scout drove Jacoby to the airport.

When Jacoby got to Redskin Park and met Gibbs, however, the new head coach — who was meeting a slew of rookies for the first time — mistakenly thought that Jacoby was a defensive tackle.

"I didn't want to correct him and ruin my chances," Jacoby said with a laugh at his Virginia auto dealership. Jacoby left the Gibbs meeting a bit bewildered, but he had signed a contract. "Five or six years later, [offensive line coach Joe] Bugel told me that Joe tried to get out of the deal because he only wanted to bring 18 offensive linemen to camp, and I was the 19th. It's amazing how these things work out."

Gibbs also had done some critical recruiting of his own. However glorious his passing credentials, Gibbs knew that he needed a dominating runner. So, months before the Class of 1981 was chosen, Gibbs went to see Riggins in Kansas. When he arrived, Riggins' wife told him that John was out and would be back the next day, so Gibbs checked into a motel and returned in the morning.

"He had a camouflage outfit on," Gibbs remembered. "He had been hunting, him and a buddy. He had a beer can in his hand. It was 10 o'clock in the morning and he's meeting his coach for the first time and I'm thinking [sarcastically], 'This guy really impresses me.' But I went in there, and I'm telling him everything. I'm telling him, 'You won't have to block, you're going to run.' I'm giving him everything. He hadn't said a word. Halfway through the conversation, he says, 'You need to get me back there. I'll make you famous.' "

"I thought to myself, 'Oh, my God, he's an egomaniac.' I thought, 'I'll get him back and then I'll trade him. I'm not putting up with a fruitcake.' So I fly back to Washington, and two days later he calls me. He says, 'Joe, I made up my mind, and I'm going to play next season.' I thought it was great. I've got him back, and I'll trade that sucker. But then he says, 'There's only one thing I want in my contract.' I ask what it was. He says, 'A no-trade clause.' "

It was one of the best concessions in the history of the franchise, and Riggins reported to training camp, telling reporters, "I'm broke, I'm bored and I'm back."

"The thing is," Gibbs said, "I tried to screw that up" with the plan to trade him. "But the bottom line is that John Riggins made me famous."

Gibbs, with a different approach from Pardee's, quickly impressed the players. "The problem with Jack was that he was too nice to a lot of guys, and several players took advantage of him, with the way they practiced and went about their jobs," Mark Moseley recalled. "Joe said he was going to build a championship team and surround himself with people who would pay the price to be the best. Those that wouldn't do that would be gone."

In Gibbs' first preseason, the Redskins went 3-1. He seemed to be making headway. But then reality hit and hit hard: The team lost its first five games of the regular season. Turnovers, injuries and penalties were the problems. In the Game 5 loss against the 49ers, for example, Metcalf had a fumble returned 80 yards for a touchdown, and running back Clarence Harmon fractured his shoulder.

The next day, when Gibbs met with Cooke, he wondered if he would be fired. Instead, Cooke reassured and encouraged him.

"He was always at his best when things were at their worst," Gibbs said of Cooke. "That tells you the guy had guts. He could sense when I needed encouragement. A lot of people panic in that situation and are ready to sell you out. He was always better when it looked like it was going to fall apart. I admired him. He was mentally tough. As we all know, he had some things about him, and he could tick people off. But he was a great owner, and I was fortunate. All of D.C. realizes that now."

In the next game, against the Bears at Soldier Field on October 11, 1981, the tide began to turn with a 24-7 Redskins victory. Two keys to that win were that the Redskins forced the turnovers (four for the game) and that Gibbs had shifted to a run-based attack. In a way, this is when Riggins first began to make Joe Gibbs famous.

Gibbs had been using Riggins, Metcalf, Harmon and Washington in combinations, depending on the circumstances. But against the Bears, Metcalf did not have a carry. Riggins rushed 23 times for 126 yards and a 2-yard touchdown. While Washington carried 21 times for 88 yards, he often went in motion from his backfield spot. The Redskins ran the ball 47 times for 227 of their total 301 yards.

In time, Riggins ended up alone in the backfield. "We had Riggins at fullback and Terry Metcalf at tailback, and we were trying to stay in an I-formation," Gibbs said. "But Riggins didn't want to block. He wanted to run with the ball. And we certainly didn't want [the smaller] Metcalf blocking for him. We made changes and went to a one-back. The other thing we did was put in another tight end, especially to put him on [New York Giant] Lawrence Taylor's nose. We made some technical changes, and that's when we made our move and took off. Richie [Petitbon] and the guys on defense gradually got better."

Petitbon had been promoted to defensive coordinator from secondary coach at Beathard's suggestion. "I thought we had a terrific operation — Joe left us alone," Petitbon said. "Joe would come in to watch film with us on Sunday, but he never told us what to play or calls to make on defense. Now, if it hadn't worked out, I'm sure he would have had more input, and he did give us ideas about what gave his offense a lot of trouble."

The Redskins offense actually had less and less trouble in 1981, with the team winning eight of its last 11 games to finish 8-8, one win shy of a playoff spot that year. Missing the post-season served as inspiration for the future. "That 0-5 motivated us for six or seven years," Gibbs said. "Guys hated it and didn't want to go back to it."

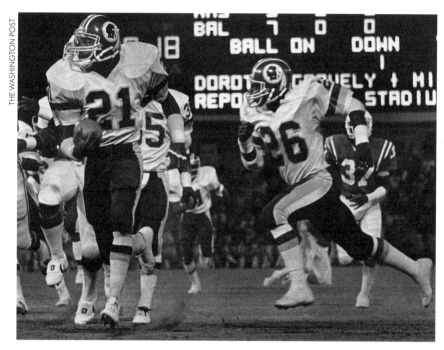

THE WASHINGTON POST

A valuable import: Mike Nelms, here returning a punt for a touchdown as Terry Metcalf (26) peels back to cut off pursuers, was an import from the Canadian Football League who made the Pro Bowl the first three years after joining the Redskins.

They certainly didn't go back to it in 1982. "That second year was like a miracle," Gibbs remarked.

Many people contributed to that miracle, not least The Hogs on the offensive line. No nickname was better. The Hogs inspired goofy costumes and made even prim-and-proper people dream of being in the slop with them. More importantly, they became a powerful, cohesive unit that provided holes for Riggins and protection for Theismann.

The original members were starting tackles Jacoby and Starke, guards Grimm and May, center Bostic, reserves Fred Dean and Ron Saul and tight ends Don Warren and Rick Walker. Riggins campaigned to get in and eventually was admitted as an Honorary Hog.

During training camp, Joe Bugel had begun what evolved into the Hogs by looking at his offensive line, which had been a weak link in 1980, and trying to figure out what to do with it. "A few of us were slightly overweight, but we carried it well," Grimm said with a laugh. Among other things, Bugel ended up making T-shirts with a pig's head on them, and they become a uniform of honor.

Honorary Hog Riggins and many of his fellow Hogs increased their tightness as members of the 5 O'Clock Club. The group met after practice in an old tool shed at Redskin Park. It had no plumbing, no electricity. There was a kerosene heater over which Riggins sometimes would warm cans of pork and beans. That delicate fare was normally washed down with frothy beverages.

"A lot of problems were solved out there," Grimm said with a chuckle.

That kind of cohesiveness was important on what became one of their signature plays, the Counter Trey. Bostic, May and Starke would block down or to the left. Grimm and Jacoby would pull and come around the right side. The running back would take a step to the left and then take the handoff going right, and it worked many times, to the dismay of opponents.

Once the Hogs got rolling, there was a reputation to protect. "You have to live up to it when you get a name like that," Grimm said.

They more than lived up to it, just as the Redskins as a whole not only lived up to but exceeded their fans' expectations that year. But that was not evident in the summer of 1982. The Redskins went 0-4 in the preseason, and fans were on edge.

The angst vanished when, in the season opener, Mark Moseley kicked a game-winning overtime field goal for a 37-34 victory over Philadelphia — a forerunner of Moseley's role in miracle-making that year.

That game settled the kicker question. The Redskins had drafted Dan Miller of the University of Miami and kept him on the team to challenge — and perhaps replace — Moseley. But after Moseley's Philadelphia heroics, Miller was cut and Moseley had no more reason to worry

On the road in Week 2, the Redskins won again, 31-13, against Tampa Bay — but then the football world stopped. The NFL Players Association (NFLPA) announced a strike, and the 1,500 union members walked out. The union was seeking a percentage of the teams' television take, establishment of a trust fund from which salaries would be drawn, and creation of a league-wide wage scale. But the owners wouldn't budge on any major issue.

The NFLPA staged a couple of games involving striking players, including one at RFK, but the crowds were small. After eight weeks, with the owners threatening to cancel the rest of the season, the players returned. *Continued on Page 145*

RIGHT

Sacked: Tackle Dan Wilkinson slips through the Bears' line to nab quarterback Cade McNown during the Redskins' October 1999 defeat of Chicago. Photo by Rich Lipski.

FAR RIGHT

In the Zone: Stephen Alexander lands in the end zone with a game-winning touchdown reception against the Panthers in December 1988. Photo by John McDonnell.

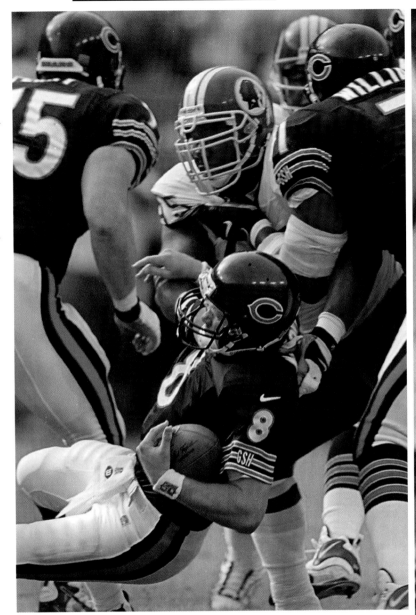

PRECEEDING PAGE

The sacking of Jim Harbaugh: Redskins defensive end Charles Mann helps bring down the Chicago Bears quarterback on October 6, 1991. The Redskins' victory at Soldier Field was the sixth straight of that 11-in-a-row season.

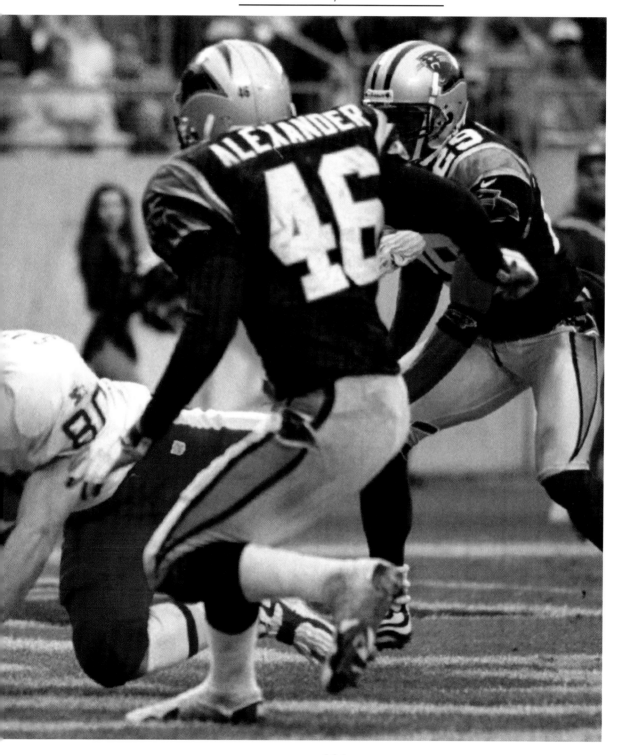

Protection in Bad Weather: In the rain and mud of the 1991 playoff against the Atlanta Falcons, quarterback Mark Rypien rolls out to throw, enjoying the kind of protection that made an important difference in that season's passing game.

Tackle Jim Lachey (79) and guard Raleigh McKenzie both ward off Falcons rushers, while rookie running back Ricky Ervins (32) prepares to do his part in the blocking pattern.

The Redskins allowed only nine sacks that season, a team record and the third lowest number of sacks in NFL history. Photo by John McDonnell.

PHOTOS BY JOEL RICHARDSON — THE WASHINGTON POST

ABOVE
The First Fan: Daniel Snyder, center, cheers the first touchdown of the first game of his first season as Redskins owner.

RIGHT
We Have Overcome: Quarterback Doug Williams becomes the first African American to win the game MVP Award after his performance in Super Bowl XXII .

FAR RIGHT
High Jump: Albert Connell leaps to catch a Brad Johnson pass during the Redskins' 27-20 victory over the New York Jets in September 1999.

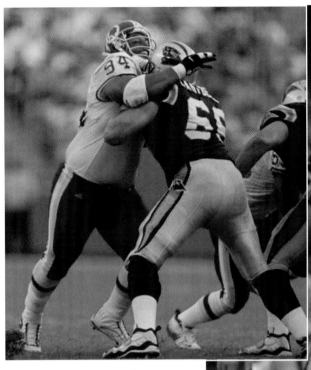

ABOVE

Defensive Struggle: Lineman Dana Stubblefield wards off Panther Frank Garcia in the Redskins' 38-36 win over the Carolina Panthers on October 3, 1999. Photo by John McDonnell.

RIGHT

Gotcha: The Redskins' Marc Boutte in November 1998 snares Raiders quarterback Donald Hollas, forcing the ball to pop into the end zone. Photo by John McDonnell.

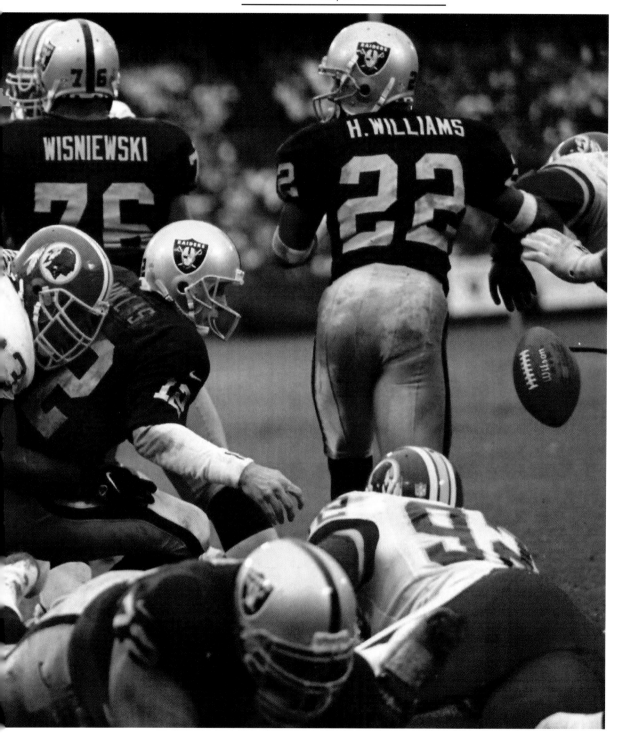

Going the Distance: Brian Mitchell stiff-arms the Chargers' Jimmy Spencer, battling for the end zone to complete a 101-yard kickoff return during the Redskins' 24-20 victory over San Diego in December 1988. Photo by John McDonnell.

ABOVE

A *Few Choice Words: Coach Norv Turner shouts from the sideline during the Redskins' January 2000 defeat of the Dolphins to end the regular season. Photo by Joel Richardson.*

RIGHT

On the Run: Redskins ground gainer Stephen Davis heads for open space during a 1999 Redskins victory over Carolina. Photo by John McDonnell.

ABOVE

Yes! Brad Johnson spikes the football after a 1999 touchdown against the Bears. Photo by Joel Richardson.

RIGHT

Ending the Drought: Brian Mitchell runs back a punt against the Lions in January 2000 as the Redskins go on to their first playoff victory in eight years. Photo by John McDonnell.

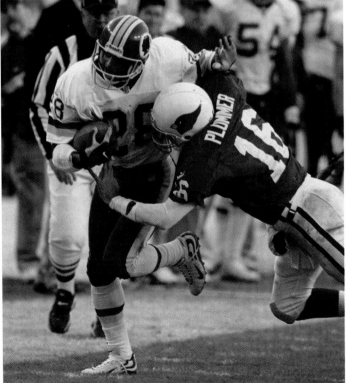

ABOVE

Flag! Wide receiver Albert Connell's face mask is snagged by Cowboy Kevin Mathis in a heartbreaking 1999 season opener that the Redskins lost in overtime. Photo by Rich Lipski.

LEFT

The Green Stuff: Darrell Green intercepts a pass from Cardinals quarterback Jake Plummer, who pushes him out of bounds. The Redskins won the October 1999 game, 24-10. Photo by Rich Lipski.

Honorary Hog and Santa Hog: John Riggins, who lobbied to become an Honorary Hog, stampedes past a downed Cowboy with Mark May (73) and Jeff Bostic (53) looking on, while Santa Hog displays one of many costumes fans donned for their favorite linemen.

"The things on the table when we left were what we came back for, except for 'now money' " paid immediately to players at the end of the strike, Jeff Bostic recalled. "There was a scale. With four or more years of experience you got $60,000. Obviously, they gave the older guys more so they would persuade the younger guys. But was it worth 57 days? No."

In the first game after the strike, the Redskins beat the Giants, 27-17, in East Rutherford, New Jersey. Even with the layoff, Theismann was sharp, completing 16 of 24 passes for 185 yards, two touchdowns and a third straight game without an interception. Then, after nearly a year between meaningful games at RFK Stadium, the Redskins defeated the Eagles, 13-9. The victory pushed the Redskins record to 4-0.

After a loss to Dallas at RFK, the Redskins regrouped, but they still were having trouble scoring. The offense had averaged just 16.6 points in the first three post-strike games.

By then, however, Moseley was on a field-goal roll, making 14 straight and providing the special care he liked to give to his kicking foot. He usually kept it in a down-lined slipper or a garbage bag. That was in addition to the six pairs of socks he always wore.

The combination was supposed to keep his foot — assuming he could still feel it under all those socks — warm and dry and safe.

That foot was becoming increasingly important to the Redskins. Indeed, in the next game, on December 12 in St. Louis, it provided the sole Redskins scoring. On his first attempt in that game, from 37 yards, Moseley slipped on the icy artificial turf at Busch Stadium. But a Cardinals penalty nullified the miss, and Moseley made it on the second try. Three more field goals later, including a knuckleball that barely dropped in, the Redskins won, 12-7.

Next, the Giants came to RFK on December 19 after winning three in a row since their home loss to the Redskins, and in that one some Redskins displayed more than their usual intensity and grit.

As part of Petitbon's continually improving defense, linebackers Rich Milot and Mel Kaufman came off the corner on blitzes — sacking Giants quarterback Scott Brunner five times. Kaufman sighed after the game and told *The Washington Post's* Ken Denlinger: "Sure wish we'd score 35 sometime, so we could let up a bit."

The game also was a tough one for Theismann, in more ways than one. He had struggled in the first half, throwing four interceptions. His best play may have been a block he threw on a Joe Washington 22-yard touchdown scramble off of a halfback option. Then it got truly painful for Theismann. Giants linebacker Byron Hunt blitzed and knocked out two of the quarterback's front teeth. Theismann called time, went to the sidelines — and came back into the game

"A lot of people said Joe was cocky," Russ Grimm said. "But I'd play for that guy anytime, because he was one of the toughest people I've ever played with."

At the start of the fourth quarter, the Redskins trailed,14-9. Then Riggins rushed eight times for 42 yards in an 11-play, 51-yard drive that set up a 31-yard Moseley field goal, cutting the Giants lead to 14-12.

Next it was Rick Walker's turn. He had 20 catches that season, but few as important as the 20-yard reception that jump-started the Redskins' last drive of the fourth quarter. The Redskins got to the Giants 25 — and let the clock run until just nine seconds were left. They would turn again to Moseley.

With two field goals so far in the game, Moseley already had tied Miami's Garo Yepremian's record of 21 consecutive field goals. As Moseley trotted on the field, snow was falling, and he remembers being exceedingly nervous: Both the playoffs and his place in football history were on the line on this 42-yard kick. Bostic's snap and Theismann's hold were fine. The Giants' Hunt got a hand on the ball — but not enough to stop it from going through the uprights for a 15-14 victory. There was bedlam at RFK. The Redskins were going to the playoffs for the first time in six years.

"I still think it was embarrassing for the organization that I was named MVP," said Moseley, whose streak ended at 23 in the last regular-season game. "Coach Gibbs was an offensive coordinator, and the offense didn't come around until later."

By defeating New Orleans and St. Louis in their last two games of the 1982 regular season to finish 8-1, the Redskins gained home-field advantage throughout the NFC playoffs, or "playoff tournament," as it was called in that strike-altered season.

What a kick: Mark Moseley earns a hug from Joe Theismann and a pat from Don Warren after kicking the winning field goal in a 27-24 victory over the San Diego Chargers on October 31, 1983. Moseley led all NFL players in scoring that season with 161 points.

For the first round, against the Lions, the Redskins had lost Monk, who was already the team's best receiver, to a broken toe. Virgil Seay also was injured. But Alvin Garrett — who had only one reception in the prior two years — caught three Theismann touchdown passes in a 31-7 rout.

The passing game, as usual, had fed off the running game, and that meant Riggins. In the week before the Detroit game, Riggins had gone to see Gibbs. "He said, 'Load the wagon. I'm going to carry it,' " Gibbs recalled. Carry it he did. The Diesel gained 119 yards on 25 carries against the Lions, the start of a fabulous playoff run. The Riggo Drill became part of Redskins history, with diesel horns the sound-effect of choice for many.

For the next playoff contest the following week against Minnesota, Riggins missed the team meeting the night before the game, according to several sources.

"In the locker room before the game," Jacoby said, "John comes over to us, the offensive linemen. He says, 'Ah, the old man is mad at me. I'm asking you to do a little more for me. I need gaping holes.' He gets halfway across the room and then walks back. He said, 'On second thought, on those gaping holes, don't make them gaping. Just big enough to get five or six yards. I don't want to get 10 or 15 yards downfield and make a fool of myself falling down.' That was John, and then he goes out and gets 185 yards."

Whatever fueled the Diesel, he ran over and through the Vikings on that day for those career-high 185 yards on 37 carries. In addition, Theismann hit Garrett for an 18-yard touchdown pass, and the defense stopped Bud Grant's Vikings twice on fourth-down plays in Redskins territory. But the day will be remembered most for Riggins and his departure from the game.

With about a minute left and the 21-7 outcome secure, Gibbs sent in a replacement for Riggins, knowing he would get a resounding ovation. Riggins was a showman, however muddy and torn his uniform was that day, so he removed his helmet. Amid the roar, he bowed to one side of the stadium, bowed to the other side, and waved to adoring masses as he went off. "It was John Wayne and things you make movies out of," Casserly said.

Archrival Dallas was next. This was the third straight NFC championship game for the Cowboys. They had lost the last two, to the Eagles in 1980 and to Bill Walsh's 49ers in 1981, but the Cowboys came to town confident. For the Redskins, it was their first championship game in a decade, and the city of Washington was on edge with excitement. "That feeling of intensity — thinking about it still sends a chill down my spine," said Darryl Grant.

The chants of "We want Dallas! We Want Dallas!" had been heard the prior two weeks, but they were deafening hours before the kickoff. "That is the loudest that stadium's ever been," Grimm said. "You could hear it in the locker room: 'We want Dallas! We want Dallas!' We were a young football team then, so everybody was pretty pumped up."

Nobody was more pumped up than some of the coaches.

"Joe Bugel never smoked the whole year, and he's in there before the game chain-smoking," Jacoby said. "He comes over to us and says, 'You guys have to keep your cool. I can't have any of you kicked out of the game.' He says this as he's lighting the next cigarette off the butt of the first. Then we're standing there for the national anthem. Russ is one side of Joe and I'm on the other. When it's over, Joe looks over to the other sideline at Ernie Stautner, who's the Cowboys defensive line coach. Joe yells over to him and then flips him off. This is the guy telling us to keep our cool."

Diesel fuel: For the January 1983 playoff against the Vikings, Riggins told The Hogs he didn't want gaping holes, just gaps big enough to gain five or six yards — and then he piled up a career-high total of 185 yards.

All parts of the Redksins engine hummed for that game. Theismann was 12 of 20 for 150 yards, with a first-quarter touchdown pass to Charlie Brown and no interceptions. The defense came through in stunning fashion. Late in the second quarter, Dexter Manley knocked down Dallas quarterback Danny White, who left the game with a concussion. Dallas backup quarterbacks had burned the Redskins before, and Gary Hogeboom threw two third-quarter touchdown passes to cut the Redskins lead to 21-17. But after a Moseley field goal, Manley, Grant and the defense came through again.

Manley sensed a delayed screen and was in perfect position to deflect Hogeboom's pass. Grant intercepted and high-stepped into the end zone for the clinching touchdown.

And, again, there was Riggins and the Hogs, who dominated Dallas' defensive front, including Randy White. Riggins had 36 carries for 140 yards and two touchdowns. Many of those yards came on a play called 50-gut, where Riggins ran left, looking for a hole between Bostic and Grimm or Grimm and Jacoby. As Gibbs tried to run out the clock, Bostic remembers running 50-gut nine straight times.

"After three or four, in the huddle I said to Russ, 'Play along with me,' " Bostic said. "I got to the line, and I said to Randy White, 'Our coaching staff loves you. We're going to run it over you again.' Then the next play Russ told him. Randy wasn't very happy, but after three or four times, he didn't say a word."

In the game's waning moments, fans were celebrating wildly in the stands, a celebration that overflowed into Washington's streets. Watching it all from his box, Jack Kent Cooke told *The Post's* Dave Kindred: "This is controlled delirium. There is a coagulation, a community of interest here that is astonishing in its depth. All over this city. The rich, the poor. The black, the white. The communists, the socialists. The affluent, the unpossessed. All are bound together in this city on this day by these Redskins."

Bostic was like many who considered the Dallas victory a defining moment. "The one game that really gave us confidence to go forward in the 1980s was that NFC championship game against Dallas," he said after retiring with three Super Bowl rings. "It was a team built with a lot of young guys, and Dallas was still thought of as the crème de la crème of the NFC."

That confidence was apparent when the Redskins ran on to the field at the Rose Bowl for Super Bowl XVII against Miami, though it did not translate into much immediate scoring.

Miami got off to a 10-3 lead, and then the score began to seesaw. Theismann hit Garrett on a 4-yard touchdown pass, and it was 10-10. Miami's Fulton Walker returned the kickoff 98 yards for a touchdown, making it 17-10. A Moseley field goal cut the Miami lead to 17-13.

In the fourth quarter, on their second possession, the Redskins faced fourth down and inches to go at the Miami 43. Gibbs decided to go for it, in part because his defense was playing well and in part because he had Riggins and The Hogs. Kim Bokamper was the Miami defensive end across from Jacoby, and it was to that corner that Riggins would run on a play called 70 Chip.

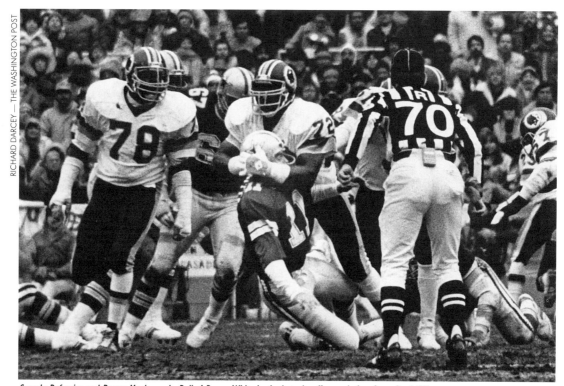

RICHARD DARCEY — THE WASHINGTON POST

Crunch: Defensive end Dexter Manley sacks Dallas' Danny White in the last playoff game before Super Bowl XVII.

"We knew we had a mismatch with Jacoby on Bokamper," Grimm said. "Usually, if Bokamper pinched in, we'd double him. If he didn't, I'd go out after the linebacker." Miami cornerback Don McNeal slipped at the snap, and his attempted arm tackle of Riggins failed miserably. Riggins rambled down the left sideline for a 43-yard touchdown to put the Redskins ahead for good, 20-17, with 10:01 left in the game.

A 6-yard touchdown catch by Garrett gave the receivers of the Fun Bunch a chance to dance and leap for a collective high-five in the Rose Bowl, but it was the running game that had dominated Miami's Killer Bees to produce the 27-17 final score. Riggins won the MVP award with 38 carries and 166 yards, both Super Bowl records at the time.

President Reagan called the Redskins's jubilant locker room after the game, but Riggins said, "At least for tonight, Ron's the president, but I'm the king."

Riggins, who had rushed for 553 yards in eight regular season games, had rolled up 610 yards in four playoff contests. For the Redskins as a whole, the four post-season wins in January of 1983 were just one shy of all post-season victories in the history of the franchise.

On February 2, an estimated 500,000 people stood in the rain along Pennsylvania Avenue for the Super Bowl parade. Though players in the future would earn more money, there might never have been a better time to be a Redskin in Washington.

"The first Super Bowl was so different," said Bostic, "because we had never been there and we had never won one. The apprehension and butterflies I felt before the first one, I never had in the second, third and fourth. The one I might appreciate the most is the one we won in 1991, because of my age. In '82, I was in my third year, and we were such a young team, we thought, 'Didn't everybody go to the Super Bowl?' You didn't have the proper appreciation for it."

That would be apparent a year later when the Redskins went to another Super Bowl after a 1983 regular season marked by an extraordinary offensive effort and by the arrival of a 5-foot, 9-inch player from Texas A&I.

Beathard usually traded down in drafts. But since he was going last in the first round that year, he kept the pick and chose a speedy, 182-pound cornerback. His name was Darrell Green, and he would be a critical part of the Redskins defense for years to come.

"I thought he was awfully small, and I didn't know how a guy his size would hold up," Petitbon said. "But Darrell got to be a big little guy. He was strong and remained healthy. He was fun to work with and has a tremendous personality. Of all the guys, Darrell enabled us to do a lot on defense. We would put him on a guy one-on-one and then play against the other 10. That was a great advantage. We had to do a lot of dogging [blitzing], and without Darrell, I'm not sure we could've done that."

In the season opener, Green impressed fans as well, but that didn't stop Dallas from beating the Redskins, 31-30 — a loss that turned out to be an important wake-up call for the Redskins. After that, the Redskins rolled over nearly every opponent, with victories in 16 of the next 17 games. Their offensive assault was stunning:

LUCIAN PERKINS — THE WASHINGTON POST

RICHARD DARCEY — THE WASHINGTON POST

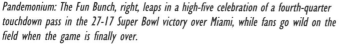

Pandemonium: The Fun Bunch, right, leaps in a high-five celebration of a fourth-quarter touchdown pass in the 27-17 Super Bowl victory over Miami, while fans go wild on the field when the game is finally over.

• The Redskins piled up 541 overall points that season, still the NFL record.

• With the best year of his career, Theismann was chosen league MVP by the Associated Press. He completed 60.1 percent of his passes for 3,714 yards and 29 touchdowns. He threw just 11 interceptions, with four of them in a meaningless game against the Giants to end the regular season. What mattered more was that Theismann had thrown only four interceptions in the previous 12 games combined.

• Also with the best year of his career, Riggins set a Redskins single-season rushing record with 1,347 yards, a mark that stood until Terry Allen gained 1,353 in 1996. Riggins also scored 24 touchdowns, breaking O.J. Simpson's record of 23. Riggins' record lasted until Dallas' Emmitt Smith scored 25 in 1995.

• Moseley made enough field goals (33 of 47 attempts) to lead all NFL players in scoring, with 161 points.

With home-field advantage and a first-round bye, the Redskins swamped the Rams,

51-7, in the divisional round. It was the most points ever scored by a Redskins team in the playoffs — and it was the largest margin of victory in any playoff game since 1957.

"It's always embarrassing to get beat that bad," Rams rookie running back Eric Dickerson told reporters after that game. The NFL's leading rusher that season, Dickerson gained only 16 yards that day. "Their defense is so odd," he said. "They do one thing one week, something different the next. Sometimes there was a linebacker on me, sometimes there was a defensive back there. I never knew."

The Redskins then defeated Bill Walsh's 49ers, 24-21, to move on to Super Bowl XVIII in Tampa. The opponent was the Raiders, a team the Redskins had beaten, 37-35, in October at RFK. The Redskins were confident — too confident, as it turned out.

"It came back to bite us, and we forgot to show up," Jacoby said.

Unlike the earlier Redskins-Raiders meeting that year, Raiders running back Marcus Allen was healthy this time. Oakland also had added cornerback Mike Haynes, and he and Lester Hayes proved how well they could cover the Redskins receivers.

"To us, the whole thing was stopping their offense, and the whole thing there was stopping Riggins," former Raiders linebacker Matt Millen said in 1997. Millen, who also played on the 1991 Redskins team that went to the Super Bowl before becoming a TV analyst, added: "Mike Haynes made us really good, and we didn't have to worry about the secondary. We could let both corners play and have the safety help against the run."

As a result, they shut down most of what the Redskins had succeeded in doing all season. They held Riggins to just 64 yards on 26 carries, ending his streak of six playoff games with at least 100 yards. Charlie Brown had only three catches in the game. Art Monk had only one. The Raiders sacked Theismann six times. The Raiders' Derrick Jensen blocked a punt and recovered it for a touchdown and a 7-0 lead — the only blocked punt against the Redskins all season. It was getting ugly.

Oakland also tripped up Washington on a play that had worked well for the Redskins in their last meeting. It happened after a touchdown catch by the Raiders' Cliff Branch made the score 14-0 and a Moseley field goal cut the lead to 14-3. That was when Jack Squirek became famous.

The Redskins had first down at their 12-yard line, with 12 seconds left in the second

THE WASHINGTON POST

Who was that? Rookie Timmy Smith runs out of the grasp of Denver's Tony Lily on his way to a 58-yard touchdown in Super Bowl XXII. The little-known Smith set a Super Bowl record with 204 overall rushing yards that day.

quarter. Gibbs didn't want to kill the clock. He called a play called Rocket Screen, in which Theismann threw a swing pass to Joe Washington in the flat. The same play to the other side had gained 67 yards in the regular-season game against the Raiders.

The problem was that Raiders defensive coordinator Charley Sumner remembered it from the first game, albeit after he had sent in the defense. He grabbed Squirek, his relatively fast linebacker, shoved him onto the field and told him to replace Millen and cover Joe Washington man-for-man, even though the rest of the Raiders were playing zone. Sure enough, Theismann lofted a pass over Lyle Alzado and intended for Washington — and Squirek intercepted it at the 5-yard line, stepping easily into the end zone for a 21-3 lead that crushed the Redskins.

"I had already called the defensive scheme in the huddle and had everybody lined up, so I come off the field grumbling, saying, 'What a stupid thing to do," Millen said in

1997. "Then Jack makes the interception, scores and I'm saying, 'What a great call.' "

If the Redskins had any hope left, Marcus Allen, who had touchdown runs of 5 yards and 74 yards, erased it. The 74-yard touchdown run, part of Allen's 191-yard day, set a Super Bowl record. It came on the last play of the third quarter. The fourth quarter was unnecessary.

That 38-9 Super Bowl rout shocked the Redskins. "Being there is not the reward," Bostic said. "It is more painful to lose a Super Bowl than it is joyous and gratifying to win one. I don't know how Buffalo could stand losing four Super Bowls."

The next year, with an 11-5 season, the Redskins still had the best record among NFC East teams. Monk caught an NFL-record 106 passes, and Riggins gained 1,239 yards. But the offensive line suffered from injuries — Bostic tore three of four ligaments to end a streak of 48 straight starts — and George Starke was in his last season at right tackle. The Redskins got a bye but then lost to the Bears, 23-19, on December 30, 1984, at RFK, the only home playoff loss in Gibbs' 12-year career.

The 1985 season signaled the end of one winning era and the building of another. The team finished 10-6, leaving it out of the playoffs for the first time since 1981. And when the season was done, so were the playing careers of Riggins and Theismann.

Riggins was 36 when the 1985 regular season began. But in April the team had traded its first-round pick to New Orleans for 26-year-old running back George Rogers and three other picks. The tenth-round and eleventh-round picks were used to add tight end Terry Orr and offensive linemen Raleigh McKenzie, both of whom would be members of the last two Redskins Super Bowl teams.

Riggins started 11 games that season, but Rogers got more and more of the work. By season's end, Riggins had 677 yards on 176 carries, while Rogers had 1,093 yards on 231 carries.

"I would make more mistakes keeping people than getting rid of them early," Gibbs said. "In Riggins' case, I pretty much had to tell him."

With Theismann the decision was less difficult for Gibbs — but it was terribly painful for Theismann, as anyone watching the Monday night game of November

JAMES A. PARCELL — THE WASHINGTON POST

Moments before the end: John Riggins pitches a flea-flicker back to Joe Theismann on November 18, 1985 — and Theismann's career would quickly be over when his leg suffered multiple fractures under the weight of three Giants pass-rushers.

18 could see. The mediocre Redskins (5-5) were playing the surging Giants (7-3) at RFK Stadium.

In the second quarter, Riggins took a handoff from Theismann, then pitched back to Theismann for a flea-flicker. But Giants Harry Carson, Lawrence Taylor and Gary Reasons arrived in succession. With all that weight on Theismann's right leg at a bad angle, the leg crumpled. Taylor, who played the game as hard as any defender, knew immediately that the injury was serious. He jumped up and waved for Redskins trainers and doctors to hurry onto the field.

Theismann lay on the ground in agony, suffering from a compound fracture. After a few minutes, he was taken from the field on a stretcher, with fans applauding him as he left. Before going into surgery at Arlington Hospital in Virginia, Theismann saw 10 minutes of the game's second half, and it had to amaze even him.

Theismann had started in 71 games in a row and was the Redskins' all-time leader in passing attempts (3,602), completions (2,044) and yards gained (25,206). Jay Schroeder, by contrast, had appeared in a total of just three previous NFL games. He had thrown eight passes, completing one to a Dallas Cowboy and four to his own teammates, for all of 51 net yards.

But Schroeder displayed a confidence that inspired his teammates that night, even if it would annoy them later. First, Schroeder declined when Gibbs asked him if he wanted trickier plays taken out of the offensive package. Then he went to work. He completed his first pass to Art Monk for 44 yards. He later found Monk for 50 more yards. In the fourth quarter, he threw a 14-yard touchdown pass that provided the decisive points in a 23-21 victory. For the game, Schroeder was 13 of 21 for 221 yards.

The next day, everyone wanted to know who Schroeder was. They found out that he had grown up in Southern California and had played two seasons at UCLA before turning to baseball with the Toronto Blue Jays organization. He had left after four seasons when the Blue Jays tried to turn him into a pitcher.

Though the Redskins were eliminated from the playoffs on the last day of the season, Schroeder had rallied the team to victories in five of their last six games to finish 10-6, a striking relief record that then turned into a wonderful starting performance in 1986. He set a franchise record in 1986, passing for 4,109 yards, and led the Redskins to a 12-4 record. His 276 completions in 541 attempts also led the NFC.

The team won its first five games that year, but then came a disturbing 30-6 loss at Dallas. The offense did nothing, the defense wasn't much better — and the kicking situation had reached a crisis stage.

In 1985, Moseley had made 22 of 34 field goals. The troubling part for Gibbs was that Moseley was just 8 of 13 between 30 and 39 yards. While coaches want kickers to make the 40-plus-yard field goals, they can't live long with misses from under 40.

The Redskins barely survived in a 14-6 win at New Orleans in which Moseley had missed both field goal attempts, from 29 yards and 45 yards. Against the Cowboys, he missed a 37-yarder and an extra point. He was cut the next day, replaced by Max Zendejas, who in turn would be replaced by Jess Atkinson for the playoffs.

After a loss to Dallas and a win over St. Louis, the Redskins went to East Rutherford. While George Rogers would finish the year with 1,203 yards, that day he gained only 30 yards on 16 carries. As a team, the Redskins mustered just 32 yards rushing, to 202 for Bill Parcells' Giants. The Giants won the game, 27-20, setting an unpleasant pattern for Redskins-Giants meetings that year.

Washington won it's next five games, but the Giants arrived at RFK Stadium on

JAMES A. PARCELL — THE WASHINGTON POST

The larger pain: Doug Williams may have twisted his knee badly in the first quarter of Super Bowl XXII, but that injury was less painful to him than the idea of Jay Schroeder taking over at quarterback.

December 7 and beat the Redskins again, 24-14. The Redskins still produced only 73 yards rushing, but the defense limited the Giants to 74. The difference this time, though, was that Schroeder tied a record — one he could have done without. Matching Sammy Baugh in 1951, Schroeder threw six interceptions. The Giants went on to win the NFC East with a 14-2 mark.

After the loss to the Giants and another to Denver, the Redskins trailed 14-0 at half-time in the regular-season finale in Philadelphia. Gibbs was not prone to locker room tantrums, but this time he overturned a table in anger. In the second half, the Redkins scored 21 points to win.

The Redskins beat the Rams, 19-7, and then the Bears, 27-13, in Chicago in the first two playoff games. That set up another matchup with the Giants — this time for a trip to the Super Bowl.

But the change in stakes had little effect. The Giants dominated again. Taylor was a force against the Redskins from his outside linebacker spot, but the whole Giant defense stuffed the Redskins' rushing attack. Rogers gained only 15 yards on nine carries, and Kelvin Bryant had just 25 yards on six runs. The dismal result was a 17-0 Redskins loss. Gibbs coached the Redskins for 205 regular season and playoff games over 12 years. That defeat, on January 11, 1987, was the only time his team was shut out.

There is nothing like a quarterback controversy to stir things up. Doug Williams or Jay Schroeder? That was the choice at the start of 1987. And the relationship between the two was, at best, chilly.

Schroeder seemed to be the future of the Redskins. He certainly thought so. "Jay was not the most well-liked guy on the team, black or white," Williams said from his head-coaching office at Morehouse College. "He was an arrogant young man."

Gibbs was, of course, familiar with Williams from his Tampa Bay days. Despite the fact that Williams was the best thing to happen to the Bucaneers, they had treated him poorly after he took them to the conference finals in 1979. So he took a year off and then played two years in the U.S. Football League before that league folded.

NFL teams did not call much, but he had more important things to worry about. In April of 1983, his wife was found to have a brain tumor. She died a week later, leaving Williams with their 3-month-old daughter.

Knowing Williams' talents, Gibbs in 1986 had talked Jack Kent Cooke into signing him, even if Williams cost $400,000 or more, which was a lot for a backup quarterback then. "A lot of owners would have said, 'You're crazy. We're not paying that for a backup, so go get somebody else,' " Gibbs said. "I was so fortunate to have him as an owner."

JAMES A. PARCELL — THE WASHINGTON POST

On the deck: Jay Schroeder being sacked during the one series in which he substituted for the injured Doug Williams in Super Bowl XXII against Denver.

Williams had thrown only one pass in 1986, but Cooke's investment paid off quickly in 1987. Schroeder sprained his shoulder in the season opener, and Williams came off the bench to throw for 272 yards and two touchdowns in a 34-24 win over the Eagles.

After the Redskins lost to Atlanta in Week 2, the football world and the quarterback controversy were interrupted by another strike, but this time only briefly. The strike began with the union seeking seven main items, including greater freedom of movement for free agents. The owners, who again would not give in, already had their general managers working on finding replacement players.

"Until a few days before the strike actually happened, we all had a hard time believing it was going to happen and that the replacement games were going to come off," Casserley said. "The day of the Atlanta game, John Cooke asked me how many we'd have on the team. I said, 'Between 30 and 60.' He said, 'Well, don't you know?' I said, 'You can call a guy thinking you have him, and by the time you call back two days later, he's committed somewhere else.' "

Other teams either did not take the replacement search seriously or failed with the mix of veterans who crossed the picket line. Casserly said it was the only time in 20 years that he hated going to work, but the job required him and Beathard to field the best squad they could.

The Redskins had 55 for the first practice. They sought players who had been in Redskins training camp or worked in similar systems. They did not want people looking for big money or expecting jobs when the strike was over (though a few got them). They figured that if players brought enthusiasm, Gibbs' staff might be able to mold them into a respectable unit.

The Redskins did not want regular players crossing the picket line. "There were some tough times and bitter feelings about missing a pay check, but we had to stay together," Jacoby said. "Joe Gibbs reinforced that. He said if people started wandering in, then we'd have problems later. We stayed together, but it wasn't easy."

Fans were in a quandary. They had difficulty sympathizing with the plight of athletes earning more than $100,000 a season. Many fans just stayed away from strike games. With only 27,728 fans at RFK, former Louisville quarterback Ed Rupert led the replacement Redskins to a 28-21 win over St. Louis, which had 11 regulars on the field. Only 9,123 were at Giants Stadium when the replacement Redskins beat the replacement Giants, 38-12.

By this point, the union was suffering from daily rank-and-file defections, at both ends of the pay spectrum, and the replacement games were making the strike impossible to sustain. "I never conceived of the possibility that they could pull off the replacement teams," Bostic said. "It certainly forced us back to work."

Eleven teams, led by the Redskins, voted to return to work even though the union said the strike was still on. When the union finally conceded, the owners tried to humiliate it, barring the regulars from playing that week. The owners claimed that they had to pay the replacement players anyway and that there wasn't enough time for the regulars to get ready. Although the union years later won back pay from the courts for that third game, Week 5 went on without them.

The Redskins had to play Dallas in that last replacement game. The Redskins, in fact, suspected that Cowboys president Tex Schramm had engineered the plan to keep the regulars out an extra week so that his Cowboys — whose stars, Tony Dorsett, Danny White, Randy White and Too Tall Jones, had crossed the picket line — could beat up on the Redskins replacements in the Monday Night game at Texas Stadium.

But the replacement Redskins stunned the Cowboys stars, winning 13-7. Tony

Turnaround artist: With the Redskins trailing in the fourth quarter of a September 11, 1988 game against the Pittsburgh Steelers, Joe Gibbs discusses offensive strategy on the sideline. The Redskins went on to win by one point, 30-29.

Robinson, who was on a work-release program from prison following a drug conviction, completed 11 of 18 passes in relief of Rupert. Lionel Vitale, from Nicholls State, outrushed Tony Dorsett, 136 yards to 81 yards, and the replacement defense made a strong fourth-quarter stand.

"Strangely enough, the most rewarding game in the 1980s was when we played Dallas on Monday night with the replacement players," Petitbon said. "They had many of their regulars. We beat them down there — and it helped us win the Super Bowl."

Indeed, while the Redskins went 3-0 in replacement games, Dallas was 2-1, Arizona 1-2, and New York and Philadelphia 0-3 each.

Once the regulars returned, so did the Redskins quarterback controversy. With time to heal during the strike, Schroeder got his job back, and the Redskins won their first two post-strike games, boosting their record to 6-1.

Schroeder then went into a slump and was replaced by Williams against Detroit. Williams in turn hurt his back and didn't play for five games, though he was again healthy for most of them. Finally, in the last regular season game, Gibbs pulled Schroeder and made Williams the playoff starter.

On a frigid day at Soldier Field, Williams led two touchdown drives, and a number of others made notable contributions to the Redskins' 27-17 victory. Defensive end Charles Mann had three sacks, the Redskins intercepted Jim McMahon three times, and Darrell Green returned a punt 52 yards, pulling rib-cage muscles in the process.

To remain in the lineup, Green took a pain-killing shot before the NFC title game against the Vikings, and his presence proved critical. The Redskins' 17-10 lead was in danger near the end of the fourth quarter. With just 56 second left in the game, the Vikings had a fourth down and 4 at the Redskins' 6-yard line. Gibbs knelt on the ground and prayed. On that Vikings last try, Green knocked away a pass to Darin Nelson to preserve the win and send the Redskins to Super Bowl XXII against Denver.

At the Super Bowl in San Diego, the Broncos were favored, and they quickly jumped to a 10-0 lead. That spooked the Redskins, who had seen the Raiders jump to an early Super Bowl lead four years earlier.

"I thought to myself, 'We've been through one of these, and I don't want to go through another one,' " Jacoby said. "The key point is when Terry Orr comes up with the fumble on the ensuing kickoff. If Denver recovers and goes up 13-0 or 17-0, we're in a real hole. And then we have that one quarter. I have never been involved in anything like that in 25 years of football."

He meant the second quarter, when Williams came back in injured, a quarter that almost defied belief.

Late in the first quarter, Williams had twisted his left knee and had left the game for two plays. But he had no thought of leaving it for good.

"When I went down, I was just thinking about finding the strength to get back up," Williams said. "Tomorrow wasn't important. One thing I could not stand was the thought that Jay Schroeder went in the game for me. The year before, in the NFC championship game against the Giants, he got banged up, and I was on the way in when he waved me off."

Williams returned to the huddle for the next series, the first of that memorable sec-

LUCIAN PERKINS — THE WASHINGTON POST

ASSOCIATED PRESS

Asking for help: Joe Gibbs kneels in prayer in the final minute of the 1988 playoff game against the Vikings — and Darrell Green, hurt and on painkillers, knocks away a pass to Minnesota's Darin Nelson to preserve the 17-10 victory.

ond quarter. On the first play, he hit Ricky Sanders for an 80-yard touchdown pass. On the next possession, he threw a 27-yard touchdown strike to Gary Clark. The Redskins moved into a 14-10 lead.

On the second play of the Redskins' third possession, Rookie Timmy Smith, a fifth-round pick from Texas Tech, made it 21-10 with a 58-yard touchdown run. The running attack helped freeze Denver safety Tony Lilly, who missed Sanders running past him to catch a 50-yard touchdown reception that widened the Redskins lead to 28-10. On the next possession, Smith busted loose for 43 yards, and then Williams hit Clint Didier for an 8-yard touchdown pass, making it 35-10.

The mind-boggling figures for the quarter had stacked up like a cord of wood. The 35 points were a post-season record for a single quarter. In 18 offensive plays, the Redskins gained 128 yards on seven rushing attempts, while Williams completed nine of 11 passes for 228 yards. Sanders had five catches for 168 yards and two touchdowns. Rookie Smith gained 122 yards on five runs in the quarter and set a Super Bowl record with 204 overall rushing yards.

When the quarter was over, Williams was in severe pain from the knee injury. "At halftime against Denver," he remembered, "Coach Bugel said we had it in hand and that we could put Jay in to finish up. I said, 'No way' and had the doctor shoot me up with painkillers. If Jay was going to get a Super Bowl ring, it was going to be because I gave it to him."

So he returned in the second half, and the score ended up at 42-10, with Denver never putting up any points after the first quarter. "It was a nightmare," Denver defensive coordinator Joe Collier said after the game.

"I was shocked we played as well as we did," Gibbs remarked. "It just happens it was in the Super Bowl."

But that made it mean so much more, especially to Williams. On January 31, 1988, he became the first African American quarterback to lead his team to a Super Bowl title and to win the game's MVP trophy. It was a resounding response to the segregationist legacy of George Preston Marshall.

"A lot of people know that the Redskins were the last team to integrate, and a lot of people told me that I put them in a bad position," Williams said. "You'd be surprised how many people said they had to cheer for the Redskins because I was playing."

Bobby Mitchell, who had paved the way for Williams as well as for so many other Redskins greats, added: "I had friends of mine in this town who knew I played for the Redskins and loved me, but hated the Redskins because of the legacy. After Doug Williams, they loved the Redskins. It made a complete transition. After Doug, some people said, 'Now, we're okay.'

The Super Bowl win over Denver gave the Redskins a 91-43-0 record in the 1980s to that point, a remarkable .677 winning percentage. But the 1988 and 1989 seasons brought another period of change for the Redskins.

In 1988, linebacker Rich Milot, running back George Rogers, tight end Clint Didier and cornerback Vernon Dean were let go. In what proved to be a steal, the Redskins traded Schroeder to the Raiders for offensive tackle Jim Lachey. By the end of the season, Lachey would replace Jacoby on the all-important left side.

Incredible quarter: On pain-killing shots for his knee injury, Doug Williams in Super Bowl XXII returned for a mind-boggling second quarter in which the Redskins piled up 35 points on 18 plays. Williams refused to let Schroeder come in for the second half.

The Redskins started 2-1, but Williams then suffered acute apendicitis. As a result, Mark Rypien made his NFL debut. Neither quarterback, however, had a great season, and neither got much running support. The Redskins went to 6-4 and were still in the play-off hunt, but they lost five of their last six to finish 7-9 — the only losing season in Gibbs' career.

The next year would end with more important departures and arrivals. It would be the last year for Dexter Manley, an important part of the 1980s miracle. In and out of drug rehabilitation, he had violated the NFL's drug policy. He later would go to prison.

Then, in May of 1989, Beathard resigned. His departure had been rumored for months. Beathard, then 52, cited a desire to return to Southern California. But, ironically, he also had had tensions with Gibbs, the coach he had recommended for the job after winning his battle with Jack Pardee nearly a decade earlier.

Beathard and his scouts had brought in players in consultation with the coaches, but Gibbs decided who made the team, and that served as a point of conflict.

"Every year there are going to be three or four guys you disagree on," Gibbs said. "The scouts are on one side, and they want to keep everybody who's a rookie and tell you how great they are. Here's the coach who's finally starting to love some of the rookies from the year before. If you have two people like we did — and it was me and Bobby and then Mr. Cooke up here — these two are going to hit . . . Yes, we had some knock-down, drag-outs . . ."

This time the coach prevailed, and Casserly took over for Beathard on May 6, 1989.

In camp that year, Rypien won the quarterback job and started the first eight games, which naturally did not make Williams happy. Williams did replace Rypien for two games, but Williams was still angry. Rypien then came around, leading the Redskins to five straight wins to end

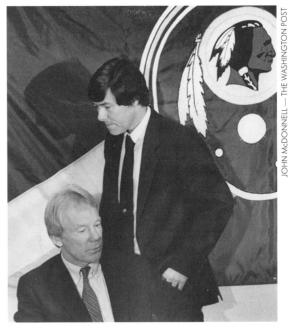

Beathard out, Casserly in: In May 1989, the seated Bobby Beathard announced his departure, and Charley Casserly — a former high school teacher and coach who had joined the Redskins as an unpaid intern in 1977 — succeeded him as general manager.

the season with a 10-6 mark, though that was not good enough to make the playoffs. Williams was released at season's end.

Before leaving, Beathard had handled the draft and had done quite well. He sent the team's 1989 second-round pick and its 1990 first-round pick to Atlanta for running back Gerald Riggs and a later 1990 pick. Riggs had been the NFL's second most productive runner the previous five years (5,895 yards), but injuries limited him to 12 games and 834 yards in 1989.

Beathard also sent Mike Oliphant to Cleveland for running back Earnest Byner, which proved to be another steal for the Redskins.

In important respects, the decade was closing as it had begun. There had been a struggle between the head coach and the general manager. The team was again in a rebuilding process. The Redskins had missed the playoffs once more — and there would be more glory ahead.

Art Monk

The Quiet Hero

By Richard Justice

Few athletes handled success with less pretense than Art Monk. Yet sometimes the goodness of the person overshadowed the magnificence of the performer. Occasionally lost in all the accolades about Monk the man and Monk the teammate and Monk the husband and father is the simple fact that Art Monk was one of the best receivers in NFL history.

He didn't have game-breaking speed, but he had the softest hands and the size and strength to muscle over cornerbacks or to jar linebackers. He also had the courage to catch balls in the middle of the field, where the collisions are the most severe.

He arrived at Redskin Park in 1980 as a quiet, unassuming wide receiver from Syracuse and departed 14 seasons later having firmly established himself as one of the best players in history at his position. His 940 career receptions are second on the all-time list. His streak of 183 consecutive games with at least one catch is an NFL record. And from 1980 until 1993, he was a key part of a magical era for the Washington Redskins.

He played 205 games and caught 888 balls. Only Sammy Baugh and Monte Coleman, with 16 seasons apiece, played more years for the Redskins. Only Coleman, with 216 games, was on the field more.

In a citywide poll on the occasion of the Redskins' 50th anniversary, Monk was voted by Washington fans as the greatest player in the franchise's history — ahead of Sonny Jurgensen, Sammy Baugh, John Riggins and Charley Taylor.

"In terms of character, he was one of the best guys I've ever been around," former Redskins coach Joe Gibbs said. "He was a role model for the youth, he was tough, he was smart and he had more talent than anyone. He made hard things look easy.

Here's a guy who probably said the least of any guy on the team, yet he was one of our best leaders. I know the couple of times he did say something, it stirred the whole team up."

Had he chosen to be more outgoing, Monk might have become a prominent personality from coast to coast. Instead, he kept to himself, gave about one interview a year and, on a veteran team that shunned the spotlight, worked harder at shunning it than almost anyone.

"I took the approach that I was going to be myself," Monk said. "I hope people appreciate someone who is honest and is themselves."

When he did speak, people listened. In 1990, when the Redskins were 6-5 and struggling to make the playoffs, Monk asked Gibbs for permission to call a players-only meeting the night before a home game against Miami. The Redskins had missed the playoffs two straight years and now were watching their season slip away after losses to Dallas and Philadelphia. Monk apparently sensed that the time was right to say something.

Words came slowly and evenly. Monk reminded his teammates that the Redskins were in danger of missing the playoffs a third straight season. He said that they had enough good players but for some reason were losing close games. He said he was re-dedicating himself to football and suggested others might do the same. He said it was time to put up or shut up.

Some of his younger teammates had heard him say barely two words. Now, here he was challenging the entire squad.

"If he was in a real good mood, he might nod to you," wide receiver Gary Clark said. "I thought he hated me the first couple of years I was around, and then I discovered that was just the way Art is. I remember one game he got real carried away. I think he said, 'Let's go' about twice. Art is the only player who can walk into a room and get absolute respect from everyone in that room."

Monk took charge of the Redskins that night, helping to pull them together at a time when they were unraveling. The Redskins credit that meeting — and the weekly ones that followed, with Monk talking less — with a lot of the good things that happened the next two seasons.

He was an example in other ways as well. Redskins assistant coach Wayne Sevier once showed his special teams film clips of Monk catching a first-down pass, then colliding with defensive backs to get an extra yard or two. Sevier told his players that Monk played the game the way it was meant to be played.

"Here's a guy going to the Hall of Fame," Sevier said. "If he's willing to do it, you've got to be willing to do it."

He provided the Redskins with memories that fans will carry for a lifetime. The record-breaking 106 catches in the 1984 season. The 13 catches against Detroit in a 1990 game. The 230 receiving yards in a game against Cincinnati in 1985. Monk became the NFL's all-time receiving leader when he caught his 820th career ball on October 12, 1992, on an emotional night at RFK Stadium. He passed Seattle's Steve Largent that night, but Monk's record later was broken by San Francisco's Jerry Rice.

Near the end of his career, he received standing ovations just for walking on the practice field at training camp. When he appeared on a radio call-in show in 1991, fans didn't ask questions so much as give testimonials, letting him know how much he was appreciated.

"We honored him at the Pigskin Club one time," Bobby Mitchell said. "It was something to see how the people felt about this guy. It's an awesome thing. When he walked in, a hush fell over the room. I've watched guys through the years — Riggo, Larry Brown, all the great ones. I've never seen this type thing. I had him on my show a couple weeks ago and it was the same thing. The calls weren't about football. They just wanted to tell him how they felt about him."

Monk grew up in White Plains, N.Y., the second cousin of the late jazz legend Thelonius Monk. He learned to play four instruments — the bass guitar, the drums, the baritone trombone and the tuba — though "I dropped all that a long time ago."

After leaving the Redskins in 1994, Monk played a season with the New York Jets and part of one with the Philadelphia Eagles. At a special 1997 event at which he signed another Redskins contract and then a release from it, Monk retired as a Redskin and will be eligible for the Pro Football Hall of Fame in 2001.

In brief remarks during a testimonial dinner in 1993, Monk told a Washington audience:

"I'm more and more amazed each time I come to this type event. I think back to my youth in New York when we'd play street ball, stickball, whatever. Guys always talked about what they're going to become. I never did that. I was never one to talk much, and that hasn't changed. Never in my wildest dreams did I ever think my career would get to this point. I think of a story of Paul at Corinth, when he said if it hadn't been for the grace of God, he would be nothing. That verse applies in my life."

TRIVIA QUIZ 4

1. Who was the only Redskin to lead the team in both rushing and receiving in a season?

2. Three of Joe Gibbs' assistants went on to become head coaches. Who were they?

3. What position did kicker Mark Moseley play in his college years at Stephen Austin?

4. When John Riggins didn't play during the 1980 season, who led the Redskins in rushing?

5. Whose complaint about the Fun Bunch's end-zone celebrations of touchdowns prompted the NFL to ban them?

6. Name the starting Redskins place kicker for Super Bowl XXII.

7. Who was the leading sacker in Redskins history?

8. In a 1987 game against the Vikings, which Redskin scored a touchdown on an interception return of 100 yards, a team record?

9. Which Redskins defensive back missed the entire 1983 season because of a drug suspension?

10. In a 1989 game against the Eagles, which Redskin rushed for the most single-game yardage in team history?

ANSWERS ON PAGE 270

CHAPTER 5
The 1990s

Another Championship — and Beyond

By Richard Justice

Joe Gibbs was mad. Sputtering mad. Red-faced mad. Punch-the-wall mad. The subject was Philadelphia Eagles Coach Buddy Ryan, and the more Gibbs talked about him, the madder he got. The words came in angry bursts, as if Gibbs were ready to deck the questioner, as if he hoped that Ryan would feel the punch in Philadelphia.

"I live to play a game like this one," Gibbs said. "I live to play this guy."

It was the first week of 1991, and the Redskins were facing a playoff game against the Eagles. While the Redskins had missed the playoffs the two previous seasons, Gibbs had lost none of his magic, especially in motivating his team. To help get the Redskins ready for the Eagles, he had taunted his players, saying:

"If you lose this game, Buddy Ryan is going to call you a bunch of fat asses like he did last time. If you don't mind being called a bunch of fat asses, that's your business."

Now it was two days before kickoff. In the parking lot at Redskin Park, Gibbs' car was still covered with snow that had fallen four days earlier. He had arrived for work late Sunday night after a meaningless December 30 victory over Buffalo to end the regular season, had spent New Year's Eve there and still had not left. During a break in a late-night meeting with his coaches, he encountered a reporter he knew well, and he finally let loose with thoughts and emotions he had long been holding back from the public.

In fact, for three days Gibbs had stood grim-faced and silent as reporters peppered him with questions about Ryan and the Eagles. That very day, Ryan had joked about how uptight Gibbs probably was, while he, Ryan, was loose and confident, knowing that he had a Super Bowl contender. Indeed, to help prepare for the Redskins, Ryan had taken his Eagles to Tampa, the site of Super Bowl XXVI, for a week of practice. "We plan to be back here," he said with a smile.

Yet when journalists pressed Gibbs to comment on Ryan, they got nothing. "Jump into the conversation at any point, Joe," one reporter joked. But Gibbs stood firm, arms folded across his chest, smiling a half-smile, simply talking about the challenge ahead.

Until that Wednesday night. Then the floodgates burst. Then the fury against Ryan poured out. Then it was clear that this would be more than a playoff game. Why? After all the big games the Redskins had played, why did this one take on such an extra dimension?

At Redskin Park, the answer was simple. Two months earlier, in a nationally televised Monday night game at Philadelphia's Veterans Stadium, the Eagles had beaten the Redskins badly. They had knocked nine Redskins, including two quarterbacks, out of the game. Five Redskins had to be carried off the field. The final score, 28-14, scarcely reflected the severity of the whipping.

Worse than the defeat were the accompanying insults. As the game wore down, an Eagle reacted to one injured Redskin lying on the turf by yelling, "Do you guys need any more body bags?" Another time an Eagle shouted, "You guys are going to need an extra bus just to carry all the stretchers!"

After the game it was even worse. The Eagles publicly poked fun at the Redskins, with Eagles defensive tackle Jerome Brown telling reporters, "They acted like they didn't want to play us anymore."

At Redskin Park, that game became known as The Body Bag Game, and it would be hard to underestimate its effect on a proud team filled with veterans like Joe Jacoby, Jeff Bostic, Earnest Byner, Art Monk and others. That game became the chief rallying cry for a stunning three-year run.

When the Redskins filed off their bus outside the Vet for that playoff game on January 4, 1991, they were stone-faced and determined. Gibbs had injected a Notre Dame-Miami hatred into them — and on the Redskins' first play from scrimmage, he was amazed by what he saw. "The line of scrimmage just exploded," Gibbs said later. "Our guys knocked Philadelphia about seven yards back. That's the kind of day it had been. In that situation, you either run and hide or you respond like a champion. Our guys responded like champions."

The Redskins, in fact, played their best game since routing Denver in Super Bowl XXII. Rypien earned his playoff spurs with two touchdown passes. Byner chalked up 126 total yards. The Redskins defense forced three turnovers. Best of all was the sweet revenge of the final score: Redskins 20, Eagles 6.

"People threw dirt on us all year," Monte Coleman said. "They didn't know we had shovels."

Surely Ryan and the Eagles had never dreamed that their words would awaken an entire organization. The Redskins would win 23 of their next 28 games. They would make three straight playoff appearances and win their first-round contest each time. The season after the Body Bag Game, they would rip through the NFL like few teams in history, winning their first 11 regular-season games and then rolling over the Buffalo Bills, 37-24, in Super Bowl XXVI.

If there had been no Buddy Ryan, would there still have been a victory in Super Bowl XXVI? That's impossible to say, since other factors also contributed to the Redskins' success. Art Monk, for example, had surprised everybody in early December with his request for a players-only meeting in which he made the rare, put-up-or-shut-up plea that moved many teammates (see profile on Page 167). But great coaches, including Gibbs, have always said that great teams have an indefinable magic. "Somewhere a team finds a spark," Gibbs said. The Redskins of 1991 — with a little help from Joe Gibbs — found their main spark in Buddy Ryan.

When the Redskins won Super Bowl XXVI, Gibbs stood atop a victory platform at a rally near the Washington Monument, holding the Lombardi Trophy aloft as thousands cheered. Surrounded by players and team officials, he wore a grin as wide as the Potomac. It was easy to think at that moment that the Redskins might always be on top of the world. But that feeling soon would fade.

Within 18 months, Gibbs would walk away, citing exhaustion and the need for a new life. His resignation would begin a series of changes, both in the front office and on the field. There would be wholesale roster changes, more changes in the coaching staff. There would be personnel mistakes and re-building projects and the kind of failure the Redskins had not suf-fered since the 1960s.

Finally, on the morning of April 6, 1997, the Redskins would suffer their most devastating blow when team owner Jack Kent Cooke, who had bankrolled three Super Bowl cham-pions and eight playoff teams, died of a heart attack.

Things can change so fast in sports that almost everything seems temporary. That was a lesson the Redskins of the 1990s learned the hard way.

The team already was in a period of slight transition as the decade began. This was not only because Doug Wil-liams, Dave Butz, Dexter Manley, Rich Milot, Vernon Dean or Clint

Last hurrahs: With Joe Gibbs holding the Lombardi Trophy aloft to the cheers of thousands, it seemed as if the Redskins couldn't lose. But in 1993 Gibbs would leave, feeling exhausted and in need of a different life. That would lead to Redskins blunders off and on the playing field and to the end of those golden years.

Didier were gone or because Bobby Beathard had resigned. Even Gibbs had changed in some surprising ways.

In a sharp departure, he had abandoned the power running game and was set to open the 1990 season with the three-wide-receiver offense that had helped win the final five games the previous year. At the time, his decision made sense. The Redskins had a rapidly improving young quarterback in Rypien and three of the league's best receivers in Monk, Gary Clark and Ricky Sanders.

But after the Body Bag Game, stuck at 5-4 and seemingly going nowhere, Gibbs, as he had so many times in the past, returned to core beliefs. The Redskins, for one thing, would go back to short, fierce practices. Gibbs had backed off a bit from harder practices for fear of burning out his veteran players. Now it was grueling practice for everyone, and if someone couldn't hold up, he didn't deserve to be there.

During the first practice after the Body Bag Game, in fact, Gibbs chewed out the entire team. Someone who was there said that Gibbs was shaking with anger, that he called his players "gutless." He told them that they had had a pretty good ride — but that the ride would be over if they didn't work much harder.

When Eric Williams was acquired from the Detroit Lions, he found out quickly what Gibbs meant. "Oh, my God, that Wednesday practice is tougher than some games I've played in," Williams said. "I wondered why we had hamburgers for lunch. I found out that was a pre-game meal."

But that was not the only change. The bigger one, the one that would carry the Redskins for the next three seasons, was a return to the power running game. With the departure of John Riggins and the injuries of Gerald Riggs, Gibbs turned to Byner, the veteran acquired in a 1989 draft-day deal with the Cleveland Browns. Gibbs decided to ride Byner, and ride him he did down the stretch in 1990. Byner had four straight 100-yard games, with the Redskins averaged a bone-jarring 176 rushing yards a game.

"We decided we could run the ball no matter what the other team is doing," guard Russ Grimm said.

The Redskins who did that weren't a bunch of high-visibility hotshots. Yes, they had their remarkable receivers. But equally if not more important was their enviable, if quieter, offensive line, with greats like Jacoby and Lachey. Mostly, though, there was a long list of workmanlike players who had been low-round draft choices and who constantly worked to prove that they belonged. If Deion Sanders and Barry Sanders are the players fans remember, Mark Rypien and Earnest Byner are the players coaches appreciate.

Byner, for example, had been a 10th-round draft choice. He arrived in Washington with a reputation as an excellent worker who had made mistakes in big games. His fumbles in the playoffs twice had helped keep Cleveland out of the running, and the Redskins wondered exactly what they were getting.

What they got was more than they could have imagined. Byner was a relentless worker, a solid performer on Sundays and a role model for every young player. He didn't give

RICH LIPSKI — THE WASHINGTON POST

No doubt about it: Two refs signal emphatically that Gary Clark has scored a touchdown on a Mark Rypien pass in an October 27, 1991 game against the Giants. The 17-13 win made it the eighth straight victory for the Redskins that remarkable season.

the Redskins the razzle-dazzle, big-burst threat they would have liked from a running back, but he was everything else. In those three straight trips to the playoffs, Byner set the tone by averaging 108.8 yards a game.

Gibbs seemed exasperated in that period when a reporter pressed him about team leaders and why the Redskins didn't seem to have any. At least there weren't Redskins who gave passionate pre-game speeches or who appointed themselves the team's public conscience. Gibbs pointed toward Monk and Warren and Coleman and said, "We're a businesslike team. We play with emotion, but just because you don't hear from guys doesn't mean they're not leaders."

They certainly were leaders now where it counted most — on the playing field. They took five of their last seven games in 1990, and they did it with a smash-mouth style that coaches and players love. They ripped Miami, 42-20, and edged Chicago, 10-9. In a cold, driving rain at New England, they clinched a playoff berth before their last two games with a 25-10 victory over the Patriots— and then savored their revenge against the Eagles.

The following week in San Francisco, however, they lost, 28-10, to Joe Montana and the 49ers. That ended a year that had been successful in many ways but unsatisfying in others, not least because the Redskins had gone 0-4 against the NFC's best teams, the Giants and the 49ers. Improved as they were, they still had given little indication of what lay ahead.

The approach to the 1991 season certainly wasn't encouraging. Rypien missed the first 10 days of training camp in a contract dispute. Once he did arrive, he looked so bad that fans in the bleachers at Dickinson College actually booed during his first practice. Nobody could remember the last time a player had been booed at a training-camp practice. That night a senior team official said: "Rip's in for a long year. This holdout was a terrible mistake. He has put all kinds of pressure on himself. What happened out there today is just the beginning."

The Redskins proceeded to lose three of their four preseason games. After one loss, Jack Kent Cooke began a conversation with Gibbs by saying: "Well, you've completely screwed this team up."

"How's that, Mr. Cooke?"

Cooke told Gibbs that he had assembled not just the wrong kind of players but the wrong kind of people. To make sure Gibbs felt the needle, Cooke added: "That Jimmy Johnson down in Dallas, he knows how to put a team together."

"Well, Mr. Cooke," Gibbs recalled saying, "I think you're wrong. I like our players."

Cooke may have felt like eating his words shortly afterward. In the season opener, those players shocked him and a lot of other people — including themselves — with their most lopsided victory in history, a 45-0 drumming of the Detroit Lions. After the ragged summer, the Redskins finally showed the world how extraordinary they would be that season — smart and tough and opportunistic and winners. Among other things, Rypien threw a pair of touchdown passes against the Lions, Brian Mitchell returned a punt for a touchdown, and cornerback Darrell Green had a pair of interceptions.

Rypien was on his way to establishing himself as, if not an artistic or stylistic quarterback, certainly a successful one. He didn't have the strong arm of John Elway or the quick release of Dan Marino or the athletic skills of Steve Young. But he was other things. The son of a cash register salesman in Spokane, Washington, Rypien never strayed far

Mountain movers: Raleigh McKenzie (63), Mark Schlereth (69), Jeff Bostic (53) and Jim Lachey (79, far right) celebrate a Gerald Riggs (37) push into the end zone behind them in a 41-10 drubbing of the Lions. The January 12, 1991 victory removed the final obstacle to Super Bowl XXVI.

from his blue-collar heritage or the solid work habits that helped a fourth-round draft choice make it. He was tough. He was patient. He almost never made a mental mistake.

He also was playing for possibly the only NFL coach who understood the importance of focusing on the things he could do instead of those he couldn't. For all his flutter balls and lack of arm strength, Rypien had a unique touch on the deep pass. He threw it with as much accuracy as any quarterback in the NFL. He also was smart enough to absorb a game plan twice as big as those of most teams. Gibbs took advantage of those talents. He built the Redskins offense around Byner's inside running. When a defense was forced to play the run, he sent Clark and Sanders down the field.

After the 1991 Detroit opener, Gibbs knew that something special was happening. "That's about as good as we've ever played," he said.

Eight days later, the Redskins went to Dallas for one of the most difficult games of the season, rallying from a 21-10 deficit to defeat the Cowboys, 33-31. On a hot, miserable Monday night in Texas, Gibbs got a magnificent effort from his players, a fitting response to the challenge of Cowboys owner Jerry Jones, who had called the game "our Super Bowl." Chip Lohmiller kicked four long field goals, Byner rushed for 104 yards, and the Redskins controlled the ball for 22 of the game's final 30 minutes.

If a team can turn a corner in Week 2, the Redskins had turned one. They would go on to win their first 11 games by an average of 20.2 points. A team-record eight Redskins, including Rypien, Byner and Clark, would be named to the Pro Bowl.

After virtually every victory, Gibbs would say that it almost seemed easy. He would tell reporters: "Well, the coaches are just kind of going along for the ride on this one. It's the players who are doing it."

It was Gibbs, however, who made sure that those players kept focused intently on the next game, that they took nothing for granted. In Game 4, the Redskins went on the road to play a winless Cincinnati team. Those kinds of games scare coaches. It's so hard to coax an emotional effort from players facing opponents who are considered easy marks. Yet by the time the Redskins got to Cincinnati, Gibbs had convinced the Redskins that they were in for the fight of their lives, and they won, 34-27.

The biggest hurdle of the first half of the season came in Game 8, when the Redskins went to the Meadowlands to face the Giants. The Redskins had lost nine consecutive non-strike games against the New Yorkers, and they knew that their 7-0 start would not mean much without a victory over the Giants. "We were 7-0, and it was like we ought to be apologizing for it — unless we beat the Giants," defensive tackle Eric Williams said.

The game didn't start well. By halftime, the Redskins were trailing 13-0. But they roared back in the second half on a pair of Rypien-to-Clark touchdown passes and a big-time effort from rookie Ricky Ervins, who subbed for Byner in the second half and gained 82 yards on 20 carries. Final score: Redskins 17, Giants 13.

"There was a monkey off our back after that," Byner said.

By the time the underdog Cowboys came to Washington for Game 12, the Redskins had extended their winning streak to 11-0. That week, Cowboys Coach Jimmy Johnson had worked his team shrewdly. The Cowboys, who arrived at RFK with a 6-5 record, were

Plotting plays: Offensive coach Jim Hanifan maps strategy with Jeff Bostic, Don Warren (85), Ralph Tamm (62) and Joe Jacoby in the October 27, 1991 game against the Giants. The Redskins' victory was the first in 10 non-strike games against the New Yorkers.

coming off close, back-to-back losses to the Oilers and the Giants. But Johnson told his team to forget their record and go have some fun against Washington. The Cowboys were going to take some chances, go for some fourth downs, let it all hang out.

"You don't hit a gorilla with a small stick," Johnson said.

He hit the Redskins hard, among other things completing a Hail Mary pass for a touchdown, recovering an onsides kick and catching the NFL's best team on a day when they were a bit off their game. Dallas ended up with a 24-21 win.

Even in that defeat, though, the Redskins found something that ultimately would help them. After falling behind by 14 points, Gibbs had gone to a no-huddle offense to get back in the game. Rypien was so proficient at it that Gibbs decided to install it as a permanent part of his playbook. The Redskins used it several more times down the stretch as well as in the Super Bowl.

They entered the final regular-season game, against the Eagles, with a 14-1 record and with home field advantage already wrapped up. After watching Rypien take a hard shot from a blitzing linebacker in the third quarter, Gibbs pulled many of his starters and allowed reserves to finish a game that ended with a 24-22 loss. The real season would begin in two weeks.

The Atlanta Falcons opened the playoffs at RFK Stadium, and Falcons Coach Jerry Glanville attempted a Buddy Ryan routine. He poked fun at the Redskins, then took his players on a carefree tour of Washington monuments on the eve of the game. At RFK, Glanville held a Redskins helmet aloft as his team gathered round him before the kick-off.

But on a rainy, bitter-cold day, the Redskins dominated from beginning to end, winning 24-7. Years later fans would not remember Glanville or the game so much as the final moments when thousands of burgundy-and-gold giveaway seat cushions flew around the stadium in spontaneous celebration.

The next day brought a big surprise: The Lions defeated the Cowboys in their playoff game. The Redskins would not be facing archrival Dallas, the only team that had beaten them in a regular-season game that counted. So the Lions came to RFK Stadium for the NFC Championship, and the Redskins again took care of business, winning 41-10. It was on to Super Bowl XXVI in Minneapolis against the Buffalo Bills.

For Gibbs, it would be his fourth Super Bowl in 11 seasons. In his first meeting with his players, he warned them to spend the first week taking care of family needs and ticket requests. He told them to be prepared to concentrate only on football once they arrived in Minneapolis. Gibbs held a series of light practices that week at Redskin Park before the team boarded a plane for the Twin Cities. Only then did players get their game plan.

What followed was a week that could not have gone better. The Redskins spent mornings doing news conferences and attending team meetings and afternoons on the field. Their practices were so fierce that on Thursday, fearing a serious injury, coaches called a halt to them. "I wouldn't want to be playing us this week," a confident assistant coach told a reporter.

He was right. Amid the roars of the fans, including the many friends and associates Jack Kent Cooke had ferried to Minnesota on a chartered Boeing 747, the Redskins played a near-perfect game. They rolled up a 24-0 lead and hung on to win, 37-24. Rypien threw a pair of touchdown passes and took home the MVP trophy, but a lot of others had contributed on a day when the Redskins rolled up 417 yards and forced four turnovers. Clark and Monk caught seven passes for 227 yards. Safety Brad Edwards intercepted a pair of Jim Kelly passes. Bills running back Thurman Thomas, who missed

JOEL RICHARDSON — THE WASHINGTON POST

Plunging for points: Earnest Byner dives for the first Super Bowl XXVI touchdown after pulling in a pass from Mark Rypien.

the first play of the game after losing his helmet, was held to a gain of just 13 yards in 10 carries.

That Super Bowl proved what a lot of people already knew: Gibbs would be remembered as one of the great coaches in history and the only one to win Super Bowls with three different starting quarterbacks. "I've never felt more humble in my life," Gibbs said. "The Good Lord has blessed me to have this owner and to be around these players."

At the end of the game, as Cooke was being escorted into the winning locker room, he turned to Casserly and said, "I can't believe we won." Years later Casserly would remark, "It was the only time I ever heard him say something like that."

Casserly himself had good cause to celebrate. He had stepped into the large chair vacated by Beathard and not only had survived but thrived. The NFL offers a limited form of free agency called Plan B in which every team allows a few players to test the open market. Casserly was brilliant in Plan B, managing to keep the players he wanted and to sift through the lists of overpaid fading stars and young unproved stars to find all sorts of gems. Beathard had put together the nucleus of the 1991 championship team, but Casserly used Plan B to acquire four defensive starters, including both starting safeties, Brad Edwards and Danny Copeland. He also got pass-rushing specialist Jumpy Geathers in Plan B. He had traded for both starting defensive tackles, Eric Williams and Tim Johnson. When Super Bowl XXVI ended, no one had a wider smile than Casserly.

Casserly had arrived at Redskin Park as an unpaid intern in 1977. He had been a high school teacher and coach in Massachusetts who wanted to give coaching on the NFL level a try. He lived in the Alexandria, Virginia, YMCA, drove a Chevy Nova with 120,000 miles on it, and typically dined on peanut butter and crackers. He fetched milk shakes for George Allen, broke down films, made scouting trips and slowly earned the respect of those around him.

When he finally drew his first NFL paycheck, he gave it to friends and schools that had helped him. By the time Beathard resigned, Cooke had so much faith in Casserly that he didn't interview anyone else.

Casserly was meticulous in organization and research, a workaholic who also found time to read a book a week and to see virtually every popular movie that came out. Once, when Cooke kept dropping the name of legendary Brooklyn Dodgers general manager Branch Rickey in conversation, Casserly bought a Rickey biography. He high-lighted a few passages like this one that could describe Casserly as well: "He was driven, as he had always been, by the ethic of work for work's sake, and also by his passionate faith in detailed and meticulous planning. Luck, as he so often informed everyone within earshot, is the residue of design."

He did the same with books on such other sports figures as basketball coaches John Wooden, Red Auerbach, Pat Riley and Rick Pitino. He kept the highlighted excerpts typed up in a loose leaf binder, and one of his goals before each training camp was to read the passages again.

Two months after the Super Bowl, Casserly took the biggest gamble of his career. He traded a pair of first-round draft choices to move into position to take wide receiver Desmond Howard, who had just won the Heisman Trophy after a dazzling season at Michigan. Casserly and Gibbs gushed over Howard on draft day, calling him an explo-sive playmaker, someone who should have a big impact for the next decade. "I've never seen a receiver who reacts as well to the ball when it's in the air," Gibbs said on draft day. "The guy makes plays."

With three veteran thirtysomething receivers, Howard was going to be the added ingre-dient in 1992 as the Redskins attempted to win a second straight Super Bowl. Other-

Follow the leaders: Rookie running back Ricky Ervins follows blockers Jim Lachey (79) and Raleigh McKenzie in a November 17, 1991 battle with the Steelers. The 41-14 rout of Pittsburgh extended the team's winning streak to 11.

wise, the Redskins wanted simply to keep things intact by signing their veterans and getting everyone into training camp on time.

The smiles faded quickly, though, after draft day. The flaw in the Redskins approach was that the special group dynamics that make up a championship team are virtually certain to have changed by the next year. Even if all the same people return, they won't be the same. They'll not only be a year older, but some will be less healthy or upset with their playing time or unhappy about their salaries. It's always something.

All of those things and more happened to the Redskins in 1992. Training camp was a disaster as Rypien, Lachey, Green and Howard all held out. Rypien was the first to show up, arriving at Redskin Park in time to catch the team's charter flight to London for a preseason game with the 49ers. But he looked terrible there. He got the four-year, $12 million deal he had been seeking, but his performance would range from inconsistent to awful. He certainly never played again at the level of 1991.

And he was the best news. Lachey, Howard and Green showed at the end of training camp, and all struggled with injuries and inconsistency in 1992. Lachey and Green promptly got hurt, and Howard began the first of three extremely disappointing seasons. The Redskins had missed badly in believing that he would be an NFL star.

That first season, Howard's performance was explained away by the fact that he had missed training camp and was playing behind Monk, Clark and Sanders. But others knew better. Gibbs himself faced the music after only a month or so of watching Howard on the practice field. He recalled saying in a meeting with Cooke: "Mr. Cooke, we blew it on this guy. It's my fault. I'll take the blame on this one. He's just not the player we thought he was."

Still, optimism was high as the Redskins flew to Dallas for a Monday night opener against the Cowboys. After the tumultuous training camp, Gibbs finally had his team intact. Even though many viewed the cocky young Cowboys as heir to the throne, Gibbs had confidence in his players. He loved their experience and work ethic, and he simply had seen them play too well too many times to feel otherwise.

Then Gibbs made one of the worst mistakes of his 12-year career. For four months, the Redskins had worked on the no-huddle offense that had been so successful at the end of 1991. He believed that with an experienced team, and especially with a quarterback as smart as Rypien, the no-huddle gave the Redskins huge advantages. It allowed the Redskins to dictate the game's pace. It prevented the defense from substituting players and adjusting to what the Redskins were doing. If Gibbs caught the Cowboys with extra defensive backs on the field, he simply would pound the ball inside to Byner and Ervins. If they were stacked to stop the run, he would send Clark down the sideline.

There was one problem that night: Texas Stadium was too noisy. Texas Stadium long had been one of the NFL's most glamorous addresses because of the mystique associated with its cheerleaders, its players and its long list of last-minute victories. But one of the untold stories was the fact that it was an easy place to play because its fans were so quiet.

Gibbs was so confident that Rypien could get the no-huddle plays called that no hand signals had been prepared — and the Redskins stepped into a bear trap. Texas Stadium was a mad, roaring place that night, and it threw the Redskins off stride. Rypien was blind-sided on the first play, and things went downhill from there until Dallas won, 23-10. What the Redskins had done was assist in the coronation of a new king. The Cowboys were on their way to back-to-back Super Bowls, and three in four seasons.

The next morning at Redskin Park, Gibbs apologized to his players for his offensive game plan. He told them that he was proud of their effort and that the defeat simply made the next week's home opener against Atlanta even more important.

He always had a knack for knowing when to push players and when to praise them.

He never forgot the need to celebrate victories and keep losses in perspective. More than once, he heard his coaches bitterly criticize this or that player in post-game staff meetings. He would sit silently, looking at the game films again and again, before stating his view. "Don't blame him for that throw," he once told an assistant. "He's got a hand in his face right there. He couldn't see the play. If our protection is better, he doesn't throw that interception."

After the Dallas defeat, the Redskins rebounded by winning six of their next eight games. But each victory exacted a toll. Jim Lachey was gone with a knee injury. Darrell Green broke an arm.

In defeating Seattle on the road in Game 9, an injured Joe Jacoby was forced to come off the bench and finish the game for an also injured Moe Elewonibi. Jacoby played despite an extremely painful pinched nerve in his neck. Around the NFL, the 16-3 score may have been seen as part of the continuing struggle of a defending Super Bowl champion. But the next day at Redskin Park, Gibbs was effusive in his praise: "What Joe Jacoby did for us yesterday is not going to be forgotten around here for a long time."

Gibbs always stressed the importance of praising players in public and criticizing them in private, one-on-one sessions. He knew that players loved to have the admiration of their peers. Fat contracts and media coverage were nice, but nothing meant more to a player than the respect of those he went to war with.

So Gibbs gave out something called the "Leather Balls" award after each victory. That was for a tough guy. He awarded reserved parking spaces for the player of the week or the special-teams star. When a player was having trouble, though, he would bring him into his office and begin the talk with something like: "Is everything okay at home?"

Another remarkable individual effort followed the next week in Kansas City, where the decimated Redskins simply were no match for the hot Chiefs. But even though they lost, 35-15, a hero emerged. After the game, cornerback Martin Mayhew approached a team doctor and said, "My arm is really hurting." He had complained about it in the first half, telling defensive coordinator Richie Petitbon that he was unable to crowd the line and make contact with a receiver because of the pain. The doctor ordered an X-ray — and it revealed that Mayhew had played the second half with a broken bone in his arm. Mayhew buried his face in his hands and cried when he heard the news.

Gibbs should have cried as well. The Redskins were missing eight starters by the time they went to New Orleans the next week, and a long list of others were playing with injuries that might have sidelined them in a normal year. In many such situations, the Redskins had risen above improbable circumstances and scored dramatic victories. Not that week. The Saints won easily, 20-3, and the Redskins were 6-5 and struggling to keep the playoffs in sight.

Three straight victories followed, including a miraculous, last-minute, 20-17 win over the Cowboys at RFK. Now at 9-5, they looked primed for another playoff run. But in Philadelphia, they lost in the final seconds to the Eagles, 17-13, and the next Saturday they were beaten by the Raiders, 21-20, when Green, with the pain-killing injection he had been taking having worn off, allowing a long Willie Gault completion.

When the Redskins left RFK after the Raiders game on December 26, it looked like the last of the season. Unless Minnesota could knock off Green Bay the next day, the Redskins were toasted. What made such an outcome so unlikely was that the Packers were playing for their playoff lives, while the Vikings had already clinched a spot.

Gibbs hugged several of his players and thanked them for their effort, seemingly a prelude to saying goodbye after the official word came the next day. But it didn't come. The Vikings upset the Packers, and the Redskins suddenly had a wild-card berth.

What followed was one more Gibbs miracle. Without depth, drained of emotion and playing a confident opponent in a hostile environment, the Redskins went to Minnesota the next weekend and beat the Vikings, 24-7. It was as thorough and surprising a beating as any Joe Gibbs' team had administered. The Vikings opened the game with a quick touchdown, but the Redskins controlled the ball for 43 of the final 55 minutes. Brian Mitchell subbed for Ervins and gained 109 yards on 16 carries. He also returned a punt 54 yards for a score. Defensive end Fred Stokes had three sacks, and Clark caught six passes for 91 yards.

The day before the game, Gibbs had shown his players George C. Scott's mesmerizing monologue at the beginning of "Patton." "That part about not dying for your country, but making the other bastard die for his country," Mayhew said. "I liked that."

"Our older guys were going to go down swinging," Gibbs said. "It was a great character check, and our guys had it."

A week later, the Redskins seemed on their way to another surprise victory when they were driving for the go-ahead touchdown in the fourth quarter at Candlestick Park. But Rypien dropped a muddy ball as he attempted to hand off to Mitchell. The 49ers recovered and went on to a 20-13 victory.

The Redskins were exhausted, physically and mentally. While they had not won the game, they had proved their mettle to Gibbs and to others with their determined, week-to-week effort despite all of their problems. Left tackle Jim Lachey had attempted to play the San Francisco game despite a torn rib cartilage. He had taken five pain-killing injections. Finally, when he requested a sixth, doctors ordered him to the sidelines. Three weeks later, Lachey was still unable to sleep through the night because of his sore ribs.

With the season over, Gibbs felt both disappointed and elated. He believed his team still capable of getting back to the Super Bowl. "I felt great about that team," he said. "I liked our quarterback. I thought we had a tough, smart group."

What few people knew was how Gibbs himself had suffered through the season. Startling, electric-like impulses had been shooting down his arms and legs, leaving him unable to sleep and worried that he was having a heart attack. But he had gutted it out, occasionally knocking off early for a nap back in his office while his assistants finished the game plan. Almost no one outside the Redskin family was aware of his trouble.

Gibbs believed that he simply was exhausted and that a couple of weeks of vacation would do the trick. Two days after the San Francisco loss, he told a reporter, "I'm definitely coming back next season."

That same day, he met with Jack Kent Cooke, executive vice president John Kent Cooke and Casserly to discuss the 1993 season. All three urged Gibbs to cut Rypien. Gibbs refused, saying Rypien would be his starter until he found someone better.

Gibbs and Casserly told Cooke that they wanted to make a run at free agent-to-be defensive end Reggie White. "Mr. Cooke agreed with us," Casserly said. "He was so adamant about getting it done that when he left I looked at Joe and said, 'We're signing Reggie White.' "

That moment should have been frozen in time. The Redskins had the NFL's best coach, an accomplished general manager and an owner who put the right decisions above profits. They had an experienced, talented team and seemed only to need a tweak here and there to get better. Reggie White would be more than a tweak.

That week, Gibbs disappeared for his usual post-season vacation. He generally would take two trips, one with just his wife Pat, the other with his sons as well. Usually he picked a resort, preferably one on the water where he could jet-ski, swim, run, play tennis, eat and rest.

Yet rest failed to stop his medical problem, and he checked himself into a clinic in Orlando, Florida, for a battery of tests. Worried that something might be seriously wrong, Gibbs was relieved when doctors discovered only a mild form of diabetes. He was ordered to eat better, to exercise more and to be mindful of getting rest.

The medical condition nonetheless had shaken Gibbs badly enough to start him thinking about walking away from football. He had had similar thoughts at other times, but thanks to a series of bad investments early in his head-coaching career, he needed the money. Now he seemed less concerned about money and more about the rest of his life.

"I was thinking more and more about taking a leap of faith, putting it in God's hands," he said. In early March, he gathered his family at a Colorado ski resort and told them that he was quitting football. Actually, he was gauging their reaction, and when his family was fully supportive, his decision seemed to have been made.

He flew back to Washington and told Jack Kent Cooke, who was stunned. As a man in his eighties who never stopped working, Cooke could not fathom retirement. He could not understand how someone who was the best in his field would even consider such a thing. He refused to accept the resignation, ordering Gibbs to take a weekend to think over his decision. Gibbs did that, returning the following week. He told Cooke then that his decision was final.

In a whirlwind 72 hours, Cooke and Casserly accepted the decision and moved forward to hire another coach. Casserly recommended longtime defensive coordinator Richie Petitbon, who was widely respected at Redskin Park. Cooke preferred a bigger name, but it was March and all of the big-name coaches already had jobs. So Cooke deferred to his general manager and hired Petitbon.

When the news of Gibbs' retirement leaked out, Washington reacted as if a king had fallen. Perhaps nobody was more shaken than his players.

"We were all devastated at the news," Rypien said. "You know nothing will ever be the same. You start thinking that the Redskins won't even play again. That's what Coach Gibbs meant to us."

At the news conference announcing his retirement, Gibbs choked back tears as he told reporters: "I've lived a dream . . . I don't know what's ahead for me, but it's tough to move on . . ." Two dozen current and former

Can't be: Adoring fans of Joe Gibbs, cheering him here, could hardly believe it when he resigned.

JOHN McDONNELL — THE WASHINGTON POST

Redskins showed up to tell their coach goodbye, and many of them shed tears as well.

Gibbs' retirement was the beginning of a long, bad summer. After ordering Casserly to cut off negotiations with several unsigned veterans midway through the 1992 season, Cooke watched as a large part of his team departed through free agency. Gary Clark, one of the NFL's top wide receivers for eight seasons, was the most prominent loss. His departure was the first sign that the Redskins had someone new in command. Petitbon didn't like Clark's temper tantrums, his abrasive personality and his ego. Gibbs hadn't either, but he had appreciated Clark's brilliance on the field even more.

Then there was the case of Art Monk. Casserly and Petitbon summoned him to their office and told him that he was no longer a starter. Just like that. After 13 seasons, he wasn't even allowed to compete for his job. The Redskins were right that Monk had lost a step and that it was time he began phasing out. But Gibbs would have let the adjustment take place gradually, on the field, not in a meeting room. Monk, proud and sensitive, reacted with fury, skipping mini-camp and attracting a summer's worth of headlines that gave the impression that the Redskins were coming apart.

It would take five years, after stints with the Eagles and the Jets, for Monk to make peace with the Redskins. On July 17, 1997, he signed a Redskins contract again — and then a release from the same contract — so that he could retire as a Redskin.

Other departures followed that summer. When linebacker Wilber Marshall demanded a $3 million salary, Cooke ordered him traded. Cornerback Martin Mayhew and defensive end Fred Stokes, a playmaker with 24 sacks in 53 games, both departed via free agency. Pass-rushing specialist Jumpy Geathers, who had performed so brilliantly in 1991, signed on with the Atlanta Falcons.

If the Redskins had had young players prepared to fill these jobs, the departures wouldn't have been so costly. Indeed, none of the departing players ever did much after leaving Redskin Park. But the Redskins didn't have the replacements. That summer, they signed a motley crew of free agents — wide receiver Tim McGee, defensive end Al Noga, linebackers Carl Banks and Rick Graf — and drafted Notre Dame cornerback Tom Carter.

The free fall had begun. With the disappearance of Gibbs, Rypien's No.1 defender, Cooke got his wish for a new quarterback. He got a lot of other wishes as well throughout the season. Benching Brian Mitchell for rookie Reggie Brooks. Benching Rypien. Benching quarterback Cary Conklin. The Redskins seemingly went out of their way to start erasing the memory of Gibbs, including removing his one-running-back offense.

Still, Petitbon had one terrific night. In his first game as coach, the Redskins pounded the Cowboys, 35-16. For a brief moment at least, the new era didn't look so bad.

But six straight defeats followed. Rypien was injured in Game 2 against Arizona. Carter was beaten on a last-second touchdown pass in Game 3. The Redskins were on their way to a disastrous 4-12 season — their worst record in three decades. Only 42,836 showed up at RFK for the regular season finale against the Minnesota Vikings, a 14-9 loss.

Before the end of the season, Cooke and Casserly had decided to fire Petitbon. They knew that the Redskins had personnel problems, but both were convinced that the team also was poorly coached. Casserly spent a large portion of his time in December evaluating Cowboys offensive coordinator Norv Turner, collecting newspaper clips, talking to his colleagues and looking at game films.

By the time that last game against Minnesota was over, Casserly had convinced Cooke that Turner should be the next Redskins coach. Four days later, Petitbon was summoned to Cooke's office for the firing. Petitbon might not have been head coach material, but

RICH LIPSKI — THE WASHINGTON POST

Awful year, awful end: Rypien closes 1993's dismal season (4-12) with a last-play fumble on a tackle by Viking Roy Barker.

it's clear in retrospect that he never had a chance. By 1993, after some poor drafts and some terrible losses in free agency, the Redskins simply were out of players.

Casserly and Turner had a long phone conversation that afternoon. Casserly would have brought Turner to town for a formal interview that weekend if NFL Commissioner Paul Tagliabue had not ordered the process stopped until the Cowboys finished the season. The Cowboys' season didn't end for another month, when Dallas won its second straight Super Bowl. Three days after that, Turner flew to Washington and met with Cooke and Casserly.

His hiring wasn't entirely the slam dunk the Redskins had expected. Turner also had been contacted by the Arizona Cardinals, who were ready to make him both coach and general manager. When he walked into Redskin Park, his intention was to delay a decision until he had talked to the Cardinals as well. But he changed his mind that day after Casserly left Turner and Cooke alone for a private chat. Some 45 minutes later Casserly was summoned back to Cooke's office. "Meet the new coach of the Washington Redskins," a smiling Cooke said.

Turner later explained: "I just decided this was where I wanted to be. I wanted to work for Mr. Cooke. There's a history and a tradition with the Redskins, and I wanted to be part of that."

Some associates had warned him not to take the job. One NFL general manager told him that the Redskins were out of players, that Casserly was overmatched in the role of general manager, and that coaching the Redskins in 1994 would be a prescription for career disaster.

Turner soon would come to agree with part of that assessment. He told Cooke: "Mr. Cooke, a lot of people warned me against coming here. They told me the Redskins didn't have any players. I wanted to be here because of you. But they're right. This is going to be a long, slow process. We've got to rebuild this team."

As part of the farewell to the old team, the Redskins said their goodbyes that summer to Mark Rypien, Art Monk, Ricky Sanders, Joe Jacoby, Jeff Bostic, Earnest Byner, Brad Edwards, Charles Mann and Eric Williams. So many more of the names and faces associated with Joe Gibbs and Super Bowls would now be gone.

On the rebuilding side, the Redskins made two sharp moves in free agency that summer in signing linebacker Ken Harvey away from the Arizona Cardinals and unwanted wide receiver Henry Ellard, last with the Los Angeles Rams. Turner also had used the third pick in the draft to get Tennessee quarterback Heath Shuler. Almost overlooked on draft day was a seventh-round pick named Gus Frerotte, a quarterback from Tulsa.

But Turner's rookie season was a 3-13 nightmare. Shuler missed half of training camp in a contract dispute, forcing Turner to change his plan to make him a starter from his first day. Not much else worked right, either, with the Redkins now a mixture of over-the-hill veterans and youngsters who weren't as good as expected.

Turner got his first NFL victory in Week 2 at New Orleans, but it would be six weeks before he won again. He stormed out of a post-game news conference after a 34-7 home loss to the Cowboys. He had watched Shuler complete just 11 of 30 passes in his first start. He had seen his offense gain only 110 total yards. He had watched running back Reggie Brooks fumble three times in the first half.

One of the few highlights of the Redskins' worst season in 31 years came in Game 8, when Turner stunned the city and his organization by giving Frerotte a start. Shuler had sprained an ankle in an overtime loss to Arizona, and instead of putting veteran John Friesz back in the lineup, Turner turned to perhaps the NFL's least known quarterback.

Cooke wondered if Turner had flipped his lid, but he was pleasantly surprised. In what might have been Frerotte's first and last chance to show the world that he belonged in the NFL, he completed 17 of 32 passes for 226 yards and two touchdowns as the Redskins defeated the Colts, 41-27.

Shuler had been booed almost from the moment he had stepped foot in RFK Stadium, and now Turner had a full-blown quarterback controversy. Frerotte, a big, raw, strong-armed kid making the minimum salary, had become the people's choice. Frerotte and Shuler split the playing time, with Shuler showing more in terms of raw talent but Frerotte more in terms of poise and arm strength. Almost to a man, the team's locker room sentiment joined the fans in favoring Frerotte.

No breaks: Norv Turner couldn't win a call against a Redskins interception in a September 25, 1994 game against the Atlanta Falcons, just as he couldn't win much else in that dreadful 3-13 year.

JOHN McDONNELL — THE WASHINGTON POST

Shuler nonetheless got back in the lineup for the final month of the season and played well enough that Turner believed he had won the job.

In the summer of 1995, there were more departures and more acquisitions. Turner showed the door to Monte Coleman, Andre Collins, Ricky Ervins, Desmond Howard, A.J. Johnson, Chip Lohmiller, Raleigh McKenzie and Mark Schlereth. Turner and Casserly also dove headlong into free agency by signing center John Gesek, tight end Scott Galbraith, safeties James Washington and Stanley Richard, linebackers Marvcus Patton and Rod Stephens and a host of others.

Their best move was one that fell in their laps. The Minnesota Vikings cut running back Terry Allen after he refused to take a pay cut, and the Redskins grabbed him for what, in the football world, was the low price of $450,000. Allen became the NFL's biggest bargain as he started by producing two consecutive 1,300-yard seasons.

Some teams had feared taking the 27-year-old Allen because both his knees had been reconstructed, and the Redskins admit they had no idea what they were getting. What they got was just about the perfect football player, one who played with an anger and recklessness that rubbed off on everyone around him. He didn't have flash, but he provided the workmanlike production that Turner wanted from his running back.

Hoping for some offensive dazzle, Turner also drafted 6-foot, 3-inch wide receiver Michael Westbrook from the University of Colorado. Turner knew the Redskins were still far from competing for a playoff spot, but if Shuler and Westbrook were as good as he hoped, they could at least make things interesting.

Even though Shuler had a poor preseason, Turner gave him the opening-day start against Arizona. He was in for just 17 plays, however, before defensive end Clyde Simmons nailed him, separating his shouler and again interrupting his career. Once more, Frerotte was in the lineup. Once more, he played decently. Once more, the Redskins were losing.

Shuler was sidelined for two months. Turner also put in Frerotte for Games 9 and 10, then started Shuler again in Game 11 against Philadelphia. He played well enough in a 14-7 loss, then a week later had the best game of his three seasons in Washington when he completed a 44-yard throw to Leslie Shepherd to spark a 24-17 upset in Dallas. Two weeks later, however, Shuler was back on the sidelines, this time with a broken finger.

After three years of turmoil, the Redskins in 1996 had a quieter off-season. They made only one dramatic trade, giving away their first-round draft choice to the St. Louis Rams for mammoth defensive tackle Sean Gilbert. Turner believed that the Redskins finally were close to being competitive after back-to-back drafts had brought guard Tré Johnson, tackle Joe Patton, center Cory Raymer, tight end Jamie Asher and defensive end Rich Owens.

But he knew that his biggest decision would be choosing between Shuler and Frerotte. So, in training camp, he staged an open competition between the two men, who had such different histories.

Shuler was a legendary athlete in tiny Bryson City, North Carolina, attracting the interest of many college coaches. He chose the University of Tennessee and was revered for his athletic skills, his boyish good looks and his Huck Finn personality. As for Frerotte, he was the son of a career worker at Pittsburgh Plate Glass, and his career almost was ended by a serious neck injury in high school. He attended Tulsa University because that was one of his few scholarship offers, and he received barely a look from NFL teams after college.

Both played decently during training camp, but Turner, already leaning heavily toward Frerotte, went with him. He believed that Frerotte would make fewer mistakes. The Redskins were going to win or lose on the strength of their running game and their defense's ability to keep things close. The last thing Turner wanted was a gambling, freewheeling quarterback.

RICH LIPSKI — THE WASHINGTON POST

New face: Gus Frerotte, the unknown quarterback who surprised everybody in 1994, soon became the people's choice.

For all practical purposes, Shuler's career in Washington was over. He was in for just one play in 1996, and when the season ended, he exercised an escape clause in his contract. He visited several teams before agreeing to a deal with the New Orleans Saints.

When the 1996 season opened, the Redskins suffered an immediate, 14-7 defeat at home against the Philadelphia Eagles. At that point, Turner, with a 9-24 record, was beginning to feel some heat.

Even Cooke, who had backed him for so long, got angry. After three straight seasons of losses, Cooke was running out of patience, especially while he was building a new stadium in a Maryland suburb outside Washington. It wasn't going to be just a stadium but a palace, complete with 78,600 seats, including luxury suites, expensive club seating and other amenities.

The problem was that Cooke may have misjudged the Washington market. His expensive seats weren't selling well, and Cooke needed the victories to spark interest. Turner got the message. "I'm not going to get into the details of what he told me," Turner said a few months later. "You can figure it out."

The Redskins then shocked the NFL by winning their next seven games. As Turner had promised, he built his offense around Terry Allen, who rushed for more than 100 yards in five of the first 10 games. Frerotte did his part, playing smartly and efficiently. And a defense that was still terribly thin in the line played better than anyone imagined possible. An ebullient Cooke said: "We're going to the playoffs. It's as certain as tomorrow, although not quite as imminent."

He had spoken too soon. The Redskins opened the second half of the season with a terrible performance, a 38-13 defeat in Buffalo. Turner was furious at his defense for allowing 476 yards, telling friends: "There's never an excuse for allowing 476 yards. Never."

A week later, things got worse when the Redskins twice blew 14-point leads in a 37-34 overtime loss to Arizona. His defense again was awful, this time allowing 615 yards. Aging Arizona quarterback Boomer Esiason passed for a mind-boggling 522 yards, including 351 in the fourth quarter and overtime. Nonetheless, had tight end Scott Galbraith not been whistled for holding on a Scott Blanton field goal attempt, the Redskins would have won anyway. Three times in the second half of the season, the Redskins would lose on the final play of a game.

Despite all of this, Turner held his team together, and, in as impressive victory as the Redskins would have all season, they went to Philadelphia and defeated the Eagles, 26-21. With an 8-3 record, they still appeared on track for the playoffs.

But not for long. The Redskins fought gallantly in a home game against the 49ers only to lose, 19-16. There was a lopsided Thanksgiving Day loss in Dallas, 21-10. Then a dismal 24-10 defeat in Tampa. Then a 27-26 loss in Arizona. All of a sudden, from 7-1 and 8-3 the Redskins had dropped to 8-7. Had they won any of those final four games, they would have made the playoffs.

Their season ended with a meaningless game against Dallas at RFK Stadium. Neither team had anything riding on the game, although it was more important for the Redskins, who were playing at their revered old RFK for the last time. Frerotte played his best game of the season, and, amid the emotion and celebration, the Redskins won, 37-10.

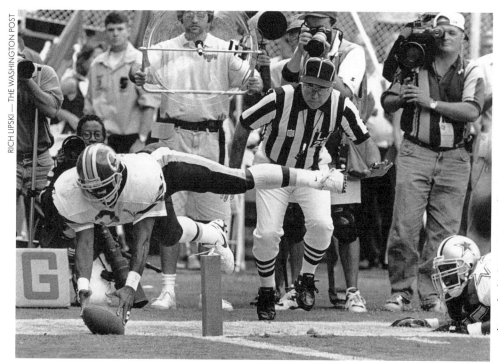

RICH LIPSKI — THE WASHINGTON POST

Big bargain: Feisty running back Terry Allen, diving here for a touchdown against Dallas on October 1, 1995, left the Vikings when they insisted on cutting his pay. He joined the Redskins at a relatively low price and with two reconstructed knees — and delivered 1,300-yard seasons.

In retrospect, the Redskins could have seen 1996 as at least a decent season, having gone from 3-13 to 6-10 to 9-7 in Turner's three years. They had found a quarterback in Frerotte and were now a solid offensive team.

But for Turner, Cooke, Casserly and others, it was not a decent season at all. Missing the playoffs again was a bitter pill to swallow. So Turner made more changes, firing defensive coordinator Ron Lynn and most of his staff and hiring the highly regarded Mike Nolan from the New York Giants. Thus began a restructuring of the NFL's 28th-ranked defense.

Turner and Cooke hoped that 1997 would be the season it all turned around, with a team headed back to the playoffs and the opening of what Cooke saw as the greatest new stadium in sports. As his team reworked its defense in the spring of 1997, Cooke took frequent drives into the suburbs to see his new stadium going up. Friends report that he would sit in his car, saying nothing as his eyes scanned the huge steel and concrete structure.

But he didn't live to see it open. On the morning of April 6, at his home in Northwest Washington, Cooke died of a heart attack. Just minutes before his death, he had summoned son John to come over and take a ride to the stadium site.

At his memorial service four days later, John Kent Cooke's brief, moving eulogy included these words: "He doted on me as a boy. He trained me as a young man. He entrusted me with the daily operation of the essence of everything he savored, the Washington Redskins." He also announced that the stadium would carry his father's name, saying: "He envisioned it a decade ago. It was his creation. It is his stadium, and it will bear his name."

He told employees and the press that he intended to keep the Redskins in the family and that things would continue to operate as they had under his father. Actually, his father's tangled will left it uncertain whether he would be able to buy the team. But even it he could, no one who knew his father believed that the Redskins ever would be the same.

Jack Kent Cooke was a loud, bullying, profane man. He had little patience, and he didn't suffer fools lightly. He also was one of the best owners in sports. The Redskins had wonderful days of glory in some of his years, and at least stayed competitive in others, while they played in the NFL's smallest stadium. They lost money virtually every year but continued to spend it because Cooke wanted to win so badly. He had strong opinions, and he challenged his coaches and general managers when they disagreed with him. But he usually followed their recommendations.

A few weeks after his father's death, John Kent Cooke described how he one day hoped to turn the Redskins over to his sons, John and Tom. He described the patch the Redskins would wear in memory of his father in 1997 and spoke about how it would be such an important season.

"I think more than any other, it's a season when I hope we go to the playoffs," he said. "It would be a fitting tribute to my father."

The Bandwagon of 1991

Trapped in a Joke

By Tony Kornheiser

O ne of my neighbors down the street has a burgundy Volvo station wagon, the official car of upper Northwest Washington, and on the rear bumper is a weatherworn sticker for The Bandwagon. I don't see many of those any-more. (I don't see many Bush-Quayle stickers anymore, either.) So when I drive home at night I often look for that Volvo and that bumper sticker, and I think about what it was like getting trapped in one of my own jokes, about the strange sensation of be-ing taken (gulp) seriously by everybody.

Everybody has his favorite Redskins team.

Mine is 1991, the year the Redskins won the Super Bowl in Minneapolis.

The year of The Bandwagon.

I first used the word "bandwagon" after the fourth game of the season. At that point the Redskins were 4-0, and scoring 36 points a game, and I was looking . . .

Excuse me, Tony, but are you going to start self-referencing here, like you did throughout that season? Your ego was bigger than Joe Jacoby — and not Joe Jacoby's ego, Joe Jacoby! Every week you wrote the same column. Ostensibly, it was about the Redskins, but it seemed like all you ever wrote about was yourself.

Like it's better if I write about Terry Orr?

I have a drawing in my office — the original drawing that accompanied the column after the Redskins won the Super Bowl. It has a likeness of me, with my big, fat, white, bald head, leading The Bandwagon, throwing rose petals in its path. Immediately behind me are two horses pulling The Bandwagon, and one of them is saying, "Let's dump Gatorade on Kornheiser!"

It's the highlight of my career.

(It could have been worse. I could have been behind The Bandwagon with a shovel.)

The whole Bandwagon thing started out as a way to make fun of the Redskins and their fans (you folks who have bought this book, and now I hope will rush out to the bookstore and pick up a copy of my hilarious new collection, *Bald As I Wanna Be*, thank you, thank you very much).

Come on, you know how out of control Redskins fans get. When I came down to Washington from New York in 1979, I couldn't believe how much the Redskins mattered here, how the entire city came to a halt on Mondays to discuss the game from the previous day. New York is a terrific sports town — there's two of everything there — but nothing, NOTHING matters as much to New Yorkers as the Redskins matter to Washingtonians. You don't really think you could get male Giants fans to put on a housedress and a pig snout, do you? I mean, unless Anna Wintour said it was okay.

So I thought I'd tap into the perennial overreaction of Redskins fans by saying right away, after the very first game (a 45-0 croaking of Detroit, you might remember), that it was time to make airline reservations for the Super Bowl in Minneapolis.

I was KIDDING!

My plan was to pump up the Redskins to ridiculous size, like a balloon in the Thanksgiving Day Parade, then blow 'em up real good as soon as they lost.

But the Redskins beat Dallas at Dallas, and then they killed Arizona, 34-0. Well, that was the Redskins' second straight shutout at home. So with weak Cincinnati coming next, the press began peppering Joe Gibbs about how good the Redskins were. And predictably, Gibbs, who is a Doomsday Machine, made the 0-3 Bengals into the 1927 Yankees. I added Gibbs to the columns as a staple character who'd say anything to cast his team in the role of massive underdog, even if they were playing one of the Seven Sisters schools.

It was after the Redskins beat Cincinnati that I started using the B word — to conjure up fair-weather fans "jumping on the bandwagon." I was just waiting to savage them for jumping off when the Redskins began losing.

But the Redskins refused to lose.

They went 4-0, 5-0, 6-0, 7-0, 8-0, 9-0, 10-0, 11-0.

They were killing me!

By now the joke was on me. The Redskins really were as good as I'd laughingly said they were. Heck, they were better.

I had two choices:

1. Admit what a dope I had been in trying to dupe people.

2. Keep dancing as fast as I could.

(Here's a clue as to which way I went. Remember *Do You Love Me?* by the Contours? It goes, "You broke my heart because I couldn't dance. You didn't even want me around. Well, now I'm back to let you know I can really shake 'em down. Watch me now!")

I rode The Bandwagon as hard as I could. If everybody suddenly thought that I had this astounding ability to call a Super Bowl winner like Babe Ruth calling a home run, that I oughta be picking stocks for Warren Buffett, who was I to say no?

So I kept making fun of Gibbs' paranoia. I kept exaggerating the Redskins' abilities — and they, incredibly, kept fulfilling my exaggerations. What could I do?

I made sure to go to the same players every week for quotes, players I thought had a sense of humor, and an appreciation for the organic quality of The Bandwagon, mostly offensive linemen, who are generally the smartest guys on a football team. I'd go to them after a game and say, "Gimme a quote for The Bandwagon." And they would. Without Russ Grimm, Jeff Bostic, Terry Orr and Mark Adickes, among others, I couldn't have sustained The Bandwagon's prediction machine. (Adickes, by the way, went on to Harvard Medical School — to be a doctor, not a patient!)

By now I was mistakenly considered such a genius that I claimed to have received a copyright for The Bandwagon from the U.S. Copyright Office. Each week I gave a different number of the copyright. Usually the number was a phone number; one week it was the address of *The New York Times*, one week it was the uniform numbers of all the Redskins pictured in the accompanying drawing. I even started soliciting fans to write in and send me stuff to use in Minneapolis, like hand warmers and lutefisk recipes. And I put their names in the columns, and officially welcomed them on The Bandwagon. I was becoming a community service columnist!

I was a shameless hustler for The Bandwagon — and my career. (Geez, this is like an HBO show: "The Making of the Bandwagon.")

By the time the Redskins finally lost a couple of games, The Bandwagon was so entrenched that the losses didn't matter. Readers kept sending in more stuff for the trek to Minneapolis: rock salt, windshield ice scrapers, jigging sticks for ice fishing, beef jerky. The players themselves would come to me in the locker room and tell me not to scrap The Bandwagon; they'd say it was just in need of a carburetor adjustment.

The good news was that The Bandwagon had taken on a life of its own.

The bad news was that when the Redskins made the Super Bowl, we actually had to drive out to Minneapolis in a 40-foot RV decorated with Bandwagon insignias. I couldn't have been any more embarrassed if Dennis Rodman had married my mother.

Three days on the road in that gargoyle with no shock absorbers. I dragged my friend Nancy and Man About Town Chip Muldoon along, swaying all over the highway. The RV had a king-sized bed in the back, but when I went to catch a nap back there I bounced like an apple in a crate. We stopped for the first night in Elkhart, Indiana, then in Tomah, Wisconsin, towns I wouldn't have stayed in on a dare.

It was so cold in Elkhart, I considered setting The Bandwagon on fire. Checking into the Signature Hotel, we found that the hotel had made me the VIP of the Day, and put my name on the message board in the lobby! As VIP of the Day I was entitled to "complimentary fruit in the room." I opened the door to find one apple, as frozen as Mrs. Paul.

And then, finally, we pulled into Minneapolis. (A few minutes before we had seen a sign on the highway: "Minneapolis 9." We weren't sure if that was mileage or temperature.)

"Do you feel it?" Man About Towns (after all, these were the Twin Cities) Chip

Muldoon asked me.

"Do I feel what?" I said, praying this wasn't an essay test.

"It! Don't you feel it?" Chip said passionately. "Here we are! That's the Metrodome! This is what we played the whole season for! This is why we changed the oil and rotated the tires! This is The Bandwagon's destiny!"

I wept.

TRIVIA QUIZ 5

1. Only four players on the 1997 Redskins roster were there before Norv Turner arrived as head coach in 1994. Name them.

2. Defensive coach Mike Nolan's father was picked as NFL head coach of the year while coaching which team?

3. In 1991, the Redskins allowed the NFL's third lowest number of sacks in a season. How many did they permit?

4. During his ill-fated three seasons with the Redskins, quarterback Heath Shuler failed to play in how many games?

5. In 1996, Shuler took just one snap from scrimmage. What was the result?

6. The Redskins in 1990 tied the greatest comeback in team history by rallying from 21 points down to beat the Lions, 41-38, in overtime. Which quarterback threw for 363 second-half yards in that game?

7. In 1992, the Redskins sent a team-record eight players to the Pro Bowl. Name them.

8. What was Brian Mitchell's NFL-leading punt-return average in 1995?

9. In 1994-95, Henry Ellard led the NFL in receptions that went for first downs. How many of his 130 catches moved the markers?

10. The Pro Football Hall of Fame has inducted 19 members who were on the Washington Redskins over the team's 60-year history. Can you name at least 15 of them?

ANSWERS ON PAGE 270

CHAPTER 6
1999 —

The Snyder Years

By Liz Clarke and Mark Maske

As a child, Daniel Snyder mostly watched Redskins games during "football picnics" in his parents' Maryland home, sitting on a blanket his mother had spread out before the TV and eating hotdogs or a sandwich or "Redskins chili." His father, though, periodically took him to Redskins games at RFK Stadium, starting when his son was 7 years old. They sat in the nosebleed section, peering through binoculars, and young Daniel sometimes glanced across the field toward the rich and powerful in Jack Kent Cooke's owner's box.

"I'd just watch and wonder what was happening in there," Snyder recalled.

When he was 34 years old, he found out. On May 25, 1999, after a tortuous, 9-month auction, Snyder himself became the Redskins' owner, buying the franchise for a record $800 million. Suddenly, the little-known Bethesda, Md., millionaire was a member of an exclusive fraternity, the youngest owner in the NFL, going from bleachers to boss of the team he had loved since childhood. It was hard to believe, "a dream come true," he said.

For Redskins fans as well, old dreams began coming true, particularly as they watched the club win the 1999 NFC East Division title, its first such victory in eight years, and then become a leading Super Bowl contender again. Those feats followed a radical retooling of the Redskins roster, a new front office staff and an aggressive team attitude to match the youthful exuberance of the new owner.

However, for everyone associated with the Redskins — fans, players and coaches alike — it was a gut-wrenching road to glory. All eyes watched as the Cooke family's quarter century of Redskins control came to an inelegant end. The transition was marked by a rancorous dispute over the team's sale, followed by months of uncertainty during which the Redskins seemed adrift. Overseeing the club were faceless trustees charged with liquidating the property. Running the show were a coach and general manager who were unsure if they would even have jobs the next season. And leading the bids for the team were out-of-towners, led by New York real estate magnate Howard Milstein, whose only previous foray into professional sports (as owner of hockey's New York Islanders) had been a major disappointment.

The unhappy chain of events was set in motion by Jack Kent Cooke's will, which required that the team be sold and that the proceeds be used to establish a foundation to dispense education aid. For fans, it seemed unfathomable that John Cooke, who had run the Redskins since his father's death, would not be the buyer. But half a dozen eager bidders emerged, and the price tag skyrocketed. Brothers Howard and Edward Milstein, whose partnership group included Bethesda's Daniel Snyder, bettered Cooke's $680 million offer by a wide margin. So on January 11, 1999, the trustees accepted the Milstein group's $800 million bid.

It became clear almost immediately, however, that some influential NFL owners had reservations about the Milstein bid, and the process dragged on for months. By April 7, Milstein, faced with certain rejection, finally withdrew his group's offer at an NFL owners' meeting in Atlanta. The Milstein brothers were whisked away from an Atlanta hotel that afternoon in a black limousine, declining comment. Few noticed that Snyder, who had managed to stay in the background of the high-profile tussle, wasn't with them.

Snyder was in his hotel suite, working the phones like a man possessed. Determined to assemble his own Redskins bid, he conferred with his closest confidantes: his sister Michele, president of the marketing firm he had founded, Snyder Communications, and his father, Gerald. In short order, Snyder lined up the other financial backers he needed in Mortimer Zuckerman, the publishing and real estate mogul, and longtime Zuckerman associate Fred Drasner. It was a bold power play that said a lot about a young man driven by a vision of returning the Redskins to the glory he had reveled in as a child.

While the maneuvering over Redskins ownership was capturing everyone's attention, there was plenty of work to be done on the field. The Redskins had rebounded from an abysmal 0-7 start in the 1998 season to win six of their last nine games. Though they had failed to make the playoffs for the sixth straight year, there was reason to think that the team was on the mend.

The first order of business in the winter of 1999 was re-signing quarterback Trent Green, who had played heroically for third-string money ($250,000) after replacing Gus Frerotte in the 1998 season opener against the New York Giants. General manager Charley Casserly prepared a budget outlining what it would take to keep Green in a Redskins jersey as well as to bring back other key players. But he quickly found himself hamstrung by the team's convoluted ownership situation.

The trustees, with authority over all expenditures, questioned the offer Casserly wanted to extend to Green, thinking the quarterback's value would come down after the NFL's free-agent signing period opened in February. And Howard Milstein, then the presumed owner-in-waiting, also wanted a voice in financial and personnel matters. The upshot: an uneasy standoff that brought off-season work to a crawl. NFL Commissioner Paul Tagliabue ultimately had to step in, restoring full authority on all Redskins matters to team president John Cooke. By then, however, the 28-year-old Green had signed a slightly more lucrative deal with the St. Louis Rams (four years, $16.5 million, including a $4.5 million signing bonus).

Members of Norv Turner's coaching staff also started departing. Quarterbacks coach Mike Martz left for the Rams. Linebackers coach Dale Lindsay went to Chicago. In time, running game coordinator Bobby Jackson would also leave.

Fearful that he might have trouble re-signing Green, Casserly had begun exploring other options as the 1998 season had drawn to a close. And within hours of Green's departure, he stunned Redskins fans by trading first-, second-, and third-round draft picks to the Minnesota Vikings for Brad Johnson, who had lost his starting job to Randall Cunningham after breaking his right leg early in the season. Some, including Milstein, thought the price was too high. But Turner was unabashed in his excitement over Johnson, who he felt had the size (6-5 and 224 pounds), accuracy and intelligence to bring Turner's offensive system to life.

With Johnson on board, work continued on the 1999 draft. The front office and coaching staffs were of a like mind on the overriding needs: a cornerback to replace Cris Dishman (who had slumped badly the previous season) and ultimately to succeed veteran Darrell Green, plus help on the offensive line, which had surrendered a team-record 61 sacks in 1998.

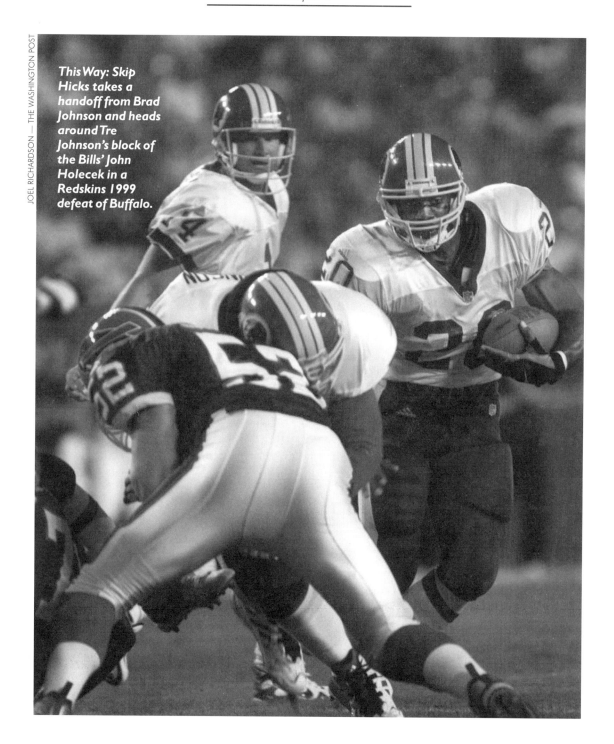

This Way: Skip Hicks takes a handoff from Brad Johnson and heads around Tre Johnson's block of the Bills' John Holecek in a Redskins 1999 defeat of Buffalo.

It would be Casserly's last draft for the Redskins, and many would argue that it was his finest. The Redskins emerged with the cornerback they wanted in Georgia's Champ Bailey, considered the best athlete in the draft. They also got right tackle Jon Jansen, a 6-6, 302-pounder from Michigan, who would start all 16 games as a rookie. And the acquisitions came at a bargain price. That was thanks to Casserly's wiles and the draft-day foolishness of New Orleans coach Mike Ditka, who traded away his entire draft for the right to move up and take running back Ricky Williams of Texas with the Redskins' fifth overall pick. When the deal-making was done, the Redskins moved down two spots in the first round and acquired an extra first-round pick in the 2000 draft, additional sixth- and seventh-round selections in the 1999 draft and still got Bailey.

"He's the guy we wanted," Turner said.

John Cooke never got to enjoy what appeared to be the Redskins' biggest draft-day coup in memory. With the Milsteins out of the picture, it seemed natural that the trustees would reopen the bidding for the team, giving Cooke one last chance to up the ante. But the trustees gave only cursory attention to Cooke's final offer of $720 million, which was deemed insufficient. So, with the trustees poised to accept Snyder's $800 million bid, including $100 million in cash, Cooke withdrew from the process on April 22. He said in a statement issued by the team: "I refuse to be used merely to increase the bids of others, since it is well known that I have always wanted to keep the Redskins in my family."

After he had fought so doggedly to keep the Redskins, Cooke's abrupt withdrawal took team officials and players by surprise. Longtime Redskins running back and return specialist Brian Mitchell said: "I guess he just got fed up with it. He didn't want any more of it. I'm sure it hurts him. His family built up the organization to where someone would offer $800 million for it. I'm sure it's hard on him. I wish him the best."

Four days later, the trustees announced that they had agreed to sell the team and Jack Kent Cooke Stadium to the Snyder-led investment group. Snyder would own about 33 percent of the team, with the rest shared by his family members, Zuckerman and Drasner. NFL approval of Snyder's group was almost perfunctory. With a 31-0 vote by the owners on May 25, 1999, the auction process that had become a black eye for the NFL mercifully came to an end.

Snyder's agenda was clear from Day One. He looked at the roster he inherited and declared that there no longer would be a place for players who were overweight, out of shape or, worse still, indifferent to the privilege of playing in a Redskins uniform. For the 1999 Redskins, he declared, nothing short of a playoff season would be acceptable. If the team under the benevolent John Cooke had resembled a football-style Club Med, as former quarterback Sonny Jurgensen had remarked, Snyder's vision was closer to boot camp, with zero tolerance for sub-par effort. Winning was all that mattered.

On the business side, Snyder's expectations were just as aggressive. The Redskins had sold out every home game since 1966 and had roughly 40,000 people still clamoring on the season-ticket waiting list. That devoted fan base helped the Redskins generated an estimated $40 million in annual cash flow. But even amid such riches, Snyder set his sights higher.

Of the stadium's 15,084 club seats, about 2,000 remained unsold. There was room to expand luxury suites beyond the existing 199. Income from advertising within the stadium bowl totaled about $3 million a year, among the lowest in the NFL. And hundreds of no-shows often contributed to a lackluster feel during home games. After touring Jack Kent Cooke Stadium countless times, Snyder declared the venue a "fixer-upper" and plunged into improving it and making game days more exciting for fans. He removed railings that obstructed many views in the upper deck. He upgraded the sound system and ordered more contemporary and upbeat pre-game music. He moved the marching band to a more prominent spot in the end zone. He added more concession stands, introduced wait service for club-seat patrons and began addressing the traffic snarls and parking woes that made attending games a headache for many.

On the personnel front, everyone, from Turner down to the groundskeepers, was on notice that job security was not to be taken for granted. When Snyder was courting NFL owners, he had promised to retain both Turner and Casserly through the 1999 season, keeping team turmoil to a minimum. That was his intent as he took the reins on July 14, just days before the team left for training camp at Frostburg State University in western Maryland. But Snyder did a quick about-face after becoming convinced that his two top people could not work well together.

Snyder's change of heart was reinforced by his own personality clash with Casserly. Aggressive and impatient, Snyder had boundless energy and liked to bounce ideas for remaking the team off Turner and Casserly. Turner typically was open to Snyder's suggestions of trade scenarios and free-agent acquisitions. Casserly, by contrast, was quicker to point out why they wouldn't be prudent — whether the topic was signing troubled running back Lawrence Phillips or acquiring aging defensive end Charles Haley.

In a matter of weeks, Snyder concluded that one of the two had to go, and Casserly, it seemed, was the more expendable. Snyder eased him out at first, making him a consultant to the owner on an interim basis. Casserly left the team for good on September 2. In Casserly's place, Snyder brought in former San Francisco 49ers player-personnel director Vinny Cerrato, who was younger and more in step with Snyder's style of doing business.

Casserly left with no outward hard feelings. "As I told Dan Snyder when he got the club," Casserly said on his last day at work, "it's his right to have anyone he wants in this position. I respect that. There's no bitterness whatsoever toward him or how he handled this."

The front-office power struggle was a clear victory for Turner. In the restructuring that followed, Turner was granted ultimate authority over personnel decisions. But with a five-year record of 32-47-1, Turner knew his victory could prove short-lived.

The Snyder message wasn't lost on players, either. Everywhere at Redskin Park, it seemed that the new era would be different. Two dozen front-office staffers were fired shortly after Snyder took control. The threadbare artificial practice field behind Redskin Park was replaced with a plush, $750,000 carpet. The subdued walls were painted bold colors and adorned with giant blowups of magazine covers extolling Redskins victories of the past. The three Super Bowl trophies from the Gibbs era, which had been gathering dust on a shelf that hardly anyone noticed any longer, were moved into the center of the building and displayed under a skylight in a custom-made trophy case.

On the day he was introduced to Redskins players, moreover, Snyder dispensed with niceties and said flat out that he had become a very wealthy man at a young age not by being a nice guy. He expected results, he said, and he was going to get them.

"It's one of two things," said defensive end Kenard Lang. "Either he's real serious about winning, or he's just trying to scare everybody. I think it's the first one. I think he's real serious."

Snyder certainly was serious. He always had been, focusing relentlessly on his goals, an impatient young man with little time for much else. Classmates at Bethesda's Charles Woodward High School had trouble even remembering him. He dabbled in college courses, first at Montgomery College and then at the University of Maryland, but he dropped out and went to work, convinced that he could make his mark in business more quickly on his own. He did, and then some.

Within a year of buying the Redskins, Snyder sold Snyder Communications to

Havas Advertising of France for stock worth about $2.1 billion. He had started the company after first striking it rich and then losing a fortune on a college magazine venture financed largely by Zuckerman. Undaunted by that failure, Snyder branched out into other marketing ventures, including selling long-distance telephone services to non-English speaking immigrants. He took his budding company public in 1996 and used the proceeds to expand his empire, buying up other advertising and marketing companies.

His passion for business had only one rival: his passion for winning a Super Bowl for the Washington Redskins.

On July 25, 1999, a new era dawned at Redskins training camp. All draft picks, including Bailey and Jansen, had signed and reported on time. Turner seemed to have extra vigor in his stride as well. After a tension-filled off-season, he was finally back on the field where he was happiest, surrounded by players as eager as he was to get the season under way.

There were questions, to be sure. Brad Johnson was noticeably favoring his surgically repaired knee, which was wrapped in a brace. Turner was so irked by the persistent questions about Johnson's readiness that he banned TV cameras from filming a morning practice session, which only drew more attention to the matter.

There was concern, too, about the Redskins' pass rush. Linebacker Ken Harvey was in uniform each day but didn't participate the first week in hopes of giving the knee injury that ended his 1998 season extra time to heal. With Harvey holding out the possibility of retirement, the linebacking corps was in the hands of three relative youngsters — second-year player Shawn Barber, third-year player Greg Jones and Derek Smith, who had taken over the leadership role at middle linebacker when Marvcus Patton left for Kansas City. Midway through camp, Harvey stunned teammates by announcing his retirement at age 34, on the eve of what would have been his 12th season in the NFL and his sixth as a Redskin. "As much as I wanted to mentally," Harvey said, "the body wasn't as good as I wanted it to be."

Snyder was a frequent presence at practices and scrimmages, his arrival heralded by the whirring of a helicopter landing on the campus' lower fields early in the morning. When he wasn't on hand, his own consultant, former NFL defensive great Jim Marshall, was on the scene as Snyder's eyes and ears. Snyder had hired Marshall to help evaluate the Redskins defense, which in 1998 had ranked 24th in the NFL. The unit was a clear disappointment to Snyder, who, shortly after completing his purchase, criticized its scheme as insufficiently aggressive. "It was as simple as vanilla ice cream," he carped.

But there was evidence of progress. Defensive end Marco Coleman, who had been signed in the off-season after his release from San Diego, brought new intensity to the underperforming front line. Sam Shade was a dramatic improvement at strong safety. And Bailey, only a rookie, flashed his potential early, returning an interception for a touchdown in the Redskins' 20-14 preseason victory over New England.

The New England win was notable for another reason. On the Redskins' fourth offensive play, left tackle Joe Patton blew a coverage that resulted in a sack of Johnson. Such a lapse typically would be overlooked, but this time the response was swift and unforgiving. Patton was demoted to third string. Within weeks, he was released, even though by most accounts he had outplayed veteran Andy Heck throughout camp. The message was heard loud and clear: no tolerance for mistakes.

Heck's ascension at left tackle wasn't the only training camp surprise. Fourth-year player Stephen Davis wrested the starting tailback's spot from second-year player Skip Hicks. Davis had had chances before, but typically on an interim basis, filling in for Terry Allen. He had made 11 starts at fullback in 1998 after Larry Bowie suffered a season-ending leg injury, then had started at tailback in the season finale at Dallas after Hicks was hurt.

Hicks had rushed for eight touchdowns as a rookie. But Davis, quiet and unassuming, now won the coaches' favor for his straight-ahead style, lowering his head and grinding out the tough yards between the tackles.

Meanwhile, the Redskins improved their lot at fullback with the acquisition of Larry Centers, who had been released by the Arizona Cardinals. A fearless receiver, Centers gave an immediate lift to the offense, practicing with the same intensity as when he played.

The release of Leslie Shepherd created an opportunity for the wiry Albert Connell to start alongside Michael Westbrook at wide receiver. Questions lingered, however, about the receiving unit. Westbrook looked strong and serious in camp, but he had yet to play a 16-game season. Three weeks before the regular season opened, the Redskins coaxed Irving Fryar out of retirement. A month shy of his 37th birthday, Fryar was the seventh-leading wide receiver in NFL history. Connell took the news poorly, his feelings already wounded by reports that the Redskins had been trying desperately to trade for a proven starting receiver. Fryar, a minister,

JOEL RICHARDSON — THE WASHINGTON POST

On Target: Wide receiver Albert Connell pulls in a Brad Johnson touchdown pass, beating the Panthers' Eric Davis, during the Redskins' 38-36 victory over Carolina on October 3, 1999.

handled the delicate situation with aplomb and proved an immediate stabilizing influence on the potentially erratic receiving corps.

The Redskins closed the preseason with a 3-1 record. But as opening day neared, plenty of questions still remained. Would Heck be able to hold up at left tackle? Would the offensive line rebound from the worst season in team history? Would the young linebacking corps, minus veterans Harvey and Patton, strike the necessary fear in opponents? Would Johnson stay healthy at quarterback? Would Snyder have the patience to stick with Turner if the team got off to a poor start?

"He understands this is it," Snyder said of Turner shortly before the regular season opened. "I think at this point, everybody on the team is pretty clear that I'm not afraid of decisions. That's how you improve and get better in everything you do: Make decisions, move forward; make decisions, move forward; make decisions, move forward."

The team that took the field on opening day had a fresh look. Of the 24 players who lined up as starters, 17 were new. Also new was the name of the venue — Redskins Stadium — after Snyder jettisoned the Jack Kent Cooke moniker. Gone too was the stadium's mythical hometown, Raljon, the honorific Cooke had bestowed on the Prince George's County spot in tribute to his two sons.

For the most part, Turner was the last significant link between the Redskins and the Cooke dynasty — and it appeared that his fate rode largely on the outcome of the season opener against the team's most reviled opponent, the Dallas Cowboys. It turned out to be as horrific a beginning as could be imagined.

A record crowd of 79,237 was on hand to cheer the start of the new Redskins era. Snyder watched it all from his elegantly refurbished owner's box above the 50-yard line. But the glorious new dawn turned into a nightmare as the Redskins lost, 41-35, in an overtime heartbreaker — suffering the worst fourth-quarter collapse in 53 years.

With a 21-point lead in the fourth quarter, the Redskins let the Cowboys reel off three unanswered touchdowns to force overtime. Just over four minutes later, Cowboys quarterback Troy Aikman hurled a 76-yard touchdown pass to virtually uncovered wide receiver Raghib Ismail for the victory. "It's devastating," said reserve cornerback Darryl Pounds. "They should never have come back. It should never have been close."

The crowd was as stunned as the players. For three quarters, the Redskins offense had looked unbeatable, as the final statistics suggested. The team piled up 504 yards. Johnson completed 20 of 33 passes for 382 yards, Westbrook had five catches for 159 yards, and Connell caught four balls for 137 yards. Davis turned in his first 100-yard performance in the NFL, with 109 yards on 24 carries. But it all unraveled in the fourth quarter.

Special teams blunders were partly to blame, as when the Cowboys recovered an onside kick in the fourth quarter. Still, the Redskins had a chance to win in regulation. With three seconds to go, kicker Brett Conway lined up for a 41-yarder that could have clinched the game. But Dan Turk's snap was slightly high, and it squirted through the hands of the holder, his brother Matt. All Conway could do was try to run with the ball, but he flipped it in the air and was credited with an incomplete pass.

In overtime the Redskins won the coin toss, but their drive stalled when Johnson was sacked on a third-and-three from the Dallas 45. With Dallas in control, the Redskins found themselves without three of their four starting defensive backs. Bailey, Shade and safety Leomont Evans all had succumbed to debilitating leg cramps, largely due to dehydration. Backup cornerback Matt Steven was fooled by Aikman's fake handoff to Emmitt Smith and was racing toward the line of scrimmage as Ismail went deep. When the game-winning pass was thrown, no Redskins defender was even close.

In the bitter aftermath, no coaches were dismissed, no players released or demoted. Snyder didn't go ballistic. He delivered a hang-in-there speech in the locker room. "It's all right," Snyder said later. "Now we'll see how tough we are."

Up next were back-to-back road games at Giants Stadium in the New Jersey Meadowlands, a venue that had long conspired against the Redskins. Game 2 was against the NFC East rival New York Giants, Game 3 against the New York Jets, who were still reeling from the loss of quarterback Vinny Testaverde.

While Turner said after the Dallas loss that he remained "absolutely" supportive of defensive coordinator Mike Nolan, Snyder's scrutiny intensified. Snyder also was dismayed over the muscle cramps that had benched five players at some point during the Dallas game — both starting wide receivers and all of the starting defensive backs except Darrell Green. "They'd better not get dehydrated next weekend," Snyder said.

After a night of soul-searching and second-guessing, the Redskins rebounded with a spirited week of practice and answered Snyder's challenge with the biggest victory of the Turner era. The team stormed into Giants Stadium and vanquished the demons of the previous week, routing the Giants 50-21.

Their 50 points — on three touchdown runs by Davis, three touchdown passes by Johnson, a 70-yard interception returned by Barber and a 48-yard field goal by Conway — were the most scored by a Redskins team on the road and the fifth most points in club history. And the game offered a stirring glimpse at the explosiveness of Turner's offense in the hands of a quarterback with Johnson's accuracy and poise. Johnson completed 20 of 28 passes for 231 yards, three touchdowns and no interceptions. Combined with his performance in the season opener, that gave him an NFL-best quarterback rating of 125.9.

Blowout: Stephen Davis scores the Redskins' first touchdown in their 50-21 rout of the New York Giants on September 19, 1999.

"Right now, everyone is feeding off Brad," Turner said. "He makes plays when they're not there, and he certainly makes plays when you're fortunate enough to call the right ones."

The game also marked the arrival of the retooled offensive line. With the veteran Heck at left tackle and the rookie Jansen at right tackle, the line didn't surrender a single sack. The feat was particularly impressive in light of the fact that Jansen drew the unenviable task of blocking defensive end Michael Strahan, who had given the Redskins fits in the teams' 1998 season opener.

While the venue was the same in Week 3, the nature of the game couldn't have been more different. The Redskins' prolific offense sputtered, but the team nonetheless found a way to make enough big plays in the fourth quarter to come away with a 27-20 victory.

The Jets had led, 14-13, entering the final period and went up 17-13 on a 37-yard field goal by John Hall with 8:10 to play. The Redskins then drove 80 yards for the go-ahead score, a four-yard run by Davis that made it 20-17 with 4:11 to play. Lang stripped the ball from Jets quarterback Rick Mirer, setting up Davis' third touchdown run of the day.

At 2-1, the Redskins' record rose above .500 for the first time since they had ended the 1997 season with an 8-7-1 mark. But it was the manner in which they won — coming from behind in the fourth quarter — that proved to Snyder and the players themselves that they were developing the sort of toughness they had lacked. "The last few years when we played a close game," Mitchell said, "we lost."

Next, the team beat the Carolina Panthers, 38-36, in the first triumph at home for Snyder, running the Redskins record to an NFC East-best of 3-1. But the wild four quarters exposed the Redskins' glaring weakness — a rickety defense — and prompted a swift response by Snyder and Turner that ultimately would salvage the season.

Before many in the sell-out crowd had settled into their seats for the game, the Redskins had fallen behind by 21 points. Carolina running back Tim Biakabutuka had torched the defense for first-quarter touchdowns of 60, 1 and 45 yards. The Panthers' assault slowed after Coach George Seifert curiously replaced Biakabutuka with Fred Lane and as Johnson seized control of the Redskins offense, throwing four touchdown passes in the second and third quarters. "There was no panic," said Johnson, who drew praise from Turner for his heroics.

The defense surrendered 481 yards in the gory win, and the Redskins stood as a statistical anomaly in the NFL: possessors of the league's top-ranked offense and its last-ranked defense. The young starting linebackers were struggling. The blitz packages worked sometimes but gave up huge plays other times. The numbers were damning. The defense was yielding 29.5 points and 433.5 yards a game.

The bye week couldn't have come at a more welcome time, and team officials used the break to make a bold move — tapping veteran defensive guru Bill Arnsparger, 72, as a consultant. Architect of the famed No-Name defense, Arnsparger maintained a low profile, deferring to Nolan and preaching a remedy as bland as tapioca pudding. "You have to line up right, know your assignment and carry that assignment out correctly."

The effect, however, was dynamic. The Redskins traveled to Arizona and staged an impressive defensive stand, holding their opponent to fewer than 20 points for the first time all season. Bailey, the rookie cornerback, had three interceptions in the 24-10 victory. And Barber took Arizona quarterback Jake Plummer out of the game with a third-quarter sack in which Plummer broke his finger after getting it stuck in the linebacker's facemask.

On the heels of their four-game winning streak, the Redskins sat atop the NFC East as they entered a rematch with Dallas at Texas Stadium, but their euphoria proved short-lived: The Cowboys soundly whipped them, 38-20. The Redskins came out flat, falling behind 17-0 in the second quarter. Cowboys cornerback Deion Sanders set the hostile tone early, flattening Davis for a four-yard loss and elbowing Connell in the jaw.

The postgame postmortem drew even more attention than the loss. Snyder, his voice hoarse from shouting throughout the game, held a half-hour meeting with Turner in the trainer's room afterward and vowed to shake up the team's lethargic attitude. As word of the meeting spread around the league, Snyder drew criticism for his unorthodox methods, which many interpreted as undercutting Turner. "I credit Mr. Snyder for his enthusiasm," Baltimore Ravens owner Art Modell said, "but enthusiasm can backfire."

Snyder declined to respond to detractors, saying simply: "I wouldn't comment on anyone else's style. Each person should have his own style. I just want to do everything I can to help this team win games and help this organization be successful. . . . Everybody knows I care."

The locker room meeting created a perception of Snyder as a meddlesome owner who wouldn't let Turner do his job. Behind the scenes, however, the relationship between the two men usually was smooth. They developed a productive give-and-take. It was Turner, not Snyder, who became most animated during the postgame meeting in Dallas, complaining that his players were being asked to make too many public appearances too late in the week. Snyder said he would fix that problem.

The meeting remained a major topic of discussion for weeks, with Turner and his players offering no objections to the timing or tone of the get-together. "The conversation I had with Dan after the game was very similar to the conversations I've had with him after each of the games," Turner said at the time. "Now the timing was different, and that probably is what has brought most attention to this." Added cornerback Darrell Green: "If I own a lawn service and I want to talk to the guy on the lawn mower while he's cutting the yard, I can talk to him. . . . Where are the rules that say when an owner can talk to you and when he can't?"

Defensive tackle Dana Stubblefield compared Snyder's leadership style to that of his former San Francisco 49ers boss, Edward DeBartolo Jr. If anything, Stubblefield said, Snyder reinforced Turner's authority in the locker room, not undermined it. He cited the speech that Snyder delivered the first time he addressed the team's players. "The owner said it in front of everybody: 'This man, what he says goes. And I got his back,'" Stubblefield recalled.

When some of Snyder's advisers told him during the season that defensive coordinator Mike Nolan should be fired, Snyder left the decision to Turner. Turner chose to retain Nolan during the season, not wanting to create an added distraction. When many in the Redskins' front office wanted to cut punter Matt Turk during the season, the decision again was left to Turner. Turk, who had been to the previous three Pro Bowls, had a poor season. He had a prolonged punting slump. He dropped the snap from his brother Dan on the field goal try that would have cinched the season opener. And he suffered a broken finger that caused him to miss the second Dallas game. Turk said the injury occurred before or during the Redskins' win at Arizona. Some suspected that Turk actually hurt his finger or worsened the injury playing recreational basketball the night after the Cardinals win. But Turner did not want the disruption of looking for another punter during the season, and the Redskins decided not to fine or release Turk. Instead, they traded him to the Miami Dolphins after the season.

At the same time, Snyder remained aggressive off the field. He played a major role in negotiating a 27-year, $205 million naming-rights deal with Federal Express that would change the stadium's name to FedEx Field. For the most part, he fixed the parking problems that had led fans to complain bitterly following the season-opening Dallas game. He poured $10 million into stadium improvements, and he protected the team's trademark by charging local television stations to use the word "Redskins" in the names of shows.

The week after the second Dallas loss was an uneasy one at Redskin Park, but the personnel changes made were minor. The Redskins signed cornerback Mark

McMillian and linebacker James Francis. They cut safety Toby Wright and placed linebacker Fred Strickland on the injured reserve list.

Turner spent the week preaching to his players that the Redskins needed to show again that they could win at home. They had to establish early in the following Sunday's game against the Chicago Bears that they were going to be the team setting the tone, he said. The players apparently listened.

On Halloween, the Redskins rolled to leads of 31-0 at halftime and 45-0 in the third quarter, and they finally overwhelmed the Bears by 48-22. The game essentially ended in the first quarter when Wilkinson huffed and puffed his way to an 88-yard interception return for a touchdown that produced a 14-0 lead. And, yes, Snyder and Turner met again, huddling after the game. "We've had a lot of good meetings," Snyder said with a grin later that day. Earlier, Turner had begun his postgame news conference by telling reporters: "Sorry I was late. I was in a meeting with Mr. Snyder."

As he celebrated the victory in the owner's box (where Turner joined the party in its final stages that night), Snyder shrugged off the week of criticism he had received. "It comes with the territory," he said. Snyder savored the Bears win in the locker room, asking Wilkinson if he intended to play fullback the following weekend.

Running back and kick returner Brian Mitchell said of Snyder in the locker room: "He cares about this team. He's cracking the whip, and that's good. I enjoy it. You do your job, and you're going to be around. As a team, we're in this together. He's in the locker room with us whether we win or lose. He's an owner, but he's been a fan for a long time."

As he walked back toward the team's locker room after leaving his news conference that day, Turner said the fallout from the previous Sunday's controversy-generating meeting helped the Redskins' preparation for the Bears. "I told our team when the season started, 'Take care of the things you can control,'" Turner said. "It wasn't negative. If anything, it was positive for our team. We all understand the sense of urgency he [Snyder] has. We have the same sense of urgency. Now we have more people who understand about coming back and competing and playing hard. We can overcome adversity."

That notion was tested in the following weeks. The Redskins could not corral quarterback Doug Flutie and lost at home to the Buffalo Bills, 34-17, the next week. Flutie made the big play whenever Buffalo needed it, throwing for 211 yards and running for 40 more. He had a pair of touchdown passes and left Redskins defenders grasping at air regularly in turning potential sacks into positive offensive plays for the Bills.

One More Time: On the third try in overtime, Brett Conway finally kicks a successful field goal to defeat the Eagles, 20-17, on November 28, 1999.

JOHN McDONNELL — THE WASHINGTON POST

"We didn't step to the plate as a whole — not as an offense, not as a defense, not on special teams," quarterback Brad Johnson said. "We knew what was at stake. We just didn't get it done."

Things got worse on November 14 on what was, as it turned out, the low point of the regular season for the Redskins. For the first time all season, the Redskins failed to respond to a crisis, losing to a team they knew they should have beaten. They committed six turnovers and lost to the Eagles, 35-28, in Philadelphia. Brad Johnson had two fumbles and three interceptions. The Eagles had two long kickoff returns and scored 11 more points than they had put on the boards in any previous game during the season.

Snyder walked, calm but grim-faced, out of the Redskins' locker room at Veterans Stadium about a half-hour after the game. As he and minority owner Fred Drasner made their way up a staircase to begin the trip home, Snyder could not even bring himself to speak, signaling to a reporter with a wave of his hand that he had nothing to say. Where would the Redskins go from there? No one in the organization, from Snyder to Turner and his staff to the players, seemed to know for certain.

With their record at 5-4, the Redskins remained tied for first place in the forgiving NFC East, but this was the furthest that their season had unraveled. The only answer, Redskins players said in the locker room, was to play with more desire and more intensity — and play better. "We're going to make the playoffs," wide receiver Michael Westbrook vowed that day.

"It wasn't any coach's fault," Westbrook remarked. "It was the players. We need to take a look at ourselves. We're a lot better than what we played like. I get tired of saying it. . . . Nobody is pointing fingers, but we all need to be held accountable for our mistakes in practice. We're going to take that upon ourselves as players to take care of our business."

Added wide receiver Albert Connell, who just had lost a fumble and had a Johnson pass bounce off his hands to Philadelphia cornerback Al Harris for a key fourth-quarter interception:" Something has got to change. I'm going to be very vocal in practice this week. We've got to take care of this as players."

The Redskins responded. The following Sunday, they celebrated the official changing of the stadium's name to FedEx Field by beating the Giants, 23-13, to reclaim sole possession of first place. An emotional day for the Redskins ended with the players presenting a cake and singing to Snyder in the locker room after they already had given him the best present of all — a victory — for his 35th birthday.

Turner was choked up during his postgame news conference as he praised his players' effort. "That's as good a win as I've been involved with, probably ever," Turner said. " . . . Our team was challenged. They responded. They responded in a big way. You can criticize this group. You can criticize me when we screw up. We call the wrong play sometimes. We go the wrong way sometimes. . . . But don't question their effort, their character, their ability to compete."

The Redskins had made plenty of mistakes against the Giants. Place kicker Brett Conway missed field goal attempts of 38, 50 and 27 yards. Connell negated a touchdown run by tailback Stephen Davis with a holding penalty. Davis and Brad Johnson botched a handoff at the Giants 1-yard line, resulting in a fumble. Westbrook, playing with a cast over a broken bone in his right wrist, caught only one pass. But thanks to Davis and the defense, the Redskins won anyway. Davis, playing with a bruised thigh, rushed for 183 yards on 33 carries.

"I was a little banged up, but I wanted to be out there," Davis said. "I wanted to suck it up and be there for this team."

The Giants had only 72 rushing yards and committed five turnovers. The Redskins, using blitzes effectively, had four sacks. The Redskins knocked Giants quarterback Kent Graham from the game with a concussion. Defensive end Ndukwe Kalu forced a fumble by backup Kerry Collins that was returned for a touchdown by Coleman to open the fourth quarter, giving the Redskins a 20-6 lead.

Another victory followed the next week, but this one didn't come easily. It took overtime and three tries at a game-winning field goal by Conway for the Redskins to beat the Eagles, 20-17, at home on November 28. "I was just trying to make it interesting," a relieved Conway said in the Redskins' locker room.

He could grin about it because he hadn't cost the Redskins a game they expected to win — and should have won far more easily than they did. The Redskins already had made things tougher on themselves than was necessary when Conway walked on the field with five seconds remaining in regulation for a 28-yard field goal attempt to win the game. They had squandered a 17-3 lead by permitting a pair of 91-yard touchdown drives in the second half. Conway added to the tension when he pushed his would-be game winner wide right as time expired, sending the game into overtime. "I wasn't nervous," Conway said. "It was a good snap. It was a good hold. I had the wind at my back. I thought I hit it good."

The Redskins won the coin toss in overtime, moved downfield again and lined up for a 20-yard try by Conway on third down. That was nothing more than an extra point. But Brad Johnson, who had served as Conway's holder since Matt Turk broke his finger, dropped the snap from Dan Turk. Johnson alertly fell on the ball and Conway had another chance on fourth down. Finally, everything went smoothly to end the most ragged of games.

"We thought we might be a little too close, so Brad took a seven-yard loss on the third-down play to get a little better angle," Turner said.

It certainly wouldn't have been a laughing matter for Conway, Turner or the Redskins if Conway had missed again. If that had happened, Tre Johnson said, Conway simply should have cleaned out his locker.

The next week, the Redskins went to Detroit and gave the sloppiest of performances. They had 14 penalties and four turnovers and were overwhelmed by the Lions' hard-charging defensive line and the din created by nearly 78,000 screaming fans in the Silverdome. The Lions ended an 18-game losing streak to the Redskins that had dated to 1965, and two of their heroes were former Redskins. Quarterback Gus Frerotte threw for 280 yards and a touchdown, and Desmond Howard provided a 68-yard punt return for a touchdown on the day after being signed by Detroit to replace injured return man Terry Fair. Davis was limited to 51 rushing yards, with only eight of them (on three carries) coming in the second half.

The game was memorable mostly for its subplots. Westbrook criticized the officiating in the locker room after the game and again the next day. He said it was as if the Redskins were facing 12 men, and he questioned the propriety of line judge Byron Boston — father of wide receiver David Boston of the Arizona Cardinals, an NFC East rival — working a game involving the Redskins.

NFL officials first told the Redskins they intended to fine Westbrook, then did an about-face. Greg Aiello, the league's vice president of public relations, said later that week that Westbrook merely would be sent a letter of reprimand informing him that any similar comments in the future would result in a fine. The decision not to fine Westbrook was made by Commissioner Paul Tagliabue, Aiello said.

"The commissioner decided the comments were so farfetched that a fine would give them more significance than they deserved," Aiello said. "We're referring to the comments that Byron Boston is making calls to help his son. Any future comments of this nature would result in a fine."

Turner, meanwhile, had to answer criticisms of his play calling in Detroit from those who felt he had abandoned the running game too soon. He pledged to get Davis more involved in the offense for the following Sunday's game against the Cardinals.

It was a soul-searching week for the Redskins. After practice on Thursday, Snyder had separate meetings in his office at Redskin Park with Johnson, Coleman, Stubblefield, wide receiver Irving Fryar and Brad Johnson. Snyder remarked later: "I said, 'Play for your teammates. Don't worry about the press, the coaches or me. Just play for yourself. Know the importance of the game and step up.' "

Snyder also planted a seed that led to a Saturday night players-only meeting at the club's hotel. "It was a wake-up call in terms of attitude," Tre Johnson said of that get-together. "Everybody had a chance to speak. People had to realize this is important. We can't live off the first four or five games of the season. That's dead and gone. Nobody cares about that now."

Snyder and the players said the meetings weren't designed to attack Turner or the team's assistant coaches. They were designed, they said, to get the players to accept accountability for their team and where it was headed. "So much is made of coaches being the reason, the scapegoats," Coleman said. "It's about the players." Added tight end Stephen Alexander: "We're all in this together — coaches, players, trainers, owner, front office. It takes us all."

The important part of the equation came on Sunday, when the Redskins gave perhaps their most complete performance of the season and beat the Cardinals, 28-3. Davis ran for 189 yards on 37 carries. The Redskins defense sacked Arizona quarterback Jake Plummer five times and limited the Cardinals to 173 total yards.

Following the triumph, Turner recalled a conversation he'd had during the week with running game coordinator Bobby Jackson. "After a game like we had last Sunday, you get as low as you can get from a standpoint of where you are as a coach [and] as a person," Turner said. " . . . [Jackson] said, 'You know, the one thing we've got going for us is this group is as resilient a group as we've had. Every time we've had a difficulty, they've responded, stepped up and really handled the adversity.' That's what our group did this week. We had good practices all week. I think the coaches put together a good plan. Our players were very determined about executing the plan. And we played awfully well."

The Redskins played well again on December 19 in Indianapolis against one of the

NFL's best teams, the Colts. They might have won, in fact, if Davis had not suffered a sprained ankle in the second quarter. He limped to the sideline and didn't return to the game, which the Redskins lost, 24-21.

The Redskins could clinch a playoff berth or even the division title the following weekend, but it was a turbulent week before their December 26 game at San Francisco. The rumors about Turner's future bubbled up again with reports that he might resign after the season. There was speculation that Turner might negotiate a buyout of his contract in the offseason in an attempt to return to Dallas, where he once was offensive coordinator, as head coach.

Those reports ignored some important facts. Even if his first year with Snyder had its frustrations, Turner has school-age children and didn't want to uproot his family. He is stubborn and wants to see things through in Washington. And even if he wanted to go to Dallas, it wasn't his decision. He had two seasons and about $2 million remaining on his contract, and Snyder was not about to negotiate a buyout so that Turner could go coach the Redskins' most bitter rival.

"I've said it before," Turner remarked that week. "I said it at the end of last year, and I'll say it now: I'm not going to resign."

The last thing the Redskins needed that week was a major controversy. "It's disappointing there's speculation," Turner said. "We're trying to get ready to win a game so we can get into the playoffs. There's been speculation about my future for a long time. This one is way out there."

By the time the Redskins took the field at 3Com Park to face the 49ers on December 26, they already had clinched their first playoff berth since the 1992 season. Losses by the Green Bay Packers and the Panthers earlier in the day ensured that. But the Redskins didn't want to back into the playoffs. They wanted to go in the front door with a victory.

For much of the game, it didn't look good. The Redskins had to go with Skip Hicks at tailback in place of the injured Davis. The 49ers led by 13-10 at halftime and by 20-10 in the third quarter. The Redskins got even on a Brad Johnson one-yard touchdown sneak with just under 3 1/2 minutes left in regulation. They got a game-saving defensive play by linebacker Shawn Barber, who forced a fumble as the 49ers maneuvered for a game-winning field goal, then won the coin toss in overtime and needed only four plays to cover 78 yards. Johnson passed to Hicks for 25 and eight yards, and fullback Larry Centers ran for 12 yards.

Happy Ending: In the final game of the regular season, Kenard Lang sacks Dolphins' quarterback Damon Huard and forces a fumble. The Redskins recovered the ball and went on to win the game, 21-10, before heading to the playoffs.

On a play from the San Francisco 33-yard line two minutes into overtime, Johnson flicked the ball to Centers in the flat against a 49ers blitz. Centers, with nothing but open field in front of him, trotted into the end zone for a 26-20 Redskins' triumph. "I couldn't believe how open I was when I turned around," Centers said. "It's a great feeling. That's the biggest play of my career."

Johnson completed 32 of his 47 throws that evening for 471 yards, breaking Sammy Baugh's 51-year-old Redskins record for passing yards in a game. "This is a great feeling," Johnson said. "I haven't been here the last six years, but I wanted to be part of helping this team make it to the next level. We could have let down tonight after the first half, but we kept battling."

As the Redskins celebrated the franchise's first NFC East crown since the 1991 season in a jubilant postgame locker room, Sndyer held a game ball aloft and yelled to the players: "Only one person deserves this!" He then handed the ball to Turner and hugged the coach as the players cheered wildly.

Turner told reporters soon thereafter: "It was a great game. I told our guys at halftime we didn't play well in the first half, and the second half would define what this team is. I think we defined it pretty well. We've been in this situation before and come up short, but we didn't come up short tonight."

Snyder drank champagne with friends and family members in his box at 3Com Park later, then celebrated late into the night at a San Francisco hotel. When the Redskins last had played a playoff game — a 20-13 defeat at San Francisco on January 9, 1993 — Joe Gibbs had been on the sideline and Snyder had been in the stands as a fan. "The players and the coaches showed they have true Washington Redskin hearts," Snyder said.

Two days later, Snyder and Turner said in a joint interview in Snyder's office at Redskin Park that Turner would return as the Redskins' coach. "Of course he'll be back," Snyder said. " . . . It wasn't a matter of making up my mind. We had a goal, and we achieved the goal. That's the first goal. There are many more. We have to play hard and play like Eastern Division champions. We have the potential to be very special, beginning this year." Turner added: "Anyone that thinks I would resign doesn't know me very well... When I came here, I came here with the idea of winning a Super Bowl. That hasn't changed."

Davis sat out the regular season finale as the Redskins beat the Dolphins, 21-10.

Then he and the Redskins spent their short preparation week fretting about whether Davis would be able to play in their January 8 playoff game against the Lions at FedEx Field. Davis looked terrible in one midweek practice but improved a bit each day after that and indeed was back in the lineup to face Detroit. He looked like he never had left. He had runs of 58 and 32 yards against the Lions en route to a 15-carry, 119-yard, two-touchdown performance. The Redskins sprinted to a 27-point, first-half lead and never looked back in a 27-13 win.

"In the first half, it was a total team effort," Centers said. "That's as good as this team has played."

Detroit fell to 0-20 all-time in Washington, including 0-3 in the postseason. Frerotte suffered a dislocated left pinkie when he was sacked by Redskins linebacker Greg Jones on the game's first play from scrimmage. It was little consolation that he threw a five-yard touchdown pass to Ron Rivers on the game's final play.

There was much to savor from their crisp outing in their first playoff game in seven years, but the news was not all good for the Redskins. Davis exited the game for good after suffering a sprained right knee in the second quarter. Veteran Andy Heck, who had stabilized the Redskins' offensive line by providing solid play at left tackle after being signed before the season as a free agent, had his season ended by a torn hamstring muscle. And Tre Johnson was ejected following a third-quarter fight that began with a scuffle between Brad Johnson and Lions defensive end Robert Porcher.

Brad Johnson had thrown an interception to Detroit linebacker Stephen Boyd on the Redskins' first possession of the third quarter. As the play ended, Porcher hit the quarterback. Johnson took exception and began wrestling with Porcher, even managing to put the defensive end on the ground. Players on both sides gathered for some pushing and shoving, and Tre Johnson was swinging both arms and fists as he was pulled away from a pile. He struck an official inadvertently and was ejected. The NFL permitted Johnson to play in the Redskins' game the following weekend at Tampa Bay but fined him $50,000 and suspended him from the team's first regular season game in 2000. That cost him just over $135,000, bringing his total penalty to about $185,000, among the largest fines for an on-field incident in league history. Fourteen Redskins were fined a total of $67,000 — including $12,500 for Brad Johnson — for the fight. Eight Lions were fined $37,000, led by a $10,000 penalty for Porcher. In all, 23 players were fined $154,000 (not including Tre Johnson's game check for his suspension) to set a league record for an on-field incident.

The Redskins' season ended in Tampa Bay on January 15 in gut-wrenching fashion. They got a 100-yard kickoff return by Mitchell and, even with Davis limping around ineffectively and their offense getting shut down, had a 13-0 lead in the third quarter. But safety John Lynch provided a momentum-changing interception of Brad Johnson, and a second-effort, two-yard touchdown run by fullback Mike Alstott

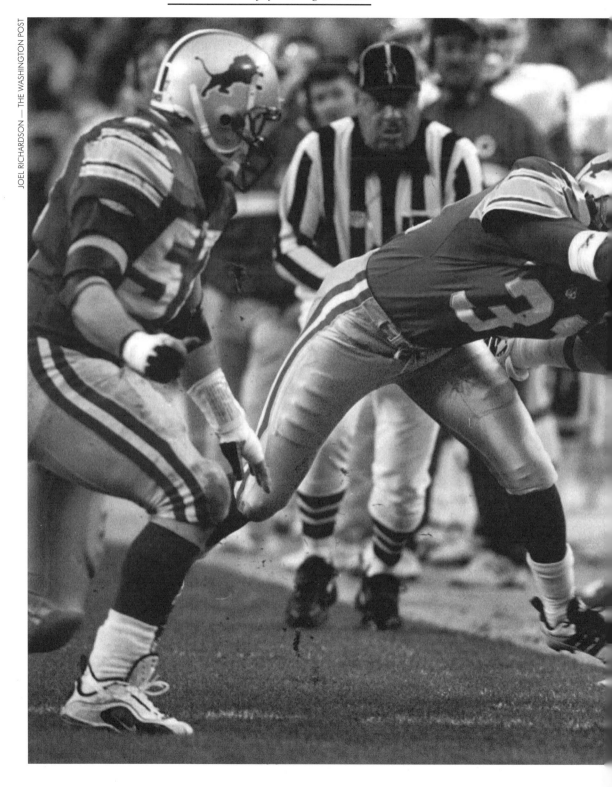

Playoff Play: Larry Centers dives for a first down as the Redskins head for their first division title in eight years, defeating the Detroit Lions, 27-13, on January 8, 2000.

got Tampa Bay to within 13-7 just over two minutes before the end of the third quarter. A fumble by Johnson led to a one-yard touchdown pass from Buccaneers rookie quarterback Shaun King to tight end John Davis with 7 1/2 minutes to play. Tampa Bay's decisive drive was kept alive when running back Warrick Dunn scooped up a fumble by King and ran for a first down.

The Redskins got the ball at their 38-yard line with 3:05 left for their last-gasp drive. They moved to the Tampa Bay 33 by the two-minute warning. But Hicks, subbing for Davis on the final drive, was stuffed for no gain on third and three. Turner turned to Conway, who had drilled field goals of 28 and 48 yards earlier, for what would have been a 52-yard attempt at a go-ahead field goal with 1:17 to play. But Dan Turk's snap bounced perhaps halfway back toward Johnson, and Conway never got a chance to kick the ball. The Tampa Bay offense ran out the clock and ended the Redskins' season.

Said Turk: "I don't know if I short-armed it or what."

It was the Redskins' first post-season defeat in 21 tries when taking a lead into the fourth quarter, and Turk did not accompany his teammates on the flight back home to Washington. "It's a 50-50 kick with a 50-yard field goal," Johnson said. "But you'd like to have a chance."

Davis, after setting a team record with 1,405 rushing yards during the regular season, headed to Hawaii with Brad Johnson and Tre Johnson for the Pro Bowl. The Redskins, meanwhile, launched quickly into an active offseason. Nolan was replaced as defensive coordinator by former Eagles and Packers head coach Ray Rhodes. Other changes were made to Turner's coaching staff, although he retained LeCharls McDaniel as special teams coach.

The Redskins were the NFL's most aggressive team once the player-acquisition phase of the offseason began. Coleman, Centers, guard Keith Sims, center Cory Raymer and Heck were re-signed as unrestricted free agents. Davis was kept off the marketplace by being named the team's franchise player after a combative set of contract negotiations failed to yield a long-term deal. The Redskins signed 11-time Pro Bowl defensive end Bruce Smith two days after Buffalo released him in a salary cap move. They signed three-time Pro Bowl safety Mark Carrier as a free agent. They added free agent tailback Adrian Murrell to back up Davis, and signed free agent quarterback Jeff George to a four-year, $18.25 million deal as an insurance policy in case Brad Johnson gets hurt.

Their splashiest move came last, when the Redskins signed cornerback Deion Sanders following his release in June by the Dallas Cowboys. Sanders, 32, was penciled in as an immediate starter, relegating Darrell Green to nickel back.

The Redskins also scored big in the 2000 draft. They had the second, 12th and 24th picks in the April college draft, and traded the 12th and 24th selections to the 49ers in February for the third overall pick. The Redskins used the second choice on Penn State linebacker LaVar Arrington and the third selection on Alabama left tackle Chris Samuels, and began gearing up for a 2000 season in which they expected to be leading Super Bowl contenders.

Snyder was asked on April 15, the day the team drafted Arrington and Samuels, whether his expectations for the first season of the new millennium included a Super Bowl title. "Not just this year," he said. "Every year."

TRIVIA QUIZ 6

1. When the Redskins moved to their new stadium in 1997, who was their first opponent, and who won?

2. The Redskins, who were victorious in their first post-season game at their new stadium in 1999, also had a strong post-season record at RFK Stadium. What was the RFK post-season tally?

3. Going into the 2000 pre-season camp, only two players from the Gibbs era remained on the Redskins. Who were they?

4. In Norv Turner's first six seasons as head coach, the Redskins had six different starting quarterbacks. Who were they — and which one started the most games?

5. In those first six Turner seasons, how many games, including playoffs, did the Redskins win?

6. Turner had 11 assistants on his initial Redskins coaching staff. Only two were still there when the team went to camp in 2000. Can you name them?

7. Stephen Davis led the team in rushing in 1999, piling up a Redskins-record 1,405 yards. In how many games, including playoffs, did he rush for more than 100 yards that year?

8. Can you name the three previous leading Redskins rushers?

9. Heath Shuler was the Redskins' first-round draft pick in 1994. Can you name the team's next six first-round picks?

10. The Redskins hold the NFL record for the most consecutive sellouts. Going into the 2000 season, how many regular-season and playoff games made up this streak?

ANSWERS ON PAGE 270

NAMES AND NUMBERS

All the Players and Games

All Washington Redskins Games

1937 (8-3)
Coach: Ray Flaherty

W	Sept.	15	New York Giants	13-3
L	Sept.	24	Chicago Cardinals	21-14
W	Oct.	3	at Brooklyn Dodgers	11-7
L	Oct.	10	Philadelphia Eagles	14-0
W	Oct.	17	Pittsburgh Steelers	34-20
W	Oct.	24	at Philadelphia Eagles	10-7
W	Oct.	31	Brooklyn Dodgers	21-0
L	Nov.	14	at Pittsburgh Steelers	21-13
W	Nov.	21	at Cleveland Rams	16-7
W	Nov.	28	Green Bay Packers	14-6
W	Dec.	5	at New York Giants	49-14

World Championship

W	Dec.	12	at Chicago Bears	28-21

1938 (6-3-2)
Coach: Ray Flaherty

W	Sept.	11	at Philadelphia Eagles	26-23
T	Sept.	18	Brooklyn Dodgers	16-16
W	Sept.	25	Cleveland Rams	37-13
L	Oct.	9	New York Giants	10-7
W	Oct.	16	at Detroit Lions	7-5
W	Oct.	23	Philadelphia Eagles	20-14
T	Oct.	30	at Brooklyn Dodgers	6-6
W	Nov.	6	at Pittsburgh Steelers	7-0
L	Nov.	13	at Chicago Bears	31-7
W	Nov.	27	Pittsburgh Steelers	15-0
L	Dec.	4	at New York Giants	36-0

1939 (8-2-1)
Coach: Ray Flaherty

W	Sept.	17	at Philadelphia Eagles	7-0
T	Oct.	1	New York Giants	0-0
W	Oct.	8	Brooklyn Dodgers	41-13
W	Oct.	15	Pittsburgh Steelers	44-14
W	Oct.	22	at Pittsburgh Steelers	21-14
L	Oct.	29	at Green Bay Packers	24-14
W	Nov.	5	Philadelphia Eagles	7-6
W	Nov.	12	at Brooklyn Dodgers	42-0
W	Nov.	19	Chicago Cardinals	28-7

W	Nov.	26	Detroit Lions	31-7
L	Dec.	3	at New York Giants	9-7

1940 (9-2)
Coach: Ray Flaherty

W	Sept.	15	Brooklyn Dodgers	24-17
W	Sept.	22	New York Giants	21-7
W	Oct.	6	at Pittsburgh Steelers	40-10
W	Oct.	13	Chicago Cardinals	28-21
W	Oct.	20	Philadelphia Eagles	34-17
W	Oct.	27	at Detroit Lions	20-14
W	Nov.	3	Pittsburgh Steelers	37-10
L	Nov.	10	at Brooklyn Dodgers	16-14
W	Nov.	17	Chicago Bears	7-3
L	Nov.	24	at New York Giants	21-7
W	Dec.	1	Philadelphia Eagles	13-6

World Championship

L	Dec.	8	Chicago Bears	73-0

1941 (6-5)
Coach: Ray Flaherty

L	Sept.	28	New York Giants	17-10
W	Oct.	5	Brooklyn Dodgers	3-0
W	Oct.	12	at Pittsburgh Steelers	24-20
W	Oct.	19	at Philadelphia Eagles	21-17
W	Oct.	26	Cleveland Rams	17-13
W	Nov.	2	Pittsburgh Steelers	23-3
L	Nov.	9	at Brooklyn Dodgers	13-7
L	Nov.	16	at Chicago Bears	35-21
L	Nov.	23	at New York Giants	20-13
L	Nov.	30	Green Bay Packers	22-17
W	Dec.	7	Philadelphia Eagles	20-14

1942 (10-1)
Coach: Ray Flaherty

W	Sept.	20	Pittsburgh Steelers	28-14
L	Sept.	27	New York Giants	14-7
W	Oct.	4	at Philadelphia Eagles	14-10
W	Oct.	11	Cleveland Rams	33-14
W	Oct.	18	at Brooklyn Dodgers	21-10
W	Oct.	25	at Pittsburgh Steelers	14-0
W	Nov.	1	Philadelphia Eagles	30-27
W	Nov.	8	Chicago Cardinals	28-0

W	Nov.	15	at New York Giants	14-7
W	Nov.	22	Brooklyn Dodgers	23-3
W	Nov.	29	at Detroit Lions	15-3

World Championship

W	Dec.	13	Chicago Bears	14-6

1943 (6-3-1)
Coach: Arthur (Dutch) Bergman

W	Oct.	10	Brooklyn Dodgers	27-0
W	Oct.	17	at Green Bay Packers	33-7
W	Oct.	24	Chicago Cardinals	13-7
W	Oct.	31	at Brooklyn Dodgers	48-10
T	Nov.	7	at Phila./Pitt. Steagles	14-14
W	Nov.	14	Detroit Lions	42-20
W	Nov.	21	Chicago Bears	21-7
L	Nov.	28	Phil.-Pitt.	27-14
L	Dec.	5	at New York Giants	14-10
L	Dec.	12	New York Giants	31-7

Eastern Title Playoff

W	Dec.	19	at New York Giants	28-0

World Championship

L	Dec.	26	at Chicago Bears	41-21

1944 (6-3-1)
Coach: Dudley DeGroot

T	Oct.	8	at Philadelphia Eagles	31-31
W	Oct.	15	at Boston Yanks	21-14
W	Oct.	22	Brooklyn Dodgers	17-14
W	Oct.	29	Chicago/Pittsburgh Stags	42-20
W	Nov.	5	Cleveland Rams	14-10
W	Nov.	12	at Brooklyn Dodgers	10-0
L	Nov.	19	Philadelphia Eagles	37-7
W	Nov.	26	Boston Yanks	14-7
L	Dec.	3	at New York Giants	16-13
L	Dec.	10	New York Giants	31-0

1945 (8-2)
Coach: Dudley DeGroot

L	Oct.	7	at Boston Yanks	28-20
W	Oct.	14	at Pittsburgh Steelers	14-0
W	Oct.	21	Philadelphia Eagles	24-14
W	Oct.	28	at New York Giants	24-14
W	Nov.	4	Chicago Cardinals	24-21
W	Nov.	11	Boston Yanks	34-7
W	Nov.	18	Chicago Bears	28-21
L	Nov.	25	at Philadelphia Eagles	16-0

W	Dec.	2	Pittsburgh Steelers	24-0
W	Dec.	9	New York Giants	17-0

World Championship

L	Dec.	16	at Cleveland Rams	15-14

1946 (5-5-1)
Coach: Turk Edwards

T	Sept.	29	Pittsburgh Steelers	14-14
W	Oct.	6	Detroit Lions	17-16
W	Oct.	13	New York Giants	24-14
W	Oct.	20	at Boston Yanks	14-6
L	Oct.	27	Philadelphia Eagles	28-24
L	Nov.	3	at Pittsburgh Steelers	14-7
W	Nov.	10	Boston Yanks	17-14
L	Nov.	17	at Chicago Bears	24-20
W	Nov.	24	at Philadelphia Eagles	27-10
L	Dec.	1	Green Bay Packers	20-7
L	Dec.	8	at New York Giants	31-0

1947 (4-8)
Coach: Turk Edwards

L	Sept.	28	at Philadelphia Eagles	42-45
W	Oct.	5	Pittsburgh Steelers	27-26
W	Oct.	12	New York Giants	28-20
L	Oct.	19	at Green Bay Packers	27-10
L	Oct.	26	Chicago Bears	56-20
L	Nov.	2	Philadelphia Eagles	38-14
L	Nov.	9	at Pittsburgh Steelers	21-14
L	Nov.	16	at Detroit Lions	38-21
W	Nov.	23	Chicago Cardinals	45-21
L	Nov.	30	at Boston Yanks	27-24
L	Dec.	7	at New York Giants	35-10
W	Dec.	14	Boston Yanks	40-13

1948 (7-5)
Coach: Turk Edwards

W	Sept.	26	Pittsburgh Steelers	17-14
W	Oct.	3	New York Giants	41-10
L	Oct.	10	at Pittsburgh Steelers	10-7
L	Oct.	17	Philadelphia Eagles	45-0
W	Oct.	24	at Green Bay Packers	23-7
W	Oct.	31	Boston Yanks	59-21
W	Nov.	7	Boston Yanks	23-7
W	Nov.	14	Detroit Lions	46-21
L	Nov.	21	at Philadelphia Eagles	42-21
L	Nov.	28	at Chicago Bears	48-13

L	Dec.	5	Los Angeles Rams	41-13	
W	Dec.	12	at Giants	28-21	

1949 (4-7-1)

Coach: John Whelchel (7 games)
Coach: Herman Ball

L	Sept.	26	at Chicago Cardinals	38-7
W	Oct.	3	at Pittsburgh Steelers	27-14
L	Oct.	9	New York Giants	45-35
W	Oct.	16	New York Bulldogs	38-14
L	Oct.	23	at Philadelphia Eagles	49-14
T	Oct.	30	at New York Bulldogs	14-14
W	Nov.	6	Pittsburgh Steelers	27-14
L	Nov.	13	Philadelphia Eagles	44-21
L	Nov.	20	Chicago Bears	31-21
L	Nov.	27	at New York Giants	23-7
W	Dec.	4	Green Bay Packers	30-0
L	Dec.	11	at Los Angeles Rams	53-27

1950 (3-9)

Coach: Herman Ball

W	Sept.	17	at Baltimore Colts	38-14
L	Sept.	24	at Green Bay Packers	35-21
L	Oct.	1	Pittsburgh Steelers	26-7
L	Oct.	8	New York Giants	21-17
L	Oct.	22	Chicago Cardinals	38-28
L	Oct.	29	at Philadelphia Eagles	35-3
L	Nov.	5	at New York Giants	24-21
L	Nov.	12	Philadelphia Eagles	33-0
L	Nov.	19	at Cleveland Browns	20-14
W	Nov.	26	Baltimore Colts	38-28
W	Dec.	3	at Pittsburgh Steelers	24-7
L	Dec.	10	Cleveland Browns	45-21

1951 (5-7)

Coach: Herman Ball (3 games)
Coach: Dick Todd

L	Sept.	30	at Detroit Lions	35-17
L	Oct.	7	New York Giants	35-14
L	Oct.	14	at Cleveland Browns	45-0
W	Oct.	21	Chicago Cardinals	7-3
W	Oct.	28	at Philadelphia Eagles	27-23
L	Nov.	4	Chicago Bears	27-0
L	Nov.	11	at New York Giants	28-14
W	Nov.	18	at Pittsburgh Steelers	27-7
W	Nov.	25	Los Angeles Rams	31-21

L	Dec.	2	Philadelphia Eagles	35-21
W	Dec.	9	at Chicago Cardinals	20-17
L	Dec.	16	at Pittsburgh Steelers	20-10

1952 (4-8)

Coach: Earl (Curly) Lambeau

W	Sept.	28	at Chicago Cardinals	23-7
L	Oct.	5	at Green Bay Packers	35-20
L	Oct.	12	Chicago Cardinals	17-6
W	Oct.	19	at Pittsburgh Steelers	28-24
L	Oct.	26	at Cleveland Browns	19-15
L	Nov.	2	Pittsburgh Steelers	24-23
L	Nov.	9	at Philadelphia Eagles	38-20
L	Nov.	16	San Francisco 49ers	23-17
L	Nov.	23	New York Giants	14-10
L	Nov.	30	Cleveland Browns	48-24
W	Dec.	7	at New York Giants	27-17
W	Dec.	14	Philadelphia Eagles	27-21

1953 (6-5-1)

Coach: Earl (Curly) Lambeau

W	Sept.	27	at Chicago Cardinals	24-13
T	Oct.	2	at Philadelphia Eagles	21-21
W	Oct.	11	New York Giants	13-9
L	Oct.	18	Cleveland Browns	30-14
L	Oct.	25	at Baltimore Colts	27-17
L	Nov.	1	at Cleveland Browns	27-3
W	Nov.	8	Chicago Cardinals	28-17
L	Nov.	15	Chicago Bears	27-24
W	Nov.	22	at New York Giants	24-21
W	Nov.	29	at Pittsburgh Steelers	17-9
W	Dec.	6	Philadelphia Eagles	10-0
L	Dec.	13	Pittsburgh Steelers	14-13

1954 (3-9)

Coach: Joe Kuharich

L	Sept.	26	at San Francisco 49ers	41-7
L	Oct.	2	at Pittsburgh Steelers	37-7
L	Oct.	10	New York Giants	51-21
L	Oct.	17	Philadelphia Eagles	49-21
L	Oct.	24	at New York Giants	24-7
W	Oct.	31	Baltimore Colts	24-21
L	Nov.	7	at Cleveland Browns	62-3
W	Nov.	14	Pittsburgh Steelers	17-14
L	Nov.	21	at Chicago Cardinals	38-16
L	Nov.	28	at Philadelphia Eagles	41-33

L	Dec.	5	Cleveland Browns	34-14
W	Dec.	12	Chicago Cardinals	37-20

1955 (8-4)
Coach: Joe Kuharich

W	Sept.	25	at Cleveland Browns	27-17
W	Oct.	1	at Philadelphia Eagles	31-30
L	Oct.	9	Chicago Cardinals	24-10
L	Oct.	16	Cleveland Browns	24-14
W	Oct.	23	at Baltimore Colts	14-13
L	Oct.	30	at New York Giants	35-7
W	Nov.	6	Philadelphia Eagles	34-21
W	Nov.	13	San Francisco 49ers	7-0
W	Nov.	20	at Chicago Cardinals	31-0
W	Nov.	27	at Pittsburgh Steelers	23-14
L	Dec.	4	New York Giants	27-20
W	Dec.	11	Pittsburgh Steelers	28-17

1956 (6-6)
Coach: Joe Kuharich

L	Sept.	30	at Pittsburgh Steelers	30-13
L	Oct.	6	at Philadelphia Eagles	13-9
L	Oct.	14	Chicago Cardinals	31-3
W	Oct.	21	Cleveland Browns	20-9
W	Oct.	28	Chicago Cardinals	17-14
W	Nov.	11	Detroit Lions	18-17
W	Nov.	18	New York Giants	33-7
W	Nov.	25	at Cleveland Browns	20-17
L	Dec.	2	at New York Giants	28-14
W	Dec.	9	Philadelphia Eagles	19-17
L	Dec.	16	Pittsburgh Steelers	23-0
L	Dec.	23	at Baltimore Colts	19-17

1957 (5-6-1)
Coach: Joe Kuharich

L	Sept.	29	at Pittsburgh Steelers	28-7
W	Oct.	6	at Chicago Cardinals	37-14
L	Oct.	13	New York Giants	24-20
L	Oct.	20	Chicago Cardinals	44-14
W	Oct.	27	at New York Giants	31-14
L	Nov.	3	at Cleveland Browns	21-17
L	Nov.	10	Baltimore Colts	21-17
T	Nov.	17	Cleveland Browns	30-30
L	Nov.	24	at Philadelphia Eagles	21-12
W	Dec.	1	at Chicago Bears	14-3
W	Dec.	8	Philadelphia Eagles	42-7

W	Dec.	15	Pittsburgh Steelers	10-3

1958 (4-7-1)
Coach: Joe Kuharich

W	Sept.	18	at Philadelphia Eagles	24-14
L	Oct.	4	at Chicago Cardinals	37-10
L	Oct.	12	New York Giants	21-14
W	Oct.	19	Green Bay Packers	37-21
L	Oct.	26	at Baltimore Colts	35-10
L	Nov.	2	at Pittsburgh Steelers	24-16
W	Nov.	9	Chicago Cardinals	45-31
L	Nov.	16	Cleveland Browns	20-10
L	Nov.	23	at New York Giants	30-0
L	Nov.	30	at Cleveland Browns	21-14
T	Dec.	7	Pittsburgh Steelers	14-14
W	Dec.	14	Philadelphia Eagles	20-0

1959 (3-9)
Coach: Mike Nixon

L	Sept.	17	at Chicago Cardinals	49-21
W	Oct.	4	at Pittsburgh Steelers	23-17
W	Oct.	11	Chicago Cardinals	23-14
L	Oct.	18	Pittsburgh Steelers	27-6
L	Oct.	25	at Cleveland Browns	34-7
L	Nov.	1	at Philadelphia Eagles	30-23
W	Nov.	8	Baltimore Colts	27-24
L	Nov.	15	Cleveland Browns	31-17
L	Nov.	22	at Green Bay Packers	21-0
L	Nov.	29	at New York Giants	45-14
L	Dec.	6	Philadelphia Eagles	34-14
L	Dec.	13	New York Giants	24-10

1960 (1-9-2)
Coach: Mike Nixon

L	Sept.	25	at Baltimore Colts	20-0
W	Oct.	9	Dallas Cowboys	26-14
T	Oct.	16	at New York Giants	24-24
T	Oct.	23	at Pittsburgh Steelers	27-27
L	Oct.	30	Cleveland Browns	31-10
L	Nov.	6	at St. Louis Cardinals	44-7
L	Nov.	13	at Philadelphia Eagles	19-13
L	Nov.	20	St. Louis Cardinals	26-14
L	Nov.	27	at Pittsburgh Steelers	22-10
L	Dec.	4	at Cleveland Browns	27-16
L	Dec.	11	New York Giants	17-3
L	Dec.	18	Philadelphia Eagles	38-28

1961 (1-12-1)
Coach: Bill McPeak

L	Sept.	17	at San Francisco 49ers	35-3
L	Sept.	24	at Philadelphia Eagles	14-7
L	Oct.	1	New York Giants	24-21
L	Oct.	8	at Cleveland Browns	31-7
L	Oct.	15	at Pittsburgh Steelers	20-0
L	Oct.	22	St. Louis Cardinals	24-0
L	Oct.	29	Philadelphia Eagles	27-24
L	Nov.	5	at New York Giants	53-0
L	Nov.	12	Cleveland Browns	17-6
T	Nov.	19	at Dallas Cowboys	28-28
L	Nov.	26	Baltimore Colts	27-6
L	Dec.	3	at St. Louis Cardinals	38-24
L	Dec.	10	Pittsburgh Steelers	30-14
W	Dec.	17	Dallas Cowboys	34-24

1962 (5-7-2)
Coach: Bill McPeak

T	Sept.	16	at Dallas Cowboys	35-35
W	Sept.	23	at Cleveland Browns	17-16
W	Sept.	30	St. Louis Cardinals	24-14
W	Oct.	8	Los Angeles Rams	20-14
T	Oct.	14	at St. Louis Cardinals	17-17
W	Oct.	21	at Philadelphia Eagles	27-21
L	Oct.	28	at New York Giants	49-34
L	Nov.	4	Dallas Cowboys	38-10
W	Nov.	11	Cleveland Browns	17-9
L	Nov.	18	at Pittsburgh Steelers	23-21
L	Nov.	25	New York Giants	42-24
L	Dec.	2	Philadelphia Eagles	37-14
L	Dec.	8	at Baltimore Colts	34-21
L	Dec.	15	Pittsburgh Steelers	27-24

1963 (3-11)
Coach: Bill McPeak

L	Sept.	15	at Cleveland Browns	37-14
W	Sept.	21	at Los Angeles Rams	37-14
W	Sept.	29	Dallas Cowboys	21-17
L	Oct.	6	New York Giants	24-14
L	Oct.	13	Philadelphia Eagles	37-24
L	Oct.	20	at Pittsburgh Steelers	38-27
L	Oct.	27	St. Louis Cardinals	21-7
L	Nov.	3	at Dallas Cowboys	35-20
L	Nov.	10	at St. Louis Cardinals	24-20
L	Nov.	17	Pittsburgh Steelers	34-28
W	Nov.	24	at Philadelphia Eagles	13-10
L	Dec.	1	Baltimore Colts	36-20
L	Dec.	8	at New York Giants	44-14
L	Dec.	15	Cleveland Browns	27-20

1964 (6-8)
Coach: Bill McPeak

L	Sept.	13	Cleveland Browns	27-13
L	Sept.	20	at Dallas Cowboys	24-18
L	Sept.	25	at New York Giants	13-10
L	Oct.	4	St. Louis Cardinals	23-17
W	Oct.	11	Philadelphia Eagles	35-20
L	Oct.	18	at St. Louis Cardinals	38-24
W	Oct.	25	Chicago Bears	27-20
W	Nov.	1	at Philadelphia Eagles	21-10
L	Nov.	8	at Cleveland Browns	34-24
W	Nov.	15	at Pittsburgh Steelers	30-0
W	Nov.	22	Dallas Cowboys	28-16
W	Nov.	29	New York Giants	36-21
L	Dec.	6	Pittsburgh Steelers	14-7
L	Dec.	13	at Baltimore Colts	45-17

1965 (6-8)
Coach: Bill McPeak

L	Sept.	19	Cleveland Browns	17-7
L	Sept.	26	at Dallas Cowboys	27-7
L	Oct.	3	at Detroit Lions	14-10
L	Oct.	10	St. Louis Cardinals	37-16
L	Oct.	17	Baltimore Colts	38-7
W	Oct.	24	at St. Louis Cardinals	24-20
W	Oct.	31	Philadelphia Eagles	23-21
W	Nov.	7	at New York Giants	23-7
L	Nov.	14	at Philadelphia Eagles	21-14
W	Nov.	21	at Pittsburgh Steelers	31-3
W	Nov.	28	Dallas Cowboys	34-31
L	Dec.	5	at Cleveland Browns	24-16
L	Dec.	12	New York Giants	27-10
W	Dec.	19	Pittsburgh Steelers	35-14

1966 (7-7)
Coach: Otto Graham

L	Sept.	11	Cleveland Browns	38-14
L	Sept.	18	at St. Louis Cardinals	23-7
W	Sept.	25	at Pittsburgh Steelers	33-27
W	Oct.	2	Pittsburgh Steelers	24-10
W	Oct.	9	Atlanta Falcons	33-20
L	Oct.	16	at New York Giants	13-10
W	Oct.	23	St. Louis Cardinals	26-20
W	Oct.	30	at Philadelphia Eagles	27-13
L	Nov.	6	at Baltimore Colts	37-10
L	Nov.	13	Dallas Cowboys	31-30
L	Nov.	20	at Cleveland Browns	14-3
W	Nov.	27	New York Giants	72-14
W	Dec.	11	at Dallas Cowboys	34-31
L	Dec.	18	Philadelphia Eagles	37-28

1967 (5-6-3)
Coach: Otto Graham

L	Sept.	17	at Philadelphia Eagles	35-24
W	Sept.	24	at New Orleans Saints	30-10
W	Oct.	1	New York Giants	38-34
L	Oct.	8	Dallas Cowboys	17-14
T	Oct.	15	at Atlanta Falcons	20-20
T	Oct.	22	at Los Angeles Rams	28-28
L	Oct.	29	Baltimore Colts	17-13
L	Nov.	5	St. Louis Cardinals	27-21
W	Nov.	12	San Francisco 49ers	31-28
W	Nov.	19	at Dallas Cowboys	27-20
L	Nov.	26	at Cleveland Browns	42-37
T	Dec.	3	Philadelphia Eagles	35-35
W	Dec.	10	at Pittsburgh Steelers	15-10
L	Dec.	17	New Orleans Saints	30-14

1968 (5-9)
Coach: Otto Graham

W	Sept.	15	at Chicago Bears	38-28
L	Sept.	22	at New Orleans Saints	37-17
L	Sept.	29	at New York Giants	48-21
W	Oct.	6	Philadelphia Eagles	17-14
W	Oct.	13	Pittsburgh Steelers	16-13
L	Oct.	20	at St. Louis Cardinals	41-14
L	Oct.	27	New York Giants	13-10
L	Nov.	3	at Minnesota Vikings	27-14
W	Nov.	10	at Philadelphia Eagles	16-10
L	Nov.	17	Dallas Cowboys	44-24
L	Nov.	24	Green Bay Packers	27-7
L	Nov.	28	at Dallas Cowboys	29-20
L	Dec.	8	Cleveland Browns	24-21
W	Dec.	15	Detroit Lions	14-3

1969 (7-5-2)
Coach: Vince Lombardi

W	Sept.	21	at New Orleans Saints	26-20
L	Sept.	28	at Cleveland Browns	27-23
T	Oct.	5	at San Francisco 49ers	17-17
W	Oct.	12	St. Louis Cardinals	33-17
W	Oct.	19	New York Giants	20-14
W	Oct.	26	at Pittsburgh Steelers	14-7
L	Nov.	2	at Baltimore Colts	41-17
T	Nov.	9	Philadelphia Eagles	28-28
L	Nov.	16	Dallas Cowboys	41-28
W	Nov.	23	Atlanta Falcons	27-20
L	Nov.	30	Los Angeles Rams	24-13
W	Dec.	7	at Philadelphia Eagles	34-29
W	Dec.	14	New Orleans Saints	17-14
L	Dec.	21	at Dallas Cowboys	20-10

1970 (6-8)
Coach: Bill Austin

L	Sept.	20	at San Francisco 49ers	26-17
L	Sept.	27	at St. Louis Cardinals	27-17
W	Oct.	4	at Philadelphia Eagles	33-21
W	Oct.	11	Detroit Lions	31-10
L	Oct.	19	at Oakland Raiders	34-20
W	Oct.	25	Cincinnati Bengals	20-0
W	Nov.	1	at Denver Broncos	19-3
L	Nov.	8	Minnesota Vikings	19-10
L	Nov.	15	at New York Giants	35-33
L	Nov.	22	Dallas Cowboys	45-21
L	Nov.	29	New York Giants	27-24
L	Dec.	6	at Dallas Cowboys	34-0
W	Dec.	13	Philadelphia Eagles	24-6
W	Dec.	20	St. Louis Cardinals	28-27

1971 (9-4-1)

Coach: George Allen

W	Sept.	19	at St. Louis Cardinals	24-17
W	Sept.	26	at New York Giants	30-3
W	Oct.	3	at Dallas Cowboys	20-16
W	Oct.	10	Houston Oilers	22-13
W	Oct.	17	St. Louis Cardinals	20-0
L	Oct.	24	at Kansas City Chiefs	27-20
W	Oct.	31	New Orleans Saints	24-14
T	Nov.	7	Philadelphia Eagles	7-7
L	Nov.	14	at Chicago Bears	16-15
L	Nov.	21	Dallas Cowboys	13-0
W	Nov.	28	at Philadelphia Eagles	20-13
W	Dec.	5	New York Giants	23-7
W	Dec.	13	at Los Angeles Rams	38-24
L	Dec.	19	Cleveland Browns	20-13

Playoffs

L	Dec.	26	at San Francisco 49ers	24-20

1972 (11-3)

Coach: George Allen

W	Sept.	18	at Minnesota Vikings	24-21
W	Sept.	24	St. Louis Cardinals	24-10
L	Oct.	1	at New England	24-23
W	Oct.	8	Philadelphia Eagles	14-0
W	Oct.	15	at St. Louis Cardinals	33-3
W	Oct.	22	Dallas Cowboys	24-20
W	Oct.	29	at New York Giants	23-16
W	Nov.	5	at New York Jets	35-17
W	Nov.	12	New York Giants	27-13
W	Nov.	20	Atlanta Falcons	24-13
W	Nov.	26	Green Bay Packers	21-16
W	Dec.	3	at Philadelphia Eagles	23-7
L	Dec.	9	at Dallas Cowboys	34-24
L	Dec.	17	Buffalo Bills	24-17

Playoffs

W	Dec.	24	Green Bay Packers	16-3
W	Dec.	31	Dallas Cowboys	26-3

Super Bowl VII in Los Angeles

L	Jan.	14	Miami Dolphins	14-7

1973 (10-4)

Coach: George Allen

W	Sept.	16	San Diego Chargers	38-0
L	Sept.	23	at St. Louis Cardinals	34-27
W	Sept.	30	at Philadelphia Eagles	28-7
W	Oct.	8	Dallas Cowboys	14-7
W	Oct.	14	at New York Giants	21-3
W	Oct.	21	St. Louis Cardinals	31-13
L	Oct.	28	at New Orleans Saints	19-3
L	Nov.	5	at Pittsburgh Steelers	21-16
W	Nov.	11	San Francisco 49ers	33-9
W	Nov.	18	Baltimore Colts	22-14
W	Nov.	22	at Detroit Lions	20-0
W	Dec.	2	New York Giants	27-24
L	Dec.	9	at Dallas Cowboys	27-7
W	Dec.	16	Philadelphia Eagles	38-20

Playoffs

L	Dec.	22	at Minnesota Vikings	27-20

1974 (10-4)

Coach: George Allen

W	Sept.	15	at New York Giants	13-10
L	Sept.	22	St. Louis Cardinals	17-10
W	Sept.	30	Denver Broncos	30-3
L	Oct.	6	at Cincinnati Bengals	28-17
W	Oct.	13	Miami Dolphins	20-17
W	Oct.	20	New York Giants	24-3
L	Oct.	27	at St. Louis Cardinals	23-20
W	Nov.	3	at Green Bay Packers	17-6
W	Nov.	10	at Philadelphia Eagles	27-20
W	Nov.	17	Dallas Cowboys	28-21
W	Nov.	24	Philadelphia Eagles	26-7
L	Nov.	28	at Dallas Cowboys	24-23
W	Dec.	9	at Los Angeles Rams	23-17
W	Dec.	15	Chicago Bears	42-0

Playoffs

L	Dec.	22	at Los Angeles Rams	19-10

1975 (8-6)

Coach: George Allen

W	Sept.	21	New Orleans Saints	41-3
W	Sept.	28	New York Giants	49-13

L	Oct.	5	at Philadelphia Eagles	26-10	
W	Oct.	13	St. Louis Cardinals	27-17	
L	Oct.	19	at Houston Oilers	13-10	
W	Oct.	26	at Cleveland Browns	23-7	
W	Nov.	2	Dallas Cowboys	30-24*	
W	Nov.	9	at New York Giants	21-13	
L	Nov.	16	at St. Louis Cardinals	20-17*	
L	Nov.	23	Oakland Raiders	26-23*	
W	Nov.	30	Minnesota Vikings	31-30	
W	Dec.	7	at Atlanta Falcons	30-27	
L	Dec.	13	at Dallas Cowboys	31-10	
L	Dec.	21	Philadelphia Eagles	26-3	

*overtime

1976 (10-4)

Coach: George Allen

W	Sept.	12	New York Giants	19-17	
W	Sept.	19	Seattle Seahawks	31-7	
W	Sept.	27	at Philadelphia	20-17*	
L	Oct.	3	at Chicago Bears	33-7	
L	Oct.	10	Kansas City Chiefs	33-30	
W	Oct.	17	Detroit Lions	20-7	
W	Oct.	25	St. Louis Cardinals	20-10	
L	Oct.	31	Dallas Cowboys	20-7	
W	Nov.	7	at San Francisco	24-21	
L	Nov.	14	at New York Giants	12-9	
W	Nov.	21	at St. Louis Cardinals	16-10	
W	Nov.	28	Philadelphia Eagles	24-0	
W	Dec.	5	at New York Jets	37-16	
W	Dec.	12	at Dallas Cowboys	27-14	

Playoffs

L	Dec.	18	at Minnesota Vikings	35-20	

*overtime

1977 (9-5)

Coach: George Allen

L	Sept.	18	at New York Giants	20-17	
W	Sept.	25	Atlanta Falcons	10-6	
W	Oct.	2	St. Louis Cardinals	24-14	
W	Oct.	9	at Tampa Bay	10-0	
L	Oct.	16	at Dallas Cowboys	34-16	
L	Oct.	23	New York Giants	17-6	

W	Oct.	30	Philadelphia Eagles	23-17	
L	Nov.	7	at Baltimore Colts	10-3	
W	Nov.	13	at Philadelphia Eagles	17-14	
W	Nov.	21	Green Bay Packers	10-9	
L	Nov.	27	Dallas Cowboys	14-7	
W	Dec.	4	at Buffalo Bills	10-0	
W	Dec.	10	at St. Louis Cardinals	26-20	
W	Dec.	17	Los Angeles Rams	17-14	

1978 (8-8)

Coach: Jack Pardee

W	Sept.	3	at New England Patriots	16-14	
W	Sept.	10	Philadelphia Eagles	35-30	
W	Sept.	17	at St. Louis Cardinals	28-10	
W	Sept.	24	New York Jets	23-3	
W	Oct.	2	Dallas Cowboys	9-5	
W	Oct.	8	at Detroit Lions	21-19	
L	Oct.	15	at Philadelphia Eagles	17-10	
L	Oct.	22	at New York Giants	17-6	
W	Oct.	29	San Francisco 49ers	38-20	
L	Nov.	6	at Baltimore Colts	21-7	
W	Nov.	12	New York Giants	16-13*	
L	Nov.	19	St. Louis Cardinals	27-17	
L	Nov.	23	at Dallas Cowboys	37-10	
L	Dec.	3	Miami Dolphins	16-0	
L	Dec.	10	at Atlanta Falcons	20-17	
L	Dec.	16	Chicago Bears	14-10	

1979 (10-6)

Coach: Jack Pardee

L	Sept.	2	Houston Oilers	29-27	
W	Sept.	9	at Detroit Lions	27-24	
W	Sept.	17	New York Giants	27-0	
W	Sept.	23	at St. Louis Cardinals	17-7	
W	Sept.	30	at Atlanta Falcons	16-7	
L	Oct.	7	at Philadelphia Eagles	28-17	
W	Oct.	14	at Cleveland Browns	13-9	
W	Oct.	21	Philadelphia Eagles	17-7	
L	Oct.	28	New Orleans Saints	14-10	
L	Nov.	4	at Pittsburgh Steelers	38-7	

W	Nov.	11	St. Louis Cardinals	30-28
W	Nov.	18	Dallas Cowboys	34-20
L	Nov.	25	at New York Giants	14-6
W	Dec.	2	Green Bay Packers	38-21
W	Dec.	9	Cincinnati Bengals	28-14
L	Dec.	16	at Dallas Cowboys	35-34

1980 (6-10)
Coach: Jack Pardee

L	Sept.	8	Dallas Cowboys	17-3
W	Sept.	14	at New York Giants	23-21
L	Sept.	21	at Oakland Raiders	24-21
L	Sept.	28	Seattle Seahawks	14-0
L	Oct.	5	at Philadelphia Eagles	24-14
L	Oct.	13	at Denver Broncos	20-17
W	Oct.	19	St. Louis Cardinals	23-0
W	Oct.	26	New Orleans Saints	22-14
L	Nov.	2	Minnesota Vikings	39-14
L	Nov.	9	at Chicago Bears	35-21
L	Nov.	15	Philadelphia Eagles	24-0
L	Nov.	23	at Dallas Cowboys	14-10
L	Nov.	30	at Atlanta Falcons	10-6
W	Dec.	7	San Diego Chargers	40-17
W	Dec.	13	New York Giants	16-13
W	Dec.	21	at St. Louis Cardinals	31-7

1981 (8-8)
Coach: Joe Gibbs

L	Sept.	6	Dallas Cowboys	26-10
L	Sept.	13	New York Giants	17-7
L	Sept.	20	at St. Louis Cardinals	40-30
L	Sept.	27	at Philadelphia	36-13
L	Oct.	4	San Francisco 49ers	30-17
W	Oct.	11	at Chicago Bears	24-7
L	Oct.	18	at Miami Dolphins	13-10
W	Oct.	25	New England Patriots	24-22
W	Nov.	1	St. Louis Cardinals	42-21
W	Nov.	8	Detroit Lions	33-31
W	Nov.	15	at New York Giants	30-27*
L	Nov.	22	at Dallas Cowboys	24-10
L	Nov.	29	at Buffalo Bills	21-14
W	Dec.	6	Philadelphia Eagles	15-13
W	Dec.	13	Baltimore Colts	38-14
W	Dec.	20	at Los Angeles Rams	30-7

*overtime

1982 (8-1)
Coach: Joe Gibbs

W	Sept.	12	at Philadelphia	37-34*
W	Sept.	19	at Tampa Bay	21-13
W	Nov.	21	at New York Giants	27-17
W	Nov.	28	Philadelphia Eagles	13-9
L	Dec.	5	Dallas Cowboys	24-10
W	Dec.	12	at St. Louis Cardinals	12-7
W	Dec.	19	New York Giants	15-14
W	Dec.	26	at New Orleans Saint	27-10
W	Jan.	2	St. Louis Cardinals	28-0

Playoffs

W	Jan.	8	Detroit Lions	31-7
W	Jan.	15	Minnesota Vikings	21-7
W	Jan.	22	Dallas Cowboys	31-17

Super Bowl XVII in Pasadena, Calif.

W	Jan.	30	Miami Dolphins	27-17

*overtime

1983 (14-2)
Coach: Joe Gibbs

L	Sept.	5	Dallas Cowboys	31-30
W	Sept.	11	at Philadelphia	23-13
W	Sept.	18	Kansas City Chiefs	27-12
W	Sept.	25	at Seattle Seahawks	27-17
W	Oct.	2	Los Angeles Raiders	37-35
W	Oct.	9	at St. Louis Cardinals	38-14
L	Oct.	17	at Green Bay	48-47
W	Oct.	23	Detroit Lions	38-17
W	Oct.	31	at San Diego Chargers	27-24
W	Nov.	6	St. Louis Cardinals	45-7
W	Nov.	13	at New York Giants	33-17
W	Nov.	20	at Los Angeles Rams	42-20
W	Nov.	27	Philadelphia Eagles	28-24
W	Dec.	4	Atlanta Falcons	37-21
W	Dec.	11	at Dallas Cowboys	31-10
W	Dec.	17	New York Giants	31-22

Playoffs

W	Jan.	1	Los Angeles Rams	51-7
W	Jan.	8	San Francisco 49ers	24-21

Super Bowl XVIII in Tampa

L	Jan.	22	Los Angeles Raiders	38-9

1984 (11-5)
Coach: Joe Gibbs

L	Sept.	2	Miami Dolphins	35-17
L	Sept.	10	at San Francisco 49ers	37-31
W	Sept.	16	New York Giants	30-14
W	Sept.	23	at New England	26-10
W	Sept.	30	Philadelphia Eagles	20-0
W	Oct.	7	at Indianapolis Colts	35-7
W	Oct.	14	Dallas Cowboys	34-14
L	Oct.	21	at St. Louis Cardinals	26-24
L	Oct.	28	at New York Giants	37-13
W	Nov.	5	Atlanta Falcons	27-14
W	Nov.	11	Detroit Lions	28-14
L	Nov.	18	at Philadelphia	16-10
W	Nov.	25	Buffalo Bills	41-14
W	Nov.	29	at Minnesota Vikings	31-17
W	Dec.	9	at Dallas Cowboys	30-28
W	Dec.	16	St. Louis Cardinals	29-27

Playoffs

L	Dec.	30	Chicago Bears	23-19

1985 (10-6)
Coach: Joe Gibbs

L	Sept.	9	at Dallas Cowboys	44-14
W	Sept.	15	Houston Oilers	16-13
L	Sept.	22	Philadelphia Eagles	19-6
L	Sept.	29	at Chicago Bears	45-10
W	Oct.	7	St. Louis Cardinals	27-10
W	Oct.	13	Detroit Lions	24-3
L	Oct.	20	at New York Giants	17-3
W	Oct.	27	at Cleveland Browns	14-7
W	Nov.	3	at Atlanta Falcons	44-10
L	Nov.	10	Dallas Cowboys	13-7
W	Nov.	18	New York Giants	23-21
W	Nov.	24	at Pittsburgh Steelers	30-23
L	Dec.	1	San Francisco 49ers	35-8
W	Dec.	8	at Philadelphia Eagles	17-12
W	Dec.	15	Cincinnati Bengals	27-24
W	Dec.	21	at St. Louis Cardinals	27-16

1986 (12-4)
Coach: Joe Gibbs

W	Sept.	7	Philadelphia Eagles	41-14
W	Sept.	14	Los Angeles Raiders	10-6
W	Sept.	21	at San Diego Chargers	30-27
W	Sept.	28	Seattle Seahawks	19-14
W	Oct.	5	at New Orleans Saints	14-6
L	Oct.	12	at Dallas Cowboys	30-6
W	Oct.	19	St. Louis Cardinals	28-21
L	Oct.	27	at New York Giants	27-20
W	Nov.	2	Minnesota Vikings	44-38*
W	Nov.	9	at Green Bay Packers	16-7
W	Nov.	17	San Francisco 49ers	14-6
W	Nov.	23	Dallas Cowboys	41-14
W	Nov.	30	at St. Louis Cardinals	20-17
L	Dec.	7	New York Giants	24-14
L	Dec.	13	at Denver Broncos	31-30
W	Dec.	21	at Philadelphia Eagles	21-14

Playoffs

W	Dec.	28	at Los Angeles Rams	19-7
W	Jan.	3	at Chicago Bears	27-13
L	Jan.	11	at New York Giants	17-0

1987 (11-4)
Coach: Joe Gibbs

W	Sept.	13	Philadelphia Eagles	34-24
L	Sept.	20	at Atlanta Falcons	21-20
W	Oct.	4	St. Louis Cardinals	28-21
W	Oct.	11	at New York Giants	38-12
W	Oct.	19	at Dallas Cowboys	13-7
W	Oct.	25	New York Jets	17-16
W	Nov.	1	at Buffalo Bills	27-7
L	Nov.	8	at Philadelphia Eagles	31-27
W	Nov.	15	Detroit Lions	20-13
L	Nov.	23	Los Angeles Rams	30-26
W	Nov.	29	New York Giants	23-19
W	Dec.	6	at St. Louis Cardinals	34-17
W	Dec.	13	Dallas Cowboys	24-20
L	Dec.	20	at Miami Dolphins	23-21
W	Dec.	26	at Minnesota Vikings	27-24*

Playoffs

W	Jan.	10	at Chicago Bears	21-17
W	Jan.	17	Minnesota Vikings	17-10

Super Bowl XXII in San Diego

W	Jan.	31	Denver Broncos	42-10

*overtime

1988 (7-9)
Coach: Joe Gibbs

L	Sept.	5	at New York Giants	27-20
W	Sept.	11	Pittsburgh Steelers	30-29
W	Sept.	18	Philadelphia Eagles	17-10
L	Sept.	25	at Phoenix Cardinals	30-21
L	Oct.	2	New York Giants	24-23
W	Oct.	9	at Dallas Cowboys	35-17
W	Oct.	16	Phoenix Cardinals	33-17
W	Oct.	23	at Green Bay Packers	20-17
L	Oct.	30	at Houston Oilers	41-17
W	Nov.	6	New Orleans Saints	27-24
L	Nov.	13	Chicago Bears	34-14
L	Nov.	21	at San Francisco 49ers	37-21
L	Nov.	27	Cleveland Browns	17-13
W	Dec.	4	at Philadelphia Eagles	20-19
L	Dec.	11	Dallas Cowboys	24-17
L	Dec.	17	at Cincinnati Bengals	20-17*

*overtime

1989 (10-6)
Coach: Joe Gibbs

L	Sept.	11	New York Giants	27-24
L	Sept.	17	Philadelphia Eagles	42-37
W	Sept.	24	at Dallas Cowboys	30-7
W	Oct.	1	at New Orleans Saints	16-14
W	Oct.	8	Phoenix Cardinals	30-28
L	Oct.	15	at New York Giants	20-17
W	Oct.	22	Tampa Bay Buccaneers	32-28
L	Oct.	29	at Los Angeles Raiders	37-24
L	Nov.	5	Dallas Cowboys	13-3
W	Nov.	12	at Philadelphia Eagles	10-3
L	Nov.	20	Denver Broncos	14-10
W	Nov.	26	Chicago Bears	38-14
W	Dec.	3	at Phoenix Cardinals	29-10
W	Dec.	10	San Diego Charger	26-21
W	Dec.	17	at Atlanta Falcons	31-30
W	Dec.	23	at Seattle Seahawks	29-0

1990 (10-6)
Coach: Joe Gibbs

W	Sept.	9	Phoenix Cardinals	31-0
L	Sept.	16	at San Francisco 49ers	26-13
W	Sept.	23	Dallas Cowboys	19-15
W	Sept.	30	at Phoenix Cardinals	38-10
L	Oct.	14	New York Giants	24-20
W	Oct.	21	Philadelphia Eagles	13-7
L	Oct.	28	at New York Giants	21-10
W	Nov.	4	at Detroit Lions	41-38*
L	Nov.	12	at Philadelphia Eagles	28-14
W	Nov.	18	New Orleans Saints	31-17
L	Nov.	22	at Dallas Cowboys	27-17
W	Dec.	2	Miami Dolphins	42-20
W	Dec.	9	Chicago Bears	10-9
W	Dec.	15	at New England	25-10
L	Dec.	22	at Indianapolis Colts	35-28
W	Dec.	30	Buffalo Bills	29-14

*overtime

1991 (14-2)
Coach: Joe Gibbs

W	Sept.	1	Detroit Lions	45-0
W	Sept.	9	at Dallas Cowboys	33-31
W	Sept.	15	Phoenix Cardinals	34-0
W	Sept.	22	at Cincinnati Bengals	34-27
W	Sept.	30	Philadelphia Eagles	23-0
W	Oct.	6	at Chicago Bears	20-7
W	Oct.	13	Cleveland Browns	42-17
W	Oct.	27	at New York Giants	17-13
W	Nov.	3	Houston Oilers	16-13*
W	Nov.	10	Atlanta Falcons	56-17
W	Nov.	17	at Pittsburgh Steelers	41-14
L	Nov.	24	at Dallas Cowboys	24-21
W	Dec.	1	at Los Angeles Rams	27-6
W	Dec.	8	at Phoenix Cardinals	20-14
W	Dec.	15	New York Giants	34-17
L	Dec.	22	at Philadelphia Eagles	24-22

Playoffs

W	Jan.	4	Atlanta Falcons	24-7
W	Jan.	12	Detroit Lions	41-10

Super Bowl XXVI in Minneapolis

W	Jan.	26	Buffalo Bills	37-24

*overtime

1992 (9-7)

Coach: Joe Gibbs

L	Sept.	7	at Dallas Cowboys	23-10
W	Sept.	13	Atlanta Falcons	24-17
W	Sept.	20	Detroit Lions	13-10
L	Oct.	4	at Phoenix Cardinals	24-17
W	Oct.	12	Denver Broncos	34-3
W	Oct.	18	Philadelphia Eagles	16-W
W	Oct.	25	at Minnesota Vikings	15-13
L	Nov.	1	New York Giants	24-7
W	Nov.	8	at Seattle Seahawks	16-3
L	Nov.	15	at Kansas City Chiefs	35-15
L	Nov.	23	at New Orleans Saints	20-3
W	Nov.	29	Phoenix Cardinals	41-3
W	Dec.	6	at New York Giants	28-10
W	Dec.	13	Dallas Cowboys	20-17
L	Dec.	20	at Philadelphia Eagles	17-13
L	Dec.	26	Los Angeles Raiders	21-20

Playoffs

W	Jan.	2	at Minnesota Vikings	24-7
L	Jan.	9	at San Francisco 49ers	20-13

*overtime

1993 (4-12)

Coach: Richie Petitbon

W	Sept.	6	Dallas Cowboys	35-16
L	Sept.	12	Phoenix Cardinals	17-10
L	Sept.	19	at Philadelphia Eagles	34-31
L	Oct.	4	at Miami Dolphins	17-10
L	Oct.	10	New York Giants	41-7
L	Oct.	17	at Phoenix Cardinals	36-6
L	Nov.	1	at Buffalo Bills	24-10
W	Nov.	7	Indianapolis Colts	30-24
L	Nov.	14	at New York Giants	20-6
L	Nov.	21	at Los Angeles Rams	10-6
L	Nov.	28	Philadelphia Eagles	17-14
W	Dec.	5	at Tampa Bay	23-17
L	Dec.	11	New York Jets	3-0
W	Dec.	19	Atlanta Falcons	30-17
L	Dec.	26	at Dallas Cowboys	38-3
L	Dec.	31	Minnesota Vikings	14-9

1994 (3-13)

Coach: Norv Turner

L	Sept.	4	Seattle Seahawks	28-7
W	Sept.	11	at New Orleans Saints	38-24
L	Sept.	18	at New York Giant	31-23
L	Sept.	25	Atlanta Falcons	27-20
L	Oct.	2	Dallas Cowboys	34-7
L	Oct.	9	at Philadelphia Eagles	21-17
L*	Oct.	16	Arizona Cardinals	19-16
W	Oct.	23	Indianapolis Colts	41-27
L	Oct.	30	Philadelphia Eagles	31-29
L	Nov.	6	San Francisco 49ers	37-22
L	Nov.	20	at Dallas Cowboys	31-7
L	Nov.	27	New York Giants	21-19
L	Dec.	4	at Tampa Bay	26-21
L	Dec.	11	at Arizona Cardinals	17-15
L	Dec.	18	Tampa Bay Buccaneers	17-14
W	Dec.	24	at Los Angeles Rams	24-21

*overtime

1995 (6-10)

Coach: Norv Turner

W	Sept.	3	Arizona Cardinals	27-7
L	Sept.	10	Oakland Raiders	20-8
L	Sept.	17	at Denver Broncos	38-31
L	Sept.	24	at Tampa Bay	14-6
W	Oct.	1	Dallas Cowboys	27-23
L*	Oct.	8	at Philadelphia Eagles	37-34
L	Oct.	15	at Arizona Cardinals	24-20
W*	Oct.	22	Detroit Lions	36-30
L	Oct.	29	New York Giants	24-15
L	Nov.	5	at Kansas City Chiefs	24-3
L	Nov.	19	Seattle Seahawks	27-20
L	Nov.	26	Philadelphia Eagles	14-7
W	Dec.	3	at Dallas Cowboys	24-17
L	Dec.	10	at New York Giants	20-13
W	Dec.	17	at St. Louis Rams	35-23
W	Dec.	24	Carolina Panthers	20-17

1996 (9-7)

Coach: Norv Turner

L	Sept.	1	Philadelphia Eagles	17-14
W	Sept.	8	Chicago Bears	10-3
W	Sept.	15	at New York Giants	31-10
W	Sept.	22	at St. Louis Rams	17-10
W	Sept.	29	New York Jets	31-16
W	Oct.	13	at New England	27-22
W	Oct.	20	New York Giants	31-21
W	Oct.	27	Indianapolis Colts	31-16
L	Nov.	3	at Buffalo Bills	38-13
L	Nov.	10	Arizona Cardinals	37-34*
W	Nov.	17	at Philadelphia Eagles	26-21
L	Nov.	24	San Francisco 49ers	19-16*
L	Nov.	28	at Dallas Cowboys	21-10
L	Dec.	8	at Tampa Bay	24-10
L	Dec.	15	at Arizona Cardinals	27-26
W	Dec.	22	Dallas Cowboys	37-10

*overtime

1997 (8-7-1)

Coach: Norv Turner

W	Aug.	31	at Carolina	24-10
L	Sept.	7	at Pittsburgh	14-13
W	Sept.	14	Arizona	19-13*
W	Sept.	28	Jacksonville	24-13
L	Oct.	5	at Philadelphia	24-10
W	Oct.	13	Dallas	21-16
L	Oct.	19	at Tennessee	28-14
L	Oct.	26	Baltimore	20-17
W	Nov.	2	at Chicago	31-8
W	Nov.	9	Detroit	30-7
L	Nov.	16	at Dallas	17-14
T	Nov.	23	New York Giants	7-7*
L	Nov.	30	St. Louis	23-20
W	Dec.	7	at Arizona	38-28
L	Dec.	13	at New York Giants	30-10
W	Dec.	21	Philadelphia	35-32

*overtime

1998 (6-10)

Coach: Norv Turner

L	Sept.	6	at New York Giants	31-24
L	Sept.	14	San Francisco 4	5-10
L	Sept.	20	at Seattle	24-14
L	Sept.	27	Denver	38-16
L	Oct.	4	Dallas	31-10
L	Oct.	11	at Philadelphia	17-12
L	Oct.	18	at Minnesota	41-7
W	Nov.	1	New York Giants	21-14
L	Nov.	8	at Arizona 29-27	
W	Nov.	15	Philadelphia	28-3
L	Nov.	22	Arizona	45-42
W	Nov.	29	at Oakland	29-19
W	Dec.	6	San Diego	24-20
W	Dec.	13	at Carolina	28-25
W	Dec.	19	Tampa Bay	20-16
L	Dec.	27	at Dallas	23-7

1999 (10-6)

Coach: Norv Turner

L	Sept.	12	Dallas	41-35*
W	Sept.	19	at New York Giants	50-21
W	Sept.	26	at New York Jets	27-20
W	Oct.	3	Carolina	38-36
W	Oct.	17	at Arizona	24-10
L	Oct.	24	at Dallas	38-20
W	Oct.	31	Chicago	48-22
L	Nov.	7	Buffalo	34-17
L	Nov.	14	at Philadelphia	35-28
W	Nov.	21	New York Giants	23-13
W	Nov.	28	Philadelphia	20-17*
L	Dec.	5	at Detroit	33-17
W	Dec.	12	Arizona	28-3
L	Dec.	19	at Indianapolis	24-21
W	Dec.	26	at San Francisco	26-20*
W	Jan.	2	Miami	21-10
W	Jan.	8	Detroit	27-13
L	Jan.	15	at Tampa Bay	14-13

*overtime

All Washington Redskins Players

A.

Absher, Dick, LB, Maryland, 1967
Adams, John, T, Notre Dame, 1945-49
Adams, Willie, LB, New Mexico State, 1965-66
Adickes, Mark, G, Baylor, 1990-91
Aducci, Nick, B, Nebraska, 1954-55
Aguirre, Joe, E, St. Mary's (CA), 1941, 1943-45
Akers, David, K, Louisville, 1998-99
Akins, Frank, B, Washington State, 1943-46
Alban, Dick, B, Northwestern, 1952-55
Aldrich, Ki, C, TCU, 1941-43, 1945-46
Alexander, Patrise, LB, SW Louisiana, 1996-98
Alexander, Stephen, TE, Oklahoma, 1998-2000
Alford, Bruce, K, TCU, 1967
Allen, Gerry, B, Nebraska-Omaha, 1967-69
Allen, Terry, RB, Clemson, 1995-98
Allen, John, C, Purdue, 1955-58
Alston, Mack, TE, Maryland State, 1970-72
Ananis, Vito, B, Boston College, 1945
Anderson, Bill, E, Tennessee, 1958-63
Anderson, Bob, RB, Colorado, 1975
Anderson, Bruce, E, Willamette, 1970
Anderson, Erick, LB, Michigan, 1994-95
Anderson, Gary, G, Stanford, 1980
Anderson, Stuart, LB, Virginia, 1982-85
Anderson, Terry, WR, Bethune-Cookman, 1978
Anderson, Willie, WR, UCLA, 1996
Andrako, Steve, C, Ohio State, 1940-41
Archer, David, QB, Iowa State, 1988
Ariri, Obed, K, Clemson, 1987
Arneson, Jim, G, Arizona, 1975
Arnold, Gerard, RB, Memphis, 2000
Arnold, Walt, TE, New Mexico, 1984
Arrington, LaVar, LB, Penn State, 2000
Asher, Jamie, TE, Louisville, 1995-98
Ashmore, Darryl, T, Northwestern, 1996-97
Atkeson, Dale, B, no college, 1954-56
Atkins, Pervis, RB, New Mexico State, 1964
Atkinson, Jess, K, Maryland, 1986-87
Audet, Earl, T, USC, 1945
Aveni, John, K, Indiana, 1961

Avery, Don, T, USC, 1946-47
Avery, Jim, E, Northern Illinois, 1966

B.

Bacon, Coy, DE, Jackson State, 1978-81
Badaczewski, John, G, Western Reserve, 1949-51
Badanjek, Rick, RB, Maryland, 1986
Badger, Brad, G/T, Stanford, 1997-99
Bagarus, Steve, RB, Notre Dame, 1945-46, 1948
Bagdon, Ed, G, Michigan State, 1952
Bailey, Champ, CB, Georgia, 1999-2000
Bailey, Robert, CB, Miami, 1995
Baker, Sam, K, Oregon State, 1953, 1956-59
Bandison, Romeo, DT, Oregon, 1995-96
Bandy, Don, G, Tulsa, 1967-68
Banks, Carl, LB, Michigan State, 1993
Banks, Willie, G, Alcorn A&M, 1968-69
Banta, Jack, RB, USC, 1941
Barber, Ernie, C, San Francisco, 1945
Barber, Jim, T, San Francisco, 1935-41
Barber, Shawn, LB, Richmond, 1998-2000
Barefoot, Ken, E, Virginia Tech, 1968
Barfield, Ken, T, Mississippi, 1954
Barker, Ed, E, Washington State, 1954
Barker, Tony, LB, Rice, 1992
Barnes, Billy Ray, RB, Wake Forest, 1962-63
Barnes, Tomur, CB, North Texas, 1996
Barnes, Walt, DT, Nebraska, 1966-68
Barnett, Doug, DE, Azusa Pacific, 1985
Barnett, Troy, DT, North Carolina, 1996
Barnett, Steve, T, Oregon, 1964
Barnhardt, Tom, P, North Carolina, 1988, 2000
Barni, Roy, B, San Francisco, 1955-56
Barnwell, Malcolm, WR, Virginia Union, 1985
Barrington, Tom, B, Ohio State, 1966
Barry, Paul, B, Tulsa, 1953
Bartkowski, Steve, QB, California, 1985
Bartos, Hank, G, North Carolina, 1938
Bartos, Joe, B, Navy, 1950
Bass, Mike, CB, Michigan, 1969-75
Bassi, Dick, G, Santa Clara, 1937

Batiste, Michael, G, Tulane, 1998
Battles, Cliff, B, West Virginia Wesleyan, 1932-37
Baugh, Sam, QB, TCU, 1937-52
Baughan, Maxie, LB, Georgia Tech, 1971
Bayless, Martin, S, Bowling Green, 1994
Beasley, Tom, DL, Virginia Tech, 1984-86
Beatty, Ed, C, Mississippi, 1961
Beban, Gary, QB, UCLA, 1968-69
Bedore, Tom, G, no college, 1944
Beinor, Ed, T, Notre Dame, 1942
Bell, Coleman, TE, Miami, 1994-95
Bell, William, RB, Georgia Tech, 1994-96
Benish, Dan, DT, Clemson, 1987
Benson, Cliff, TE, Purdue, 1987
Berrang, Ed, E, Villanova, 1949-52
Berschet, Merve, G, Illinois, 1954-55
Bigby, Keiron, WR, Brown, 1987
Biggs, Verlon, DE, Jackson State, 1971-75
Bingham, Guy, C, Montana, 1992-93
Birlem, Keith, B, San Jose State, 1939
Bishop, Harold, TE, LSU, 1996
Blanchard, Cary, K, Oklahoma State, 1998
Blanton, Scott, K, Oklahoma, 1996-98
Boensch, Fred, G, Stanford, 1947-48
Boll, Don, T, Nebraska, 1953-59
Bond, Chuck, T, Washington, 1937-38
Bond, Randal, B, Washington, 1938
Bonner, Brian, LB, Minnesota, 1989
Bosch, Frank, DT, Colorado, 1968-70
Bosseler, Don, B, Miami, 1957-64
Bostic, Jeff, C, Clemson, 1980-93
Boutte, Marc, DT, LSU, 1994-99
Bowie, Larry, FB, Georgia, 1996-99
Bowles, Todd, S, Temple, 1986-90, 1992-93
Boykin, Deral, S, Louisville, 1994
Braatz, Tom, DE, Marquette, 1957-59
Bradley, Harold, E, Elon, 1938
Bragg, Mike, P, Richmond, 1968-79
Branch, Reggie, RB, East Carolina, 1985-89
Brandes, John, TE, Cameron, 1990-92
Brantley, John, LB, Georgia, 1992-93
Breding, Ed, LB, Texas A&M, 1967-68
Breedlove, Rod, LB, Maryland, 1960-64
Brewer, Homer, B, Mississippi, 1960
Briggs, Bill, DE, Iowa, 1966-67
Briggs, Bob, B, Central Oklahoma State, 1965

Brilz, Darrick, G, Oregon State, 1987
Brito, Gene, DE, Loyola (CA), 1951-53, 1955-58
Britt, Ed, B, Holy Cross, 1937
Britt, Oscar, G, Mississippi, 1946
Brohm, Jeff, QB, Louisville, 1995
Brooks, Bill, WR, Boston University, 1996
Brooks, Perry, DT, Southern, 1978-84
Brooks, Reggie, RB, Notre Dame, 1993-95
Brown, Buddy, G, Arkansas, 1951-52
Brown, Charlie, WR, South Carolina St., 1982-84
Brown, Dan, E, Villanova, 1950
Brown, Doug, DT, Simon Fraser, 1998-99
Brown, Eddie, S, Tennessee, 1975-77
Brown, Hardy, LB, Tulsa, 1950
Brown, Jamie, T, Florida A&M, 1999
Brown, Larry, RB, Kansas State, 1969-76
Brown, Ray, G, Arkansas State, 1989-95
Brown, Tom, DB, Maryland, 1969
Brownlow, Darrick, LB, Illinois, 1995-96
Brueckman, Charley, C, Pittsburgh, 1958
Brundige, Bill, DE, Colorado, 1970-77
Brunet, Bob, RB, Louisiana Tech, 1968, 1970-77
Bryant, Kelvin, RB, North Carolina, 1986-88, 1990
Bryant, Trent, CB, Arkansas, 1981
Buck, Jason, DE, BYU, 1991-93
Buckley, Curtis, CB, East Texas State, 1999-2000
Budd, Frank, WR, Villanova, 1963
Buggs, Danny, WR, West Virginia, 1976-79
Bukich, Rudy, QB, USC, 1957-58
Buksar, George, B, Purdue, 1951-52
Bunch, Derek, LB, Michigan State, 1987
Burks, Shawn, LB, LSU, 1986
Burkus, Carl, T, George Washington, 1948
Burman, George, G, Northwestern, 1971-72
Burmeister, Danny, S, North Carolina, 1987
Burnett, Chester, LB, Arizona, 1998
Burrell, John, WR, Rice, 1966-67
Butkus, Carl, T, George Washington, 1948
Butsko, Harry, LB, Maryland, 1963
Butz, Dave, DT, Purdue, 1975-88
Byner, Earnest, RB, East Carolina, 1989-93

C.

Cafego, George, QB, Tennessee, 1943
Caldwell, Ravin, LB, Arkansas, 1987-92

Campbell, Jesse, S, North Carolina State, 1997-98
Campofreda, Nick, C, Western Maryland, 1944
Campora, Don, T, Pacific, 1953
Caravello, Joe, TE, Tulane, 1987-88
Carlson, Mark, T, S. Connecticut State, 1987
Carpenter, Brian, CB, Michigan, 1983-84
Carpenter, Preston, E, Arkansas, 1964-66
Carr, Jim, LB, Morris Harvey, 1964-65
Carrier, Mark, FS, USC, 2000
Carroll, Jim, LB, Notre Dame, 1966-68
Carroll, Leo, DE, San Diego State, 1969-70
Carroll, Vic, T, Nevada, 1936-42
Carson, John, E, Georgia, 1954-59
Carter, Tom, CB, Notre Dame, 1993-96
Casares, Rick, RB, Florida, 1965
Caster, Rich, TE, Jackson State, 1981-82
Castiglia, Jim, B, Georgetown, 1947-48
Catanho, Al, LB, Rutgers, 1996
Centers, Larry, RB, Stephen F. Austin, 1999-2000
Cherry, Raphel, S, Hawaii, 1985
Cheverko, George, B, Ohio State, 1948
Christensen, Erik, E, Richmond, 1956
Churchwell, Don, T, Mississippi, 1959
Cichowski, Gene, B, Indiana, 1958-59
Cifers, Ed, E, Tennessee, 1941-42, 1946
Clair, Frank, E, Ohio State, 1941
Claitt, Rickey, FB, Bethune-Cookman, 1980-81
Clark, Gary, WR, James Madison, 1985-92
Clark, Jim, G, Oregon, 1952-53
Clark, Mike, DE, Florida, 1981
Clay, Billie, B, Mississippi, 1966
Clay, Ozzie, B, Iowa State, 1964
Clifton, Gregory, WR, Johnson C. Smith, 1993
Cloud, John, B, William & Mary, 1952-53
Cochran, Tom, B, Auburn, 1949
Cofer, Joe, S, Tennessee, 1987
Coffey, Ken, S, SW Texas State, 1983-86
Coia, Angelo, WR, USC, 1964-65
Coleman, Greg, P, Florida A&M, 1988
Coleman, Marco, DE, Georgia Tech, 1999-2000
Coleman, Monte, LB, Central Arkansas, 1979-94
Collier, Jim, E, Arkansas, 1963
Collins, Andre, LB, Penn State, 1990-94
Collins, Shane, DE, Arizona State, 1992-94
Condit, Merle, B, Carnegie Tech, 1945
Conklin, Cary, QB, Washington, 1990-93

Conkright, Bill, C, Oklahoma, 1943
Connell, Albert, WR, Texas A&M, 1997-2000
Connell, Mike, P, Cincinnati, 1980-81
Conway, Brett, K, Penn State, 1998-2000
Cook, Anthony, DE, South Carolina St., 1999
Copeland, Anthony, LB, Louisville, 1987
Copeland, Danny, S, Eastern Kentucky, 1991-93
Corbitt, Don, C, Arizona, 1948
Coupee, Al, B, Iowa, 1946
Cowne, John, C, Virginia Tech, 1987
Cox, Bill, B, Duke, 1951-52, 1955
Cox, Steve, P, Arkansas, 1985-88
Coyle, Eric, C, Colorado, 1987-88
Crabb, Claude, CB, Colorado, 1962-63
Crane, Dennis, DT, USC, 1968-69
Crews, Terry, LB, Western Michigan, 1995
Crisler, Harold, E, San Jose State, 1948-49
Crissy, Cris, WR, Princeton, 1981
Croftcheck, Don, G, Indiana, 1965-66
Cronan, Peter, LB, Boston College, 1981-85
Cronin, Gene, DE, Pacific, 1961-62
Crossan, Dave, C, Maryland, 1965-69
Crotty, Jim, B, Notre Dame, 1960-61
Crutchfield, Buddy, CB, N. Carolina Central, 1998
Cudzik, Walt, C, Purdue, 1954
Cunningham, Doug, RB, Mississippi, 1974
Cunningham, Jim, RB, Pittsburgh, 1961-63
Curtis, Bobby, LB, Savannah State, 1987
Curtis, Mike, LB, Duke, 1977-78
Curtis, Travis, S, West Virginia, 1988, 1991
Cvercko, Andy, G, Northwestern, 1963

D.

Dahl, Bob, G, Notre Dame, 1996-97
Dale, Roland, E, Mississippi, 1950
Daniels, Calvin, LB, North Carolina, 1986
Darre, Bernie, G, Tulane, 1961
Davidson, Ben, DT, Washington, 1962-63
Davis, Andy, B, George Washington, 1952
Davis, Brian, CB, Nebraska, 1987-90
Davis, Fred, T, Alabama, 1941-42, 1945
Davis, Jack, G, Maryland, 1959
Davis, Stephen, RB, Auburn, 1996-2000
Davis, Wayne, DB, Indiana State, 1989-90
Davlin, Mike, T, San Francisco, 1955

Day, Eagle, QB, Mississippi, 1959-60
Deal, Rufus, B, Auburn, 1942
Dean, Fred, G, Texas Southern, 1978-82
Dean, Vernon, CB, San Diego State, 1982-87
DeCarlo, Art, DB, Georgia, 1956-57
DeCorrevont, Bill, B, Northwestern, 1945
Dee, Bob, DE, Holy Cross, 1957-58
Deeks, Don, T, Washington, 1947
DeFrance, Chris, WR, Arizona State, 1979
DeFruiter, Bob, B, Nebraska, 1945-47
Dekker, Al, WR, Michigan State, 1953
Deloplaine, Jack, RB, Salem College, 1978
DeMao, Al, C, Duquesne, 1945-53
Dennison, Glenn, TE, Miami, 1987
Denson, Moses, RB, MD Eastern Shore, 1974-75
Denton, Tim, CB, Sam Houston State, 1998-99
Dess, Darrell, G, North Carolina State, 1965-66
Didier, Clint, TE, Portland State, 1982-87
Didion, John, LB, Oregon State, 1969-70
Dishman, Cris, CB, Purdue, 1997-98
Doll, Don, DE, USC, 1953
Donnalley, Rick, C, North Carolina, 1984-85
Doolan, John, B, Georgetown, 1945
Dorow, Al, QB, Michigan State, 1954-56
Dow, Ken, B, Oregon State, 1941
Dowda, Harry, DB, Wake Forest, 1949-53
Dowler, Boyd, WR, Colorado, 1971
Drake, Troy, T, Indiana, 1998
Drakeford, Tyronne, CB, Virginia Tech, 2000
Drazenovich, Chuck, LB, Penn State, 1950-59
Dubinetz, Greg, G, Yale, 1979
DuBois, Phil, TE, San Diego State, 1979-80
Duckworth, Joe, E, Colgate, 1947
Dudley, Bill, RB, Virginia, 1950-51, 1953
Duff, Jamal, DE, San Diego State, 1997-98
Dugan, Fred, WR, Dayton, 1961-63
Duich, Steve, G, San Diego State, 1969
Dukes, Chad, RB, Pittsburgh, 1999-2000
Duncan, Leslie, DB, Jackson State, 1971-73
Dunn, Coye, B, USC, 1943
Dunn, K.D., TE, Clemson, 1987
Dupard, Reggie, RB, SMU, 1989-90
Dusek, Brad, LB, Texas A&M, 1974-81
Dwyer, Jack, DB, Loyola (CA), 1951
Dye, Les, E, Syracuse, 1944-45
Dyer, Henry, RB, Grambling, 1969-70

E.

Ecker, Enrique, T, John Carroll, 1952
Edwards, Brad, S, South Carolina, 1990-93
Edwards, Turk, T, Washington State, 1932-40
Edwards, Weldon, T, TCU, 1948
Eilers, Pat, DB, Notre Dame, 1992-94
Elewonibi, Moe, T, BYU, 1990-93
Ellard, Henry, WR, Fresno State, 1994-98
Elliott, Matt, C, Michigan, 1992
Ellis, Ed, T, Buffalo, 2000
Ellstrom, Marv, B, Oklahoma, 1943
Elmore, Doug, DB, Mississippi, 1962
Elter, Leo, RB, Duquesne, 1955-57
Emtman, Steve, DT, Washington, 1997
Erhardt, Clyde, C, Georgia, 1946-49
Erickson, Carl, C, Washington, 1938-39
Ervins, Ricky, RB, USC, 1991-94
Etherly, David, CB, Portland State, 1987
Evans, Charles, RB, USC, 1974
Evans, Greg, S, TCU, 1998
Evans, Leomont, S, Clemson, 1996-99
Evans, Reggie, RB, Richmond, 1983

F.

Fanucci, Mike, DE, Arizona State, 1972
Farkas, Andy, FB, Detroit, 1938-44
Farman, Dick, G, Washington State, 1939-43
Farmer, Tom, B, Iowa, 1947-48
Faulkner, Jeff, DE, Southern, 1993
Feagin, Tom, G, Houston, 1963
Felton, Ralph, LB, Maryland, 1954-60
Ferris, Neil, DB, Loyola (CA), 1951-52
Filchock, Frank, QB, Indiana, 1938-41, 1944-45
Fiorentino, Al, G, Boston College, 1943-44
Fischer, Mark, C, Purdue, 1998-2000
Fischer, Pat, CB, Nebraska, 1968-77
Fisher, Bob, T, USC, 1940
Flemister, Zeron, TE, Iowa, 2000
Flick, Tom, QB, Washington, 1981
Flores, Mike, DT, Louisville, 1995
Foltz, Vernon, C, St. Vincent's, 1944
Forte, Ike, RB, Arkansas, 1978-80
Foxx, Dion, LB, James Madison, 1995
Frain, Todd, TE, Nebraska, 1986

Francis, Dave, FB, Ohio State, 1963
Francis, James, LB, Baylor, 1999
Frazier, Frank, G, Miami, 1987
Freeman, Bob, DB, Auburn, 1962
Frerrote, Gus, QB, Tulsa, 1994-98
Friesz, John, QB, Idaho, 1994
Frisch, Dave, TE, Colorado State, 1997
Fritsch, Ted, C, St. Norbert, 1976-79
Fryar, Irving, WR, Nebraska, 1999-2000
Fryer, Brian, WR, Alberta (Canada), 1976-78
Fugett, Jean, TE, Amherst, 1976-79
Fulcher, Bill, G, Georgia Tech, 1956-58
Fuller, Larry, B, no college, 1944-45

G.

Gaffney, Jim, B, Tennessee, 1945-46
Gage, Steve, S, Tulsa, 1987-88
Gaines, William, DT, Florida, 1995-97
Galbraith, Scott, TE, USC, 1995-96
Gannon, Rich, QB, Delaware, 1993
Garner, Dwight, RB, California, 1986
Garrett, Alvin, WR, Angelo State, 1981-84
Garzoni, Mike, B, USC, 1947
Geathers, James, DT, Wichita State, 1990-92
Gentry, Lee, B, Tulsa, 1941
George, Jeff, QB, Illinois, 2000
German, Jim, QB, Centre College, 1939
Gesek, John, C, Cal State Sacramento, 1994-95
Giaquinto, Nick, RB, Connecticut, 1981-83
Gibson, Alec, DT, Illinois, 1987
Gibson, Joe, B, Tulsa, 1943
Gilbert, Sean, DT, Pittsburgh, 1996
Gilmer, Harry, QB, Alabama, 1948-52, 1954
Givens, Reggie, LB, Penn State, 2000
Glick, Gary, DB, Colorado A&M, 1959-61
Gob, Art, E, Pittsburgh, 1959-60
Gogolak, Charlie, K, Princeton, 1966-68
Goodburn, Kelly, P, Emporia State, 1990-93
Goode, Bob, RB, Texas A&M, 1949-51, 1954-55
Goodnight, Clyde, E, Tulsa, 1949-50
Goodyear, John, B, Marquette, 1942
Goosby, Tom, G, Baldwin-Wallace, 1966
Gouveia, Kurt, LB, BYU, 1987-94, 1999
Graf, Dave, LB, Penn State, 1981
Graf, Rick, LB, Wisconsin, 1993

Graham, Don, LB, Penn State, 1989
Grant, Alan, CB, Stanford, 1994
Grant, Bob, LB, Wake Forest, 1971
Grant, Darryl, DT, Rice, 1981-90
Grant, Frank, WR, S. Colorado State, 1973-78
Gray, Bill, G, Oregon State, 1947-48
Green, Darrell, CB, Texas A&I, 1983-2000
Green, Robert, RB, William & Mary, 1992
Green, Tony, RB, Florida, 1978
Green, Trent, QB, Indiana, 1995-98
Griffin, Keith, RB, Miami, 1984-88
Grimm, Dan, C, Colorado, 1969
Grimm, Russ, G, Pittsburgh, 1981-91
Guglielmi, Ralph, QB, Notre Dame, 1955, 1958-60
Gulledge, David, FS, Jacksonville State, 1992

H.

Hackbart, Dale, DB, Wisconsin, 1961-63
Hageman, Fred, C, Kansas, 1961-64
Haight, Mike, T, Iowa, 1992
Haines, Kris, WR, Notre Dame, 1979
Haji-Sheikh, Ali, K, Michigan, 1987
Haley, Dick, DB, Pittsburgh, 1959-60
Hall, Galen, QB, Penn State, 1962
Hall, Windlan, DB, Arizona State, 1977
Ham, Derrick, DE, Miami, 1999-2000
Hamel, Dean, DT, Tulsa, 1985-88
Hamilton, Malcolm, LB, Baylor, 1998-99
Hamilton, Rick, LB, Central Florida, 1993-94
Hamilton, Steve, DE, East Carolina, 1985-88
Hamlin, Gene, C, Western Michigan, 1970
Hammond, Bobby, RB, Morgan State, 1979-80
Hanburger, Chris, LB, North Carolina, 1965-78
Hancock, Mike, TE, Idaho State, 1973-75
Hanna, Zip, G, South Carolina, 1945
Hansen, Ron, G, Minnesota, 1954
Harbour, Dave, C, Illinois, 1988-89
Hardeman, Buddy, RB, Iowa State, 1979-80
Hare, Cecil, FB, Gonzaga, 1941-42, 1945
Hare, Ray, QB, Gonzaga, 1940-43
Harlan, Jim, T, Howard Payne, 1978
Harmon, Clarence, RB, Mississippi State, 1977-82
Harold, George, B, Allen, 1968
Harraway, Charley, RB, San Jose State, 1969-73

Harris, Don, S, Rutgers, 1978-79
Harris, Hank, G, Texas, 1947-48
Harris, Jim, DB, Howard Payne, 1970
Harris, Joe, LB, Georgia Tech, 1977
Harris, Rickie, DB, Arizona, 1965-70
Harrison, Kenny, WR, SMU , 1980
Harrison, Lloyd, CB, North Carolina State, 2000
Harrison, Nolan, DE, Indiana, 2000
Harry, Carl, WR, Utah, 1989, 92
Hart, Jim, QB, Southern Illinois, 1984
Hartley, Howard, B, Duke, 1948
Hartman, Bill, B, Georgia, 1938
Harvey, Ken, LB, California, 1994-98
Harvin, Allen, RB, Cincinnati, 1987
Hatcher, Ron, FB, Michigan State, 1962
Hauss, Len, C, Georgia, 1964-77
Haws, Kurt, TE, Utah, 1994
Hayden, Ken, C, Arkansas, 1943
Hayes, Jeff, P, North Carolina, 1982-85
Haymond, Alvin, DB, Southern, 1972
Haynes, Hall, DB, Santa Clara, 1950, 1953-55
Haynes, Reggie, TE, UNLV, 1978
Hazelwood, Ted, T, North Carolina, 1953
Heath, Leon, FB, Oklahoma, 1951-53
Heck, Andy, T, Notre Dame, 1999-2000
Hecker, Norb, DB, Baldwin-Wallace, 1955-57
Heenan, Pat, E, Notre Dame, 1960
Hegarty, Bill, T, Villanova, 1960
Heinz, Bob, DT, Pacific, 1978
Hendershot, Larry, LB, Arizona State, 1967
Henderson, Jon, WR, Colorado State, 1970
Hendren, Bob, T, USC, 1949-51
Hennessey, Jerry, DE, Santa Clara, 1952-53
Hermeling, Terry, T, Nevada, 1970-80
Hernandez, Joe, WR, Arizona, 1964
Hickman, Dallas, DE, California, 1976-81
Hickman, Donnie, G, USC, 1978
Hicks, Skip, RB, UCLA, 1998-2000
Hill, Calvin, RB, Yale, 1976-77
Hill, Nate, DE, Auburn, 1989
Hitchcock, Ray, C, Minnesota, 1987
Hoage, Terry, S, Georgia, 1991
Hobbs, Stephen, WR, North Alabama, 1990-92
Hochertz, Martin, DE, Southern Illinois, 1993
Hodgson, Pat, TE, Georgia, 1966
Hoelscher, David, DT, Eastern Kentucky, 1998

Hoffman, Bob, QB, USC, 1940-41
Hoffman, John, DE, Hawaii, 1969-70
Hogeboom, Gary, QB, Central Michigan, 1990
Hollar, John, B, Appalachian State, 1948-49
Hollinquest, Lamont, LB, USC, 1993-94
Holloway, Derek, WR, Arkansas, 1986
Holly, Bob, QB, Princeton, 1982-83
Holman, Walter, RB, West Virginia State, 1987
Holman, Willie, DE, South Carolina State, 1973
Horner, Sam, B, VMI, 1960-61
Horton, Ethan, TE, North Carolina, 1994
Hostetler, Jeff, QB, West Virginia, 1997
Houghton, Jerry, T, Washington State, 1950
Houston, Ken, S, Prairie View, 1973-80
Houston, Walt, G, Purdue, 1955
Hover, Don, LB, Washington State, 1978-79
Howard, Desmond, WR, Michigan, 1992-94
Howell, Dixie, B, Alabama, 1937
Hudson, Bob, G, Clemson, 1959
Huff, Ken, G, North Carolina, 1983-85
Huff, Sam, LB, West Virginia, 1964-67, 1969
Hughley, George, FB, Central Oklahoma State, 1965
Hull, Mike, RB, USC, 1971-74
Humphries, Stan, QB, NE Louisiana, 1989-91
Huntington, Greg, C, Penn State, 1993
Hunter, Bill, DB, Syracuse, 1965
Husak, Todd, QB, Stanford, 2000
Hyatt, Fred, WR, Auburn, 1973

I.

Imhof, Martin, DE, San Diego State, 1974
Irwin, Don, FB, Colgate, 1936-39
Izo, George, QB, Notre Dame, 1961-64

J.

Jackson, Charles, S, Texas Tech, 1987
Jackson, Leroy, RB, Western Illinois, 1962-63
Jackson, Steve, LB, Texas-Arlington, 1966-67
Jackson, Trenton, WR, Illinois, 1967
Jackson, Wilbur, FB, Alabama, 1980-82
Jacobs, Jack, QB, Oklahoma, 1946
Jacoby, Joe, T/G, Louisville, 1981-93
Jaffurs, John, G, Penn State, 1946
Jagielski, Harry, T, Indiana, 1956

James, Dick, RB, Oregon, 1956-63
Janowicz, Vic, B, Ohio State, 1954-55
Jansen, Jon, T, Michigan, 1999-2000
Jaqua, Jon, S, Lewis & Clark, 1970-72
Jefferson, Roy, WR, Utah, 1971-76
Jencks, Bob, K/E, Miami (OH), 1965
Jenkins, Jacque, FB, Vanderbilt, 1943, 1946
Jenkins, James, TE, Rutgers, 1991-2000
Jenkins, Ken, RB, Bucknell, 1985-86
Jessie, Tim, RB, Auburn, 1987
Johnson, AJ, SW Texas State, 1989-94
Johnson, Andre, T, Penn State, 1996
Johnson, Billy, WR, Widener, 1988
Johnson, Brad, QB, Minnesota, 1999-2000
Johnson, Dennis, DT, Delaware, 1974-77
Johnson, Jimmie, TE, Howard, 1989-91
Johnson (Howard), Joe, WR, Notre Dame, 1989-91
Johnson, Larry, C, Haskell Indian, 1944
Johnson, Mitch, T, UCLA, 1966-68, 1972
Johnson, Randy, QB, Texas A&I, 1975-76
Johnson, Richard, WR, Colorado, 1987
Johnson, Sidney, CB, California, 1990-92
Johnson, Tim, DT, Penn State, 1990-95
Johnson, Tré, T, Temple, 1994-2000
Johnston, Jim, B, Washington, 1939-40
Jones, Anthony, TE, Wichita State, 1984-88
Jones, Chuck, E, George Washington , 1955
Jones, David, C, Texas, 1987
Jones, Deacon, DE, Mississippi Vocational, 1974
Jones, Greg, LB, Colorado, 1997-2000
Jones, Harvey, B, Baylor, 1947
Jones, Jimmie, DE, Wichita State, 1971-73
Jones, Joe, DE, Tennessee State, 1979-80
Jones, Larry, WR, NE Missouri State, 1974-77
Jones, Larry, FB, Miami, 1995
Jones, Melvin, G, Houston, 1981
Jones, Stan, DT, Maryland, 1966
Jordan, Curtis, FS, Texas Tech, 1981-86
Jordan, Jeff, RB, Washington, 1971-72
Junker, Steve, E, Xavier, 1961-62
Junkin, Trey, LB, Louisiana Tech, 1984
Jurgensen, Sonny, QB, Duke, 1964-74
Justice, Charlie, RB, North Carolina, 1950, 1952-54
Justice, Ed, B, Gonzaga, 1936-42
Juzwik, Steve, B, Notre Dame, 1942

K.

Kahn, Ed, G, North Carolina, 1935-37
Kalaniuvalu, Alai, G, Oregon State, 1994
Kalu, Ndukwe, DE, Rice, 1998-2000
Kammerer, Carl, DE, Pacific, 1963-69
Kane, Rick, RB, San Jose State, 1984
Kantor, Joe, RB, Notre Dame, 1966
Karamatic, George, B, Gonzaga, 1938
Karas, Emil, E, Dayton, 1959
Karcher, Jim, G, Ohio State, 1936-39
Karras, Lou, T, Purdue, 1950-51
Karras, Ted, DT, Northwestern, 1987
Katrishen, Mike, T, Southern Mississippi, 1948-49
Kaufman, Mel, LB, Cal Poly SLO, 1981-88
Kawal, Ed, C, Illinois, 1937
Keating, Chris, LB, Maine, 1985
Keenan, Jack, T, South Carolina, 1944-45
Kehr, Rick, G, Carthage, 1987-88
Kelley, Gordon, LB, Georgia, 1962-63
Kelly, John, T, Florida A&M, 1966-67
Kerr, Jim, DB, Penn State, 1961-62
Khayat, Bob, K, Mississippi, 1960, 1962-63
Khayat, Ed, DT, Tulane, 1957, 1962-63
Kiick, Jim, RB, Wyoming, 1977
Kilmer, Bill, QB, UCLA, 1971-78
Kimball, Bruce, G, Massachusetts, 1983-84
Kimble, Garry, CB, Sam Houston State, 1987
Kimmel, J.D., T, Houston, 1955-56
Kimmel, John, LB, Colgate, 1987
Kincaid, Jim, B, South Carolina, 1954
Kinney, Kelvin, DE, Virginia State, 1997-98
Kirk, Randy, LB, San Diego State, 1990
Kitts, Jim, FB, Ferrum, 1998
Knight, Curt, K, Coast Guard, 1969-73
Koch, Markus, DE, Boise State, 1986-91
Koniszewski, John, T, Geo. Wash., 1945-46, 1948
Kopay, Dave, RB, Washington, 1969-70
Kovatch, John, E, Notre Dame, 1942-46
Krakoski, Joe, B, Illinois, 1961
Krakoski, Joe, LB, Washington, 1986
Krause, Max, FB, Gonzaga, 1937-40
Krause, Paul, DB, Iowa, 1964-67
Krause, Red, C, St. Louis, 1938
Kreuger, Al, RB, USC, 1941-42

Krouse, Ray, T, Maryland, 1960
Kruczek, Mike, QB, Boston College, 1980
Kubin, Larry, LB, Penn State, 1982-84
Kuchta, Frank, C, Notre Dame, 1959
Kuehl, Ryan, DT, Virginia, 1996-97
Kupp, Jake, G, Washington, 1966
Kuziel, Bob, G, Pittsburgh, 1975-80

L.

Laaveg, Paul, G, Iowa, 1970-75
Lachey, Jim, T, Ohio State, 1988-95
Lane, Skip, S, Mississippi, 1987
Lang, Kenard, DE, Miami, 1997-2000
Lapka, Ted, E. St. Ambrose, 1943-44, 1946
Larson, Bill, TE, Colorado State, 1977
Larson, Pete, RB, Cornell, 1967-68
Lasse, Dick, LB, Syracuse, 1960-61
Lathrop, Kit, DT, Arizona State, 1987
Laster, Donald, T, Tennessee State, 1982-83
Laufenberg, Babe, QB, Indiana, 1983-85
Lavender, Joe, CB, San Diego State, 1976-82
Law, Dennis, WR, East Tennessee State, 1979
Lawrence, Don, T, Notre Dame, 1959-61
LeBaron, Eddie, QB, Pacific, 1952-53, 1955-59
Leeuwenburg, Jay, G, Colorado, 2000
Lemek, Ray, T, Notre Dame, 1957-61
Lennan, Reid, G, no college, 1945
Leon, Tony, G, Alabama, 1943
Lewis, Dan, RB, Wisconsin, 1965
Lewis, Ron, G, Washington State, 1995
Liebenstein, Todd, DE, UNLV, 1982-85
Lipscomb, Paul, T, Tennessee, 1950-54
Livingston, Howie, B, Fullerton JC, 1948-50
Lockett, J.W., B, Central Oklahoma State, 1964
Logan, Marc, FB, Kentucky, 1995-97
Lohmiller, Chip, K, Minnesota, 1988-94
Lolatai, Al, G, Weber State, 1945
Long, Bob, WR, Wichita State, 1969
Lookabaugh, John, E, Maryland, 1946-47
Looney, Joe Don, RB, Oklahoma, 1966-67
Lorch, Karl, DT, USC, 1976-81
Love, John, WR, North Texas State, 1967
Lowe, Gary, B, Michigan State, 1956-57
Lowry, Quentin, LB, Youngstown State, 1981-83

Luce, Lew, B, Penn State, 1961
Lynch, Dick, B, Notre Dame, 1958

M.

MacAfee, Ken, E, Alabama, 1959
Macioszczck, Art, FB, Western Michigan, 1948
Madarik, Elmer, B, Detroit, 1948
Malinchak, Bill, WR, Indiana, 1970-74, 1976
Malone, Benny, RB, Arizona State, 1978-79
Malone, Charley, E, Texas A&M, 1934-40, 1942
Mandeville, Chris, DB, Cal-Davis, 1989
Manley, Dexter, DE, Oklahoma State, 1981-89
Mann, Charles, DE, Nevada-Reno, 1983-93
Manton, Tillie, FB, TCU, 1938
Manusky, Greg, LB, Colgate, 1988-90
Marciniak, Ron, C, Kansas State, 1955
Marcus, Pete, E, Kentucky, 1944
Marshall, Leonard, DT, LSU, 1994
Marshall, Rich, T, Stephen F. Austin, 1966
Marshall, Wilber, LB, Florida, 1988-92
Martin, Aaron, DB, North Carolina College, 1968
Martin, Jamie, QB, Weber State, 1997
Martin, Jim, K, Notre Dame, 1964
Martin, Steve, DE, Jackson State, 1987
Mason, Eddie, LB, North Carolina, 1999-2000
Mason, Tommy, RB, Tulane, 1971-72
Masterson, Bob, E, Miami, 1938-43
Maston, Le'Shai, FB, Baylor, 1998
Matich, Trevor, C, BYU, 1994-96
Mattson, Riley, T, Oregon, 1961-64
Mauti, Rich, WR, Penn State, 1984
May, Mark, T, Pittsburgh, 1981-89
Mayhew, Martin, CB, Florida State, 1989-92
Mays, Alvoid, CB, West Virginia, 1990-94
Mays, Damon, WR, Missouri, 1996
Mazurek, Fred, B, Pittsburgh, 1965-66
McCabe, Dick, B, Pittsburgh, 1959
McCloud, Tyrus, LB, Louisville, 2000
McChesney, Bob, E, UCLA, 1936-42
McCrary, Greg, TE, Clark, 1978, 1981
McDaniel, John, WR, Lincoln, 1978-80
McDaniel, Le Charls, CB, Cal Poly SLO, 1981-82
McDole, Ron, DE, Nebraska, 1971-78
McDonald, Ray, RB, Idaho, 1967-68
McEwen, Craig, TE, Utah, 1987-88

McGee, Tim, WR, Tennessee, 1993
McGee, Tony, DE, Bishop (TX), 1982-84
McGrath, Mark, WR, Montana State, 1983-85
McGriff, Curtis, DT, Alabama, 1987
McKee, Paul, E, Syracuse, 1947-48
McKeever, Marlin, LB, USC, 1968-70
McKenzie, Raleigh, G, Tennessee, 1985-94
McKinney, Zion, WR, South Carolina, 1980
McLinton, Harold, LB, Southern, 1969-78
McMillan, Mark, CB, Alabama, 1999
McNeil, Clifton, WR, Grambling, 1971-72
McQuaid, Dan, T, UNLV, 1985-87
McQuilken, Kim, QB, Lehigh, 1978-80
McRae, Stan, E, Michigan State, 1946
Meade, Jim, B, Maryland, 1939-40
Meads, Johnny, LB, Nicholls State, 1992
Meadows, Ed, DB, Duke, 1959
Melinger, Steve, E, Kentucky, 1956-57
Mendenhall, Mat, DE, BYU, 1981-82
Merkle, Ed, G, Oklahoma A&M, 1944
Mercein, Chuck, RB, Yale, 1969
Metcalf, Terry, RB, San Diego State, 1981
Michaels, Ed, G, Villanova, 1937
Micka, Mike, FB, Colgate, 1944
Mickles, Joe, RB, Mississippi, 1989
Middleton, Ron, TE, Auburn, 1988, 1990-93
Millen, Matt, LB, Penn State, 1991
Miller, Allen, LB, Ohio, 1962-63
Miller, Clark, DE, Utah State, 1969
Miller, Dan, K, Florida, 1982
Miller, Fred, T, Pacific, 1955
Miller, John, T, Boston College, 1956, 1958-59
Miller, Norman, RB, Texas A & M, 1999
Miller, Tom, B, Hampden-Sydney, 1945
Millner, Wayne, E, Notre Dame, 1936-41, 1945
Mills, Lamar, DT, Indiana, 1994
Milot, Rich, LB, Penn State, 1979-87
Milstead, Rod, G, Delaware State, 1998-99
Mims, Chris, DT, Tennessee, 1997
Mingo, Gene, K, no college, 1967
Mitchell, Bobby, FL, Illinois, 1962-68
Mitchell, Brian, RB, SW Louisiana, 1990-99
Mitchell, Kevin, LB, Syracuse, 2000
Mitchell, Michael, CB, Howard Payne, 1987
Modzelewski, Dick, DT, Maryland, 1953-54
Mojsiejenko, Ralf, P, Michigan State, 1989-90

Momsen, Tony, C, Michigan, 1952
Monachino, Jim, B, California, 1955
Monaco, Ray, G, Holy Cross, 1944
Monasco, Don, B, Texas, 1954
Monk, Art, WR, Syracuse, 1980-92
Mont, Tommy, QB, Maryland, 1947-49
Moore, Chuck, G, Arkansas, 1962
Moore, Darryl, G, UTEP, 1992-93
Moore, Jeff, RB, Jackson State, 1984
Moore, Michael, G, Troy State (AL), 2000
Moore, Wilbur, B, Minnesota, 1939-46
Morgan, Bob, DT, Maryland, 1954
Morgan, Boyd, S, USC, 1939-40
Morgan, Mike, LB, LSU, 1968
Morley, Sam, E, Stanford, 1954
Morris, Jamie, RB, Michigan, 1988-89
Morrison, Darryl, S, Arizona, 1993-96
Morrison, Tim, CB, North Carolina, 1986-87
Mortensen, Fred, QB, Arizona State, 1979
Morton, Michael, RB, UNLV, 1985
Moseley, Mark, K, Stephen F. Austin, 1974-86
Moss, Eddie, RB, SE Missouri State, 1977
Moss, Joe, T, Maryland, 1952
Muhammad, Calvin, WR, Texas Southern, 1984-85
Mul-Key, Herb, RB, no college, 1972-74
Murphy, Mark, S, Colgate, 1977-84
Murray, Eddie, K, Tulane, 1995
Murrell, Adrian, RB, West Virginia, 2000
Musgrove, Spain, DT, Utah State, 1967-69
Myslinski, Tom, G, Tennessee, 1992

N

Natowich, Andy, B, Holy Cross, 1944
Nelms, Mike, KR, Baylor, 1980-84
Nelson, Ralph, RB, no college, 1975
Niemi, Laurie, T, Washington State, 1949-53
Nichols, Gerald, DT, Florida State, 1993
Ninowski, Jim, QB, Michigan State, 1967-68
Nisby, John, G, Pacific, 1962-64
Nix, Doyle, B, SMU, 1958-59
Nobile, Leo, G, Penn State, 1947
Noble, James, WR, Stephen F. Austin, 1986
Nock, George, RB, Morgan State, 1972
Noga, Al, DE, Hawaii, 1993
Norman, Jim, T, no college, 1955

Norris, Hal, B, California, 1955-56
North, Jim, T, Central Washington, 1944
Norton, Jim, T, Washington, 1969
Nottage, Dexter, DE, Florida A&M, 1994-96
Nugent, Dan, G, Auburn, 1976-78, 1980
Nussbaumer, Bob, E, Michigan, 1947-48

O.

O'Brien, Fran, T, Michigan State, 1960-66
O'Dell, Stu, LB, Indiana, 1974-76
Ogrin, Pat, DT, Wyoming, 1981-82
Oliphant, Mike, RB, Puget Sound, 1988
Oliver, Muhammad, CB, Oregon, 1995
Olkewicz, Neal, LB, Maryland, 1979-89
Olsson, Les, G, Mercer, 1934-38
Olszewski, John, B, California, 1958-60
Orr, Terry, TE, Texas, 1986-92
Osborne, Tom, WR, Hastings (NE), 1960-61
Ostrowski, Chet, E, Notre Dame, 1954-59
Osterhout, Jon, G, Cal St. (Sacramento), 2000
Owen, Tom, QB, Wichita State, 1982
Owens, Brig, DB, Cincinnati, 1966-77
Owens, Don, T, Southern Mississippi, 1957
Owens, Rich, DE, Lehigh, 1995-97

P.

Paine, Jeff, LB, San Jose State, 1986
Paluck, John, DE, Pittsburgh, 1956, 1959-65
Palmer, Sterling, DE, Florida State, 1993-96
Papit, John, B, Virginia, 1951-53
Pardee, Jack, LB, Texas A&M, 1971-72
Parks, Mickey, C, Oklahoma, 1938-40
Parrish, Lemar, CB, Lincoln, 1978-81
Pasqua, Joe, T, SMU, 1943
Paternoster, Angelo, G, Georgetown, 1943
Patton, Joe, T, Alabama A&M, 1994-98
Patton, Marvcus, LB, UCLA, 1995-98
Paul, Tito, CB, Ohio State, 1999
Pebbles, Jim, E, Vanderbilt , 1946-49, 1951
Peete, Rodney, QB, USC, 1999
Peiffer, Dan, C, Southeast Missouri State, 1980
Pellegrini, Bob, LB, Maryland, 1962-65
Pepper, Gene, G, Missorui, 1950-53
Pergine, John, LB, Notre Dame, 1973-75

Perrin, Lonnie, RB, Illinois, 1979
Peters, Floyd, T, San Francisco State, 1970
Peters, Tony, S, Oklahoma, 1979-82, 1984-85
Peters, Volney, T, USC, 1954-57
Peterson, Nelson, RB, West Virginia Wesleyan, 1937
Pettey, Phil, G, Missouri, 1987
Petitbon, Richie, S, Tulane, 1971-72
Phillips, Joe, WR, Kentucky, 1985-87
Piasecky, Al, E, Duke, 1943-45
Pierce, Dan, RB, Memphis State, 1970
Pinckert, Erny, FB, USC, 1937-40
Planutis, Jerry, B, Michigan State, 1956
Podoley, Jim, RB, Central Michigan, 1957-60
Poillon, Dick, B, Canisius, 1942, 1946-49
Polsfoot, Fran, E, Washington State, 1953
Ponds, Antwaune, LB, Syracuse, 1998
Porter, Juan,C, Ohio State, 1999
Pounds, Darryl, CB, Nicholls State, 1995-99
Pourdanish, Shar, T, Nevada, 1996-98
Pottios, Myron, LB, Notre Dame, 1971-73
Presley, Leo, C, Oklahoma, 1945
Prestel, Jim, T, Idaho, 1966-67
Promuto, Vince, G, Holy Cross, 1960-70

Q.

Query, Jeff, WR, Millikin, 1995
Quinlan, Bill, DE, Michigan State, 1965
Quirk, Ed, B, Missouri, 1948-51

R.

Raab, Marc, C, USC, 1993
Raba, Bob, TE, Maryland, 1981
Rae, Mike, QB, USC, 1981
Ramsey, Knox, G, William & Mary, 1952-53
Raymer, Cory, C, Wisconsin, 1995-2000
Reaves, Willard, RB, Northern Arizona, 1989
Rector, Ron, B, Northwestern, 1966
Reed, Alvin, TE, Prairie View, 1973-75
Reed, Bob, G, Tennessee State, 1965
Reem, Matt, T, Minnesota, 1996
Reger, John, LB, Pittsburgh, 1964-66
Renfro, Will, T, Memphis State, 1957-59
Reynolds, Mack, QB, LSU, 1960
Ribar, Frank, G, Duke, 1943

Ricca, Jim, C, Georgetown, 1951-54
Richard, Stanley, S, Texas, 1995-98
Richardson, Grady, TE, Cal St. Fullerton, 1979-80
Richardson, Huey, LB, Florida, 1992
Richter, Pat, WR, Wisconsin, 1963-70
Riggins, John, RB, Kansas, 1976-79, 1981-85
Riggs, Gerald, RB, Arizona State, 1989-91
Riggs, Jim, TE, Clemson, 1993
Roberts, Walter, WR, San Jose State, 1969-70
Robinson, Dave, LB, Penn State, 1973-74
Robinson, Lybrant, DE, Delaware State, 1989
Robinson, Tony, QB, Tennessee, 1987
Roby, Reggie, P, Iowa, 1993-94
Rock, Walter, T, Maryland, 1968-73
Rocker, Tracy, DT, Auburn, 1989-90
Roehnelt, Bill, LB, Bradley, 1960
Rogers, George, RB, South Carolina, 1985-87
Rosato, Sal, B, Villanova, 1945-47
Rose, Carlton, LB, Michigan, 1987
Rosso, George, B, Ohio State, 1954
Roussel, Tom, LB, Southern Mississippi, 1968-70
Roussos, Mike, T, Pittsburgh, 1948-49
Rowe, Ray, TE, San Diego State, 1992
Rubbert, Ed, QB, Louisville, 1987
Rucker, Keith, DT, Ohio Wesleyan, 1997
Runnels, Tom, RB, North Texas State, 1956-57
Rush, Tyrone, RB, North Alabama, 1994
Russell, Bo, T, Auburn, 1939-40
Russell, Twan, LB, Miami, 1997-99
Rutgens, Joe, DT, Illinois, 1961-69
Ruthstrom, Ralph, B, SMU, 1947
Rutledge, Jeff, QB, Alabama, 1990-92
Ryan, Frank, QB, Rice, 1969-70
Ryczek, Dan, C, Virginia, 1973-75
Rykovich, Jules, B, Illinois, 1952-53
Rymkus, Lou, T, Notre Dame, 1943
Rypien, Mark, QB, Washington State, 1987-93
Rzempoluch, Ted, DB, Virginia, 1963

S.

Saenz, Eddie, RB, USC, 1946-51

Sagnella, Anthony, DT, Rutgers, 1987
Salem, Ed, B, Alabama, 1951
Salter, Bryant, S, Pittsburgh, 1974-75
Sample, Johnny, DB, Maryland State, 1963-65
Samuels, Chris, T, Alabama, 2000
Sanchez, John, T, San Francisco, 1947-49
Sanders, Chris, TE, Texas A&M, 1997
Sanders, Deion, CB, Florida State, 2000
Sanders, Lonnie, DB, Michigan State, 1963-67
Sanders, Ricky, WR, SW Texas State, 1986-93
Sandifer, Dan, DB, LSU, 1948-49
Sanford, Haywood, E, Alabama, 1940
Sardisco, Tony, G, Tulane, 1956
Sasa, Don, DT, Washington State, 1997
Saul, Ron, G, Michigan State, 1976-81
Savage, Sebastian, CB, North Carolina State, 1995
Sawyer, John, TE, Southern Mississippi, 1983
Scanlan, Jerry, T, Hawaii, 1980-81
Scarbath, Jack, QB, Maryland, 1953-54
Schick, Doyle, LB, Kansas, 1961
Schilling, Ralph, E, Oklahoma City, 1946
Schlereth, Mark, G, Idaho, 1989-94
Schoenke, Ray, G, SMU, 1966-75
Schrader, Jim, C, Notre Dame, 1954, 1956-61
Schroeder, Jay, QB, UCLA, 1984-88
Scissum, Williard, G, Alabama, 1987
Scott, Jake, S, Georgia, 1976-78
Scotti, Ben, DB, Maryland, 1959-61
Scudero, Joe, B, San Francisco, 1954-58
Scully, Mike, C, Illinois, 1988
Seals, George, G, Missouri, 1964
Seay, Virgil, WR, Troy State, 1981-84
Sebek, Nick, B, Indiana, 1950
Sedoris, Chris, C, Purdue, 1996
Seedborg, John, E, Arizona State, 1965
Sellers, Mike, TE, Walla Walla, 1999-2000
Seno, Frank, B, George Washington, 1943-44, 1949
Settles, Tony, LB, Elon, 1987
Severson, Jeff, DB, Long Beach State, 1972
Shade, Sam, S, Alabama, 1999-2000
Seymour, Bob, B, Oklahoma, 1940-45
Sharp, Everett, T, California Tech, 1944-45
Shepard, Derrick, WR, Oklahoma, 1987-88
Shepherd, Leslie, WR, Temple, 1994-98
Shiner, Dick, QB, Maryland, 1964-66
Shoener, Herb, E, Iowa, 1948-49

Shorter, Jim, DB, Detroit, 1964-67
Shugart, Clyde, G, Iowa State, 1939-43
Shula, Don, DB, John Carroll, 1957
Shuler, Heath, QB, Tennessee, 1994-96
Siegert, Herb, G, Illinois, 1949-51
Siever, Paul, T, Penn State, 1992-93
Simmons, Ed, T, Eastern Washington, 1987-97
Simmons, Roy, G, Georgia Tech, 1983
Sims, Keith, G, Iowa State, 1997-2000
Sistrunk, Manny, DT, Arkansas AM&N, 1970-75
Slivinski, Steve, G, Washington, 1939-43
Smith, Ben, E, Alabama, 1937
Smith, Bruce, DE, Virginia Tech, 2000
Smith, Cedric, FB, Florida, 1994-95
Smith, Chris, TE, Texas, 2000
Smith, Derek G., T, Virginia Tech, 1999-2000
Smith, Derek M., LB, Arizona State, 1997-2000
Smith, Dick, DB, Northwestern, 1967-68
Smith, George, C, California, 1937, 1941-43
Smith, Hugh, E, Kansas, 1962
Smith, Jack, E, Stanford, 1943
Smith, Jerry, TE, Arizona State, 1965-77
Smith, Jim, DB, Oregon, 1968
Smith, Jimmy, RB, Elon, 1984
Smith, John, WR, North Texas State, 1978
Smith, Larry, RB, Florida, 1974
Smith, Paul, DE, New Mexico, 1979-80
Smith, Ricky, CB, Alabama State, 1984
Smith, Riley, QB, Alabama, 1937-38
Smith, Timmy, RB, Texas Tech, 1987-88
Smith, Vernice, G, Florida A&M, 1993-95
Snead, Norm, QB, Wake Forest, 1961-63
Sneddon, Bob, B, St. Mary's (CA), 1944
Snidow, Ron, DE, Oregon, 1963-67
Snipes, Angelo, LB, West Georgia, 1986
Snowden, Jim, T, Notre Dame, 1965-72
Sobolenski, Joe, G, Michigan, 1949
Sommer, Mike, B, Geo. Wash., 1958-59, 1961
Sommers, John, C, UCLA, 1947
Spaniel, Frank, B, Notre Dame, 1950
Sparks, Dave, G, South Carolina, 1954
Spirida, John, E, St. Anselm's, 1939
Stacco, Ed, T, Colgate, 1948
Stallings, Don, E, North Carolina, 1960
Stanfel, Dick, G, San Francisco, 1956-58

Stanley, Walter, WR, Mesa (CO), 1990
Starke, George, T, Columbia, 1973-84
Stasica, Leo, B, Colorado, 1943
Staton, Jim, T, Wake Forest, 1951
Steber, John, G, Georgia Tech, 1946-50
Steffen, Jim, DB, UCLA, 1961-65
Stenn, Paul, T, Villanova, 1946
Stensrud, Mike, DT, Iowa State, 1989
Stephens, Louis, G, San Francisco, 1955-60
Stephens, Rod, LB, Georgia Tech, 1995-96
Stevens, Matt, S, Appalachian State, 1998-2000
Stief, Dave, WR, Portland State, 1983
Stits, Bill, DB, UCLA, 1959
Stock, Mark, WR, VMI, 1993
Stokes, Fred, DE, Georgia Southern, 1989-92
Stokes, Tim, T, Oregon, 1975-77
Stone, Ken, S, Vanderbilt, 1973-75
Stout, Pete, B, TCU, 1949-50
Stovall, Dick, C, Abilene Christian, 1949
Stowe, Tyrone, LB, Rutgers, 1994
Stralka, Clem, G, Georgetown, 1938-42, 1945-46
Strickland, Fred, LB, Purdue, 1999
Stuart, Jim, T, Oregon, 1938
Stubblefield, Dana, DT, Kansas, 1998-2000
Sturt, Fred, G, Bowling Green, 1974
Stynchula, Andy, DT, Penn State, 1960-63
Suminski, Dave, G, Wisconsin, 1953
Sutton, Ed, B, North Carolina, 1957-59
Sutton, Eric, CB, San Diego State, 1996
Sweeney, Walt, G, Syracuse, 1974-75
Sykes, Bob, B, San Jose State, 1952
Symonette, Josh, S, Tennessee Tech, 2000
Szafaryn, Len, T, North Carolina, 1949

T

Talbert, Diron, DT, Texas, 1971-80
Tamm, Ralph, T, West Chester, 1991
Tanner, Barron, DT, Oklahoma, 1999
Taylor, Charley, WR, Arizona State, 1964-77
Taylor, Hugh (Bones), E, Oklahoma City, 1947-54
Taylor, Keith, S, Illinois, 1994-96
Taylor, Mike, T, USC, 1971
Taylor, Roosevelt, DB, Grambling, 1972
Temple, Mark, B, Oregon, 1936
Tereshinski, Joe, E, Georgia, 1947-54

Terrell, David, CB, Texas-El Paso, 2000
Theismann, Joe, QB, Notre Dame, 1974-85
Theofiledes, Harry, QB, Waynesburg, 1968
Thibodeaux, Keith, CB, NW Louisiana, 1997
Thielemann, R.C., G, Arkansas, 1985-88
Thomas, Chris, WR, Cal Poly San Luis Obispo, 1997-99
Thomas, Duane, RB, West Texas State, 1973-74
Thomas, George, B, Oklahoma, 1950-51
Thomas, Johnny, CB, Baylor, 1988-90, 92-94
Thomas, Mike, RB, UNLV, 1975-78
Thomas, Ralph, E, San Francisco, 1955-56
Thomas, Spencer, S, Washburn, 1975
Thompson, Derrius, WR, Baylor, 1999
Thompson, Ricky, WR, Baylor, 1978-81
Thompson, Steve, DT, Minnesota, 1987
Thrash, James, WR, Missouri Southern, 1997-2000
Thure, Brian, T, California, 1995
Thurlow, Steve, RB, Stanford, 1966-68
Tice, Mike, TE, Maryland, 1989
Tillman, Rusty, LB, Northern Arizona, 1970-77
Tilton, Ron, G, Tulane, 1986
Titchenal, Bob, C, San Jose State, 1940-42
Todd, Dick, RB, Texas A&M, 1939-42, 1945-48
Toibin, Brendan, K, Richmond, 1987
Toneff, Bob, DT, Notre Dame, 1959-64
Torgeson, LaVern, LB, Washington State, 1955-57
Towns, Morris, T, Missouri, 1984
Tracy, Tom, B, Tennessee, 1963-64
Truitt, Dave, TE, North Carolina, 1987
Truitt, Olanda, WR, Mississippi State, 1994-95
Tuckey, Dick, FB, Manhattan, 1938
Turk, Dan, C, Wisconsin, 1997-99
Turk, Matt, P, Wisconsin-Whitewater, 1995-99
Turley, Doug, E, Scranton, 1944-48
Turner, J.T., G, Duke, 1984
Turner, Jay, B, George Washington, 1938-39
Turner, Kevin, LB, Pacific, 1981
Turner, Scott, CB, Illinois, 1995-97
Tyrer, Jim, T, Ohio State, 1974

U.

Ucovich, Mitchell, T, San Jose State, 1944
Uhlenhake, Jeff, C, Ohio State, 1996-97

Ulinski, Harry, C, Kentucky, 1950-51, 1953-56
Ungerer, Joe, T, Fordham, 1944-45

V.

Vactor, Ted, DB, Nebraska, 1969-74
Vanderbeek, Matt, LB, Michigan State, 1995-96
Varty, Mike, LB, Northwestern, 1974
Vaughn, Clarence, S, Northern Illinois, 1987-91
Venuto, Sam, B, Guilford, 1952
Verdin, Clarence, WR, SW Louisiana, 1986-87
Vereb, Ed, RB, Maryland, 1960
Vickers, Kipp, T, Miami, 1999
Vital, Lionel, RB, Nicholls State, 1987
Voytek, Ed, G, Purdue, 1957-58

W.

Waddy, Ray, CB, Texas A&I, 1979-80
Wade, Bob, DB, Morgan State, 1969
Waechler, Henry, DT, Nebraska, 1987
Wahler, Jim, DT, UCLA, 1992-93
Walker, Brian, S, Washington State, 1996-97
Walker, Marquis, CB, SE Missouri State, 1996
Walker, Rick, TE, UCLA, 1980-85
Walters, Tom, DB, Southern Mississippi, 1964-67
Walton, Alvin, S, Kansas, 1986-91
Walton, Frank, G, Pittsburgh, 1944-45
Walton, Joe, E, Pittsburgh, 1957-60
Ward, Bill, G, Washington State, 1946-47
Warren, Don, TE, San Diego State, 1979-92
Washington, Anthony, CB, Fresno State, 1983-84
Washington, Fred, T, North Texas State, 1968
Washington, James, S, UCLA, 1995
Washington, Joe, RB, Oklahoma, 1981-84
Washington, Mickey, CB, Texas A&M, 1992
Watson, Jim, C, Pacific, 1945
Watson, Sid, B, Northwestern, 1958
Watts, George, T, Appalachian State, 1942
Weatherall, Jim, T, Oklahoma, 1958
Weaver, Charlie, LB, USC, 1981
Weil, Jack, P, Wyoming, 1989
Welch, Herb, DB, UCLA, 1989
Weldon, Casey, QB, Florida St, 1999
Weldon, Larry, QB, Presbyterian, 1944-45
Wells, Billy, B, Michigan State, 1954, 1956-57

Westbrook, Michael, WR, Colorado, 1995-2000
Whisenhunt, Ken, TE, Georgia Tech, 1990
White, Jeris, CB, Hawaii, 1980-82
Whited, Marvin, G, Oklahoma, 1942-45
Whitfield, A.D., RB, North Texas State, 1966-68
Whitlow, Bob, C, Arizona, 1960-61
Wiggins, Paul, T, Oregon, 1998
Wilbur, John, G, Stanford, 1971-73
Wilburn, Barry, CB, Mississippi, 1985-89
Wilde, George, B, Texas A&M, 1947
Wilder, James, RB, Missouri, 1990
Wilkin, Willie, T, St. Mary's (CA), 1939-43
Wilkins, Roy, LB, Georgia, 1960-61
Wilkinson, Dan, DT, Ohio State, 1998-2000
Williams, Clarence, RB, South Carolina, 1982
Williams, Doug, QB, Grambling, 1986-89
Williams, Eric, DT, Washington State, 1990-93
Williams, Fred, T, Arkansas, 1964-65
Williams, Gerard, DB, Langston, 1976-78
Williams, Greg, FS, Mississippi State, 1982-84
Williams, Jamel, S, Nebraska, 1997-98
Williams, Jeff, T, Rhode Island, 1978-80
Williams, John, B, USC, 1952-53
Williams, Kevin, CB, Iowa State, 1985, 1988
Williams, LaFann, CB, South Florida, 2000
Williams, Marvin, TE, Fullerton State, 1987
Williams, Michael, TE, Alabama A&M, 1982-84
Williams, Robert, CB, Baylor, 1993
Williams, Sid, LB, Southern, 1967
Williamson, Ernie, T, North Carolina, 1947
Willis, Keith, DT, Northeastern, 1993
Willis Larry, S, Texas-El Paso, 1973
Wilson, Bobby, DT, Michigan State, 1991-94
Wilson, Eric, LB, Maryland, 1987
Wilson, Ted, WR, Central Florida, 1987
Wilson, Wayne, RB, Shepard, 1987
Winans, Tydus, WR, Fresno State, 1994-95
Windham, David, LB, Jackson State, 1987
Wingate, Heath, C, Bowling Green, 1967
Winslow, Doug, WR, Drake, 1976-77
Witucki, Casimir, G, Indiana, 1950-51, 1953-56
Wonsley, Otis, RB, Alcorn State, 1981-85
Woodberry, Dennis, CB, S. Arkansas, 1987-88
Woods, Tony, DE, Pittsburgh, 1994-96
Woodward, Dick, C, Iowa, 1952
Wooten, John, G, Colorado, 1968

Wooten, Mike, C, VMI, 1987
Wright, Steve, T, Alabama, 1970
Wright, Toby, CB, 1999
Wulff, Jim, B, Michigan State, 1960-61
Wyant, Fred, QB, West Virginia, 1956
Wyche, Sam, QB, Furman, 1971-73
Wycheck, Frank, TE/FB, Maryland, 1993-94
Wynne, William, DE, Tennessee State, 1977
Wysocki, Pete, LB, Western Michigan, 1975-80

Y

Yarber, Eric, WR, Idaho, 1986-87
Yehobah-Kodie, Phil, LB, Penn State, 1995
Yonaker, John, E, Notre Dame, 1952
Youel, Jim, B, Iowa, 1946-48
Young, Bill, T, Alabama, 1937-42, 1946
Young, Roy, T, Texas A&M, 1938
Young, Wilburn, DE, William Penn, 1981
Youngblood, Jim, LB, Tennessee Tech, 1984
Yowarsky, Walt, E, Kentucky, 1951-54

Z

Zagers, Bert, B, Michigan State, 1955, 1957-58
Zelenka, Joe, TE, Wake Forest, 2000
Zendejas, Max, K, Arizona, 1986
Zeno, Joe, G, Holy Cross, 1942-44
Zorich, Chris, DT, Notre Dame, 1997
Zimmerman, Roy, B, San Jose State, 1940-42

TRIVIA QUIZ ANSWERS

QUIZ 1

1. b) Newark.

Under pressure from the young NFL, which wanted to move games to larger towns and cities, the Duluth Eskimos in 1927 sold their franchise right back to the league. That right was awarded first to a group representing Orange, New Jersey, and then to another from Newark. Marshall used Newark's franchise in Boston in 1932. Some mistakenly believe that he acquired the Duluth franchise, others that it was Pottsville's. The Pottsville franchise was used to establish a different Boston team, the Bulldogs, which folded in the late 1920s.

2. Running back Steve Bagarus.

3. Team captain Turk Edwards. He went on to become a Redskins line coach and then head coach for three seasons, 1946 through 1948.

4. Running back Cliff Battles, quarterback Sammy Baugh, tackle Turk Edwards, head coach Ray Flaherty, owner George Preston Marshall and end Wayne Milner.

5. b) First downs.

6. In an October 10, 1948 game against the Steelers at Pittsburgh, when the Redskins went 160 yards in reverse on 17 penalties. For that season as a whole, the Redskins were called for 122 penalties, another team record.

7. a) Auto racing and b) basketball. Marshall participated in a failed venture to popularize auto racing at Roosevelt Raceway in New York. His laundry chain also sponsored a basketball team in Washington called the Palace Big Five.

8. Running back Cal Rossi. The first year's pick was nullified because he was still a junior in college. So the Redskins drafted him No. 1 again the next year. But Rossi, who decided not to pursue a pro football career, never played.

9. In 1949, John Whelchel, a former admiral who had coached for Navy, lasted just seven games.

10. *King of the Texas Rangers.*

TRIVIA QUIZ 2

1. The American Oil Company, or Amoco.

2. Herman Ball with a record of 4-16-0, or a winning percentage of .200. A close runner-up was Mike Nixon, whose record was 4-18-2, or .208.

3. Running back Johnny Olszewski.

4. Bobby Mitchell, who gained 1,436 receiving yards in 1963.

5. Roy Barni

6. Chris Hanburger, who went to nine Pro Bowl games. Second was Charley Taylor, who appeared in eight.

7. Bill Dudley. He returned a punt 96 yards for a touchdown against the Steelers in December 1950.

8. c) 113 points (the score was 72-41).

9. In 1959 the No. 1 pick was Bob Allard of Boston College, who went to Canada, and in 1960 Richie Lucas of Penn State, who went to Buffalo in the AFL.

10. Billy Wells. He ran 88 yards from scrimmage for a touchdown against the Cardinals in November 1954.

TRIVIA QUIZ 3

1. Diron Talbert.

2. The assistants: Charlie Waller (Chargers), Charley Winner (Cardinals), Marv Levy (Bills), Ted Marchibroda (Colts and Ravens) and Mike McCormack (Eagles and Colts). The players: Richie Petitbon (Redskins); Jack Pardee (Oilers, Redskins and Bears) and Sam Wyche (Bengals and Bucaneers).

3. Charley Harraway.

4. Cornerback Pat Fischer, who stood up for him when McDole converted to Catholicism while they were at the University of Nebraska.

5. Frank Grant. He gained 776 receiving yards to Taylor's 744 and scored eight touchdowns to Taylor's six. Taylor, however, had more catches, 53 to 41.

6. Sam Wyche.

7. Sammy Baugh, Monte Coleman and Don Warren.

8. Mark Moseley, with 1,207.

9. Eight. While three, not surprisingly, are from the 1940s (guard Tom Bedore and backs Larry Fuller and Reid Lennan), two played in the 1950s (back Dale Atkeson and tackle Jim Norman), one in the 1960s (kicker Gene Mingo) and two in the 1970s (running back Ralph Nelson in addition to Mul-Key).

10. Brig Owens and Sammy Baugh

TRIVIA QUIZ 4

1. Joe Washington, in 1981.

2. Richie Petitbon (Redskins), Joe Bugel (Cardinals and Raiders) and Dan Henning (Chargers).

3. Quarterback.

4. Wilber Jackson, with 708 yards.

5. Cowboys coach Tom Landry.

6. Ali Haji-Sheikh.

7. Dexter Manley, with 97.5.

8. Barry Wilburn.

9. Tony Peters.

10. Gerald Riggs, who gained 221 yards rushing in 29 attempts.

TRIVIA QUIZ 5

1. Darrell Green, James Jenkins, Brian Mitchell and Ed Simmons.

2. The San Francisco 49ers.

3. 9

4. 28.

5. A fumble.

6. Jeff Rutledge.

7. Earnest Byner, Gary Clark, Darrell Green, Jim Lachey, Chip Lohmiller, Charles Mann, Mark Rypien and Mark Schlereth.

8. 12.6 yards.

9. 122.

10. The Redskins Hall of Famers are running back Cliff Battles, quarterback Sammy Baugh, running back Bill Dudley, tackle Turk Edwards, coach Ray Flaherty, coach Joe Gibbs, coach Otto Graham, safety Ken Houston, linebacker Sam Huff, defensive end David (Beacon) Jones, defensive tackle Stan Jones, quarterback Sonny Jurgensen, coach Curly Lambeau, coach Vince Lombardi, founder George Preston Marshall, end Wayne Milner, flanker Bobby Mitchell, running back John Riggins and wide receiver Charley Taylor.

TRIVIA QUIZ 6

1. The Arizona Cardinals. The Redskins won in overtime, 19-13.

2. At RFK, the Redskins won 11 games and lost one in post-season play.

3. Darrell Green and James Jenkins.

4. John Friesz, Heath Shuler, Gus Frerotte, Jeff Hostetler, Trent Green and Brad Johnson. Frerotte started the most games, 46.

5. Turner's teams won 43 games in his first six years, one in a playoff.

6. Russ Grimm and Terry Robiskie.

7. Davis rushed for more than 100 yards seven times in 1999, including in the playoff game against Detroit.

8. Jerry Allen (19995-98), Ricky Ervins (1994) and Reggie Brooks (1993).

9. Michael Westbrook (1995), Andre Johnson (1996), Kennard Lang (1997), nobody in 1998, Champ Bailey (1999) and LaVar Arrington and Chris Samuels (2000).

10. As the 2000 season began, the Redskins had sold out 267 regular-season and playoff games over 33 years, dating back to the start of the 1966 season.

Index